THE METAPHYSICAL SAGA

A Speck in the Quest of Dune

THE METAPHYSICAL SAGA

A SPECK IN THE QUEST OF DUNE

MADHUSUDAN SAINI

Bigfoot Publications
Because, there's a writer in everyone.

INDIA
MALAYSIA
UNITED KINGDOM

Bigfoot Publications
Because, there's a writer in everyone.

The Metaphysical Saga: A Speck in the Quest of Dune
Author: Madhusudan Saini

First Published by:
Bigfoot06 Publications (OPC) Pvt. Ltd.
1st floor, BSR Building near Vishal Mega Mart,
Daultabad Flyover, Laxman Vihar Phase 3,
Gurugram, Haryana (122001)
Website: www.bigfootpublications.in
Email: info@bigfootpublications.in

First Edition: January 2025

ISBN Print Book- 978-93-6347-113-9

Typeset in Sabon at 11.5pt
By Yachika Prajapati for Bigfoot06 Publications

Printed in India

In the Lotus Feet of the Supreme Being

'I bow to the source of this magnificent creation,
The Source that dwells within its own manifestation.
Wherever my eyes wander, your presence I perceive,
You are as close as my heartbeat, yet as distant as eternity.
But in shedding illusions and embracing truth's light,
One can find you instantly, in every moment's sight.
I bow to the Absolute, in whom I find reflection,
In your boundless embrace, I seek my true connection.'

CONTENTS

INTRODUCTION

If you sit quietly for a moment and keenly observe this physical world, you will realize that all of humanity is driven by their desires. In this era, people are blindly racing in an endless pursuit to fulfill their ambitions and yearnings. Every individual craves recognition, fame, success, wealth, and all forms of prosperity.

However, even those who possess these things to some extent are not content and yearn to enhance them further, driven by the pervasive belief that accumulating material wealth defines life's ultimate purpose. Excluding merely one percent, every individual holds the belief that attaining prosperity is equivalent to attaining success in life.

Amidst the pursuit of earthly possessions, there comes a moment in nearly every individual's life when suddenly, everything grinds to a halt, and nothing seems to make sense. Life proceeds smoothly until, unexpectedly, the whole world turns upside down. A cascade of crises descends upon us and we find ourselves in uncharted territory.

This period is commonly labelled as the dark phase of life. During this phase, we exert every effort to find solutions, yet none seem to work. Gradually, everything accumulated over the years starts to appear futile; even the will to live diminishes, and life itself begins to feel faded and meaningless.

During that crucible of adversity, many people raise their hands and ruin their lives by turning to drugs and intoxicants, while other courageous individuals opt to restart everything and a few seek solace in the Divine. Among those who turn to the Divine, a few surrender themselves thoroughly at its feet, and receive abundant grace.

Then through the benevolence of the Almighty, unexpectedly an individual becomes aware of their true selves and begins to inquire: What is the purpose of life? Why are we born? Do humans exist only to suffer? Is there a path to enduring peace and joy in life? What is our true identity? Is there truly a supreme power orchestrating everything? Does God exist, or is it merely a figment of our imagination? What is the ultimate truth?

These relentless 'what' and 'why' queries persist within one. It is only when such queries disturb their peace during the day and disrupt their sleep at night they begin seeking answers. Every individual seeks light only when darkness looms.

When an individual realizes that they know nothing about themselves, or that what they know is not absolute truth, and the pain of ignorance steals away their serenity, then a seeker is born.

This is the saga of an ordinary man named Madhusudan who, like many others, chasing his dreams and desires. He aspired to achieve social status and immense wealth because, like most people, he equated earthly prosperity with success. However, the cosmos had different plans for him. Initially, everything was occurring in a composed manner in Madhusudan's life but abruptly, his small world became flooded with crises.

When all else fails, humans often turn to God, hoping for a miracle. Speaking from my personal experience, prayers are always answered if they are in our best interest. Eventually, Madhusudan turned to God for solace and guidance. This marked the beginning of his journey on the path of self-discovery.

The Divine's grace transformed the course of Madhusudan's life miraculously, leading him into the mystical realms of metaphysics. Along his journey, Madhusudan encountered an extraordinary saint whose profound influence opened his eyes to the spiritual world. These experiences shattered all his preconceived beliefs and notions and led him on a quest for the ultimate truth.

As you journey through this saga, you may encounter various phenomena that challenge belief and are hard to swallow. I myself initially found these incidents hard to accept. However, rest assured, every word in this narrative holds profound truth—a truth that I have personally experienced and lived.

I have striven to woven remarkable anecdotes and folklore throughout the chapters to heighten the reader's thrill and foster a deeper understanding regarding certain profound concepts. Each word in this saga reflects my heartfelt dedication to creating something meaningful for you. You can trust that investing your time and money in this book will be rewarding. Furthermore, I'm certain that this narrative will permanently transform your perspective toward the world around you.

Before we begin, I want to articulate that this book is not affiliated with any specific religion or sect, nor does it advocate for or adhere to any particular belief system. Rather, this book is for all those on the path of self-realization, seeking answers, and striving to understand their true identity.

Whether you are aware of it or not, if you are reading this, you are a genuine seeker, and this book is dedicated to all seekers around the world. Now, I invite you to gear up yourself and join me, as we embark on an extraordinary journey that may challenge everything you have come to know thus far.

CHAPTER 1

AN ESOTERIC SCRIPTURE

Typically, only two types of individuals embark on the journey of self-realization. One group comprises those driven by a deep longing for Nirvana (salvation). These individuals are inherently exceptional, exhibiting remarkable abilities from an early age. They immerse themselves in acts of devotion, worship, chanting, meditation, and other spiritual disciplines, unaffected by the allure of worldly pleasures. Over time, they gracefully renounce material pursuits and retreat to secluded places to engage in intense penance. In the yogic lore, these beings are referred to as 'Mumukshu', the seeker of ultimate truth; they are incredibly rare, with only one appearing in perhaps a million people.

And then come those who find themselves deeply disenchanted with their lives, battling inner turmoil. These individuals reach a certain juncture in their lives where the idea of death holds greater allure than the continuation of their current existence. Caught amidst a tumultuous sea of crises, they come to the stark realization that there is no way out. Eventually, they turn to God for solace and guidance.

Following this, they raise their hands and submit themselves at the feet of the Divine. In response, the Divine showers them with compassion and reveals a beacon of hope. This beacon serves as their guide on a transformative journey of self-discovery. The vast majority of people fall into this category, and I was no exception. Like many others, I reached a certain point where life's challenges wore me down, leading me to seek solace in the embrace of the Divine.

It all began several years back. During that time, I was driven by strong ambition and passion. Just like any typical person, I had lofty dreams despite my modest beginnings. I yearned to hold the luxuries of the material world in my hands. Therefore, while pursuing my undergraduate degree, I opted to embark on a startup journey alongside one of my close friends.

Before bringing an idea to fruition, individuals usually engage in mental visualization. They create a conceptual framework in their minds, envisioning the desired outcome and every step of the journey from inception to destination. This process fuels their enthusiasm as they embark on working towards their goal. In technical terminology, this mental visualization process is frequently labelled as 'planning'. Formulating plans mentally is akin to shooting an arrow in the dark; there is no guarantee that your plan will succeed, yet you proceed with it. The reality is, everything in this world is uncertain; you can't even foresee what will transpire in the next moment.

With my friend by my side, I meticulously planned every aspect, utilizing my intelligence to its fullest, and then commenced the tasks accordingly. Primarily, I convinced my father to become an angel investor in the startup. My aim was to rapidly amplify the funds and repay him promptly. Things were going smooth as butter in the initial days. My father and the rest of the family were over the moon to witness my progress. However, as time passed, everything began to deteriorate. Our planning didn't yield the anticipated results, and we struggled to pinpoint what was lacking in our efforts. Meanwhile, conflicts between my colleague and me regarding tasks became frequent, leading to a rapid deterioration of our bond.

With time, the fervor I once possessed to achieve everything began to wane, leading me to feel increasingly melancholic. The dreams I had once woven in my eyes started to crumble before me. It seemed as though everything was coming to a halt, and I felt thoroughly incapable of remedying the situation. My peace during the day and sleep at night vanished. Whenever I crossed paths with acquaintances, I felt compelled to wear a fake smile, unwillingly pretending that everything was going well. You can't reveal your struggles to everyone, especially to those who have faith in you, and who believe that you are destined for great achievements in life. At that time, I stayed in the village with my family due to vacations after the second-year exams, and also because my workplace was located in a nearby town; just one hour away from the village.

One evening, as I made my way home from work, my mind buzzed with a million thoughts. Amidst this mental flurry, I rode my motorbike. Frequently, you may have noticed that when we are lost in our thoughts or deeply contemplating something, our ability to see and hear things around us becomes momentarily dulled. It feels like the world around us momentarily fades away. Unintentionally, while engrossed in my mind, I slipped into a state of numbness amidst the bustling road. My senses temporarily ceased to function, rendering everything invisible and inaudible to me. It was as if the traffic and its noise ceased to exist around me. Out of the blue, a roar fell into my ears: 'Hey…!!!' Before I could regain consciousness, it was quite late, and I bumped into an autorickshaw; that uproar emanated from the passengers inside the autorickshaw. Although the driver strived to turn the handle briskly, I couldn't escape it entirely, and my right hand slammed into the autorickshaw with force. The collision was intense; however, what truly astounded me was that I managed to control my motorbike and avoid falling; neither I nor the autorickshaw driver suffered any damage. You may consider it fortunate, but I must acknowledge that some unworldly force protected me. Considering the force of the impact, it seemed inevitable that I would have fallen to the road. The injury was minor; I only had some light scratches and swelling on my arm. Hence, I didn't feel the need to mention it to anyone after arriving home.

As the night settled in and all living beings drifted into a peaceful sleep, my mind became consumed by a myriad of troubling thoughts. I found myself reflecting: Why did our endeavors yield no fruit despite our earnestness? How will I face my father? Will I become a subject of ridicule for all? How do I navigate this situation now?

In a flash, these questions instilled an unsettling fear within me; I began to feel suffocated, as though these questions were driving me to madness. Despite my efforts to shake them off, I found no relief. I yearned to scream aloud, yet it felt as though my voice was trapped in my throat. A monstrous specter of worries and uncertainties haunted me, while the dread of failure consumed me from within. I yearned to escape to a place far away, away from the torment, where I could seek solace.

Experiencing significant agitation, I find myself contemplating: 'It would have been preferable if I had perished on the road today.' Living in such a manner feels more burdensome than death. Unable to find an escape from that dreadful condition, I reached out to the Almighty for assistance. With a soul weighed down by sorrow, I cried out in my mind, "O Lord! You comprehend the depths of my plight. I surrender myself entirely to you, for I am devoid of strength, and you are my final beacon of hope. Illuminate my path, I beseech you. Please, prevent my life from descending into darkness."

In the meantime, my gaze shifted towards my father, who lay asleep at a distance from me. Habitually during summer nights in rural Bharat (India), people often gather their beds closely together under the starlit sky. My father rested on his opposite side; his back turned away from me. Through some effort, I positioned myself onto my father's bed and gently embraced him from behind, aiming to avoid disturbing his slumber. Yet, my efforts proved futile as I ended up waking him. Father shifted slightly, seeking to identify the presence behind him, before inquiring in a sleepy tone, "Is everything alright?"

As he inquired, a tear escaped from my left eye, tracing a path down my cheek, and landed gently on his pillow. It symbolized a tear of relief, held captive within my eyes for an extended period, now finding its long-awaited freedom. After a while, I collected myself and responded in a grave tone, "Hmm..."

My father didn't pursue further questioning. It seemed that my brief response was adequate for him to grasp the entirety of the situation. You may strive to portray yourself as blissfully happy to the world, but you can't maintain that facade with your parents. No matter how adept you are at stretching the truth, your parents will eventually see through it. In my view, within the grand narrative of existence, a father embodies an enigmatic presence. He resembles the vital underground network of a tree—the roots—often overlooked amidst the admiration for the tree's visible splendor: its leaves, trunk, flowers, and fruits. Yet, it's the roots that provide the necessary support, enabling the tree to stand tall and steadfast, reaching toward the sky.

I have observed a noticeable difference in how fathers interact with their adult children compared to mothers. A father tends not to ask many questions or feel obligated to respond to everything. Verbal communication isn't typically his preference; instead, he often conveys his sentiments through gestures, particularly with his eyes and facial expressions. Even if a father doesn't seek explanations for everything and doesn't interact much with his children, it doesn't imply a lack of care or tenderness in his heart for his children, much like a mother. While he might not openly display it, a father loves his children immensely, cherishing them above all else. In essence, your father knows you inside out; he can discern from your face, your eyes, and the way you speak when something troubles you, even if he doesn't openly acknowledge it.

Truthfully, embracing my father in such a heartfelt manner was a challenge for me, as I wasn't accustomed to showing him such affection or being openly affectionate towards him. This could be attributed to the fact that I hadn't been particularly close to my father before. I believe this sentiment might resonate especially with those born in the 90s or earlier. Our generation tends to be less forthcoming with our elders compared to those who came after us.

My father, Shri Praveen Saini, is a naive and generous person. Nevertheless, I find myself slightly uncomfortable when it comes to speaking up or asking him anything. However, when I proposed the idea of a startup to my father, he didn't dwell on it much nor did he pose numerous questions. Instead, he simply gave me his blessing to pursue it. I admit I was lucky in this instance because it can be quite difficult to persuade traditional Bhartiya parents about such matters. After all, they typically view a government job as the ultimate achievement.

That night, I enjoyed a peaceful sleep after a long period. The next morning, while I was having breakfast, my father approached me and took a seat beside me. Immediately, I paused mid-chew and averted my gaze, hoping to avoid any discussion about the previous night. Yet, he tenderly placed his hand on my shoulder and uttered, "Son, if things are not progressing as you hoped, there is no shame in stepping back. You have your entire future ahead of you for such endeavors. But for now, prioritize accomplishing your graduation."

Unable to find the right words, I remained silent, staring at my plate. After some time, my father left, and I too left for work. Upon arriving at the workplace, I found myself deep in thought, pondering over my father's words. His words left me speechless, as I had been preoccupied with concerns about how to explain everything to him and what his reaction might be. Yet, upon learning the situation, my father stood firmly by my side, offering me some solace. Nevertheless, the issue still loomed, and I found myself uncertain about what steps to take next to navigate through the situation.

As I contemplated these thoughts, abruptly a cascade of profound questions surged through my mind: Is this the undeniable truth of existence? Are we fated to meet our end in such a manner, or does life harbor a greater meaning? Why does the world abound with so much anguish and despair? Where is the Divine's assistance in my time of need? Could it be that my fate is predetermined, leading me down this path?

Lacking answers, I sought solace and quieted the turmoil in my mind by turning to motivational videos on my mobile phone. While watching a video, I came across a motivational speaker discussing essential books that everyone should read at least once in their lifetime. Among the titles mentioned were the Bhagavad Gita, the Holy Bible, Think and Grow Rich, Vedanta, Autobiography of a Yogi, and a few others. Among these titles, I had some familiarity with the Bhagavad Gita and the Holy Bible, perhaps from hearing about them during my school days.

A few days later, one morning, as my father was preparing to go to Haridwar for some errands, I found myself suddenly reminded of something. Just as he was about to leave, I asked him if he could bring the Bhagavad Gita from the Gita Press Gorakhpur store.

"Hmm... I will see if I can manage it," my father replied, walking away.

Back then, I had casually requested the scripture from him, but looking back now, I must attribute it to the Divine's grace. Until then, I was familiar with the Bhagavad Gita as a revered text of Hinduism, I had no inkling that it would soon become the catalyst for a profound transformation in my life.

Throughout the day, while sitting at my workplace, I found myself repeatedly checking my watch, eager for time to pass quickly so I could return home. However, doubts persisted regarding whether my father would fulfill my request for the scripture. You might assume that I had a natural inclination towards studying scriptures, but that wasn't the case. I wasn't much of a book person until I came across the Bhagavad Gita.

Upon arriving home in the evening, I headed straight to my father's room to check if he had returned. Well, I found him seated there, engrossed in some paperwork. Upon exchanging greetings, I inquired, "Did you bring the book for me?"

"The storekeeper mentioned wrapping it in a red fabric after reading," my father responded, handing me a black color polybag.

I nodded my head and came out of the room. Although I didn't have much idea about the Bhagavad Gita, I was exuberant to have it. For reasons beyond my comprehension, I felt a deep resonance with this scripture in my heart. It seemed to resonate deeply with what I needed in my life.

The next morning, in addition to my usual items, I packed the Bhagavad Gita in my backpack before heading to work. My mind was consumed with the anticipation of delving into the scripture as soon as I could. Upon arriving at work, I swiftly completed my routine tasks and then settled down to leisurely go through it.

Now allow me to express vividly that I'm entirely inadequate to narrate or expound upon even a single aspect of the Bhagavad Gita in a proficient manner. It is only the Divine who possesses the ability to do so, for this text transcends the ordinary—it is believed that each word within it emanates from the Divine itself. However, it would be unjust to proceed without endeavoring to offer a brief glimpse into the essence of this enigmatic scripture. Therefore, I humbly beseech the Almighty to illuminate us all with a brief understanding. With your permission, my Lord...

The Sanskrit word 'Bhagavad' translates to 'God' and 'Gita' to 'a Song'. Hence, the Bhagavad Gita is also known as 'The Song of God'. It holds a significant place within the Sanskrit epic 'Mahabharata', which stands as the largest and most esteemed epic in the world. Comprising 18 chapters and a total of 700 verses, the Bhagavad Gita unfolds in the form of a dialogue between the Pandava prince, the mighty warrior Arjun, and Lord Vasudeva Krishna, on the battlefield of Kurukshetra.

A clash of righteousness unfolded, with individuals from the same lineage ready to confront each other in battle. On one side stood the Pandavas, defending righteousness and ethics, while on the other side stood the Kauravas, opposing righteousness and ethics.

As the battle was on the brink of commencing, Arjun implored the Lord, "Vasudeva, position the chariot between the two armies; I wish to closely observe all the warriors." In response to his request, the Lord stationed the chariot between the two armies and remarked, "Dear Arjun, observe all these warriors assembled here meticulously, their hearts filled with a desire for battle." Following that, Arjun attentively surveyed both armies and recognized his own grandfather, teacher, uncle, brothers, nephews, and other relatives standing against him. As he beheld them, a disturbing thought emerged in his mind: 'To emerge victorious in this battle, I must confront and defeat them all.' However, amidst these contemplations, a wave of fear washed over him, causing him to recoil from the impending conflict. His powerful bow slipped from his grasp, and he was overcome with anguish. Arjun found himself in a state of perplexity, offering various justifications to Lord Vasudeva for his reluctance to engage in battle. He conveyed to the Lord, "It would be against righteousness to slaughter our own people for the sake of kingship. Such an act would be profoundly sinful. I am certain that this battle will lead us all to damnation. I refuse to seek victory at the expense of the lives of our own kin."

"Arjun, why do you entertain such cowardly thoughts at this critical moment?" inquired Lord Vasudeva. He continued, "Such notions are not befitting a mighty warrior. Therefore, stand up and fight."

Despite employing various methods to persuade him, including mockery, teasing, and even harsh words, when all else failed, the Lord eventually introduced Arjun to the profound wisdom of the Bhagavad Gita.

The Bhagavad Gita outlines three primary paths of yoga that lead one to liberation and union with the Supreme Being: *Sankhya Yoga, Karma Yoga, and Bhakti Yoga.*

Sankhaya Yoga – It is also referred to as *'Gyana Yoga'* or the path of knowledge. At the onset of Sankhya Yoga, Arjun submits himself to Lord Vasudeva and seeks His guidance. The Lord then elucidates that the wise neither mourn for the dead nor the living, for they understand the truth. The physical body is impermanent, but the soul (Aatma) is eternal, thus there is no cause for sorrow. While describing the nature and various attributes of the soul the Lord says:

'na jayate mriyate va kadachi
nayam bhutva bhavita va na bhuyah
ajo nityah shasvato aym purano
na hanyate hanyamane sharire'

Bhagavad Gita: Chapter 2, verse 20

The soul is neither born, nor ever die; it is eternal, immortal, changeless, and ageless. It does not perish when the body is perished. The one who knows the soul to be eternal cannot be struck down. One ought not to mourn the things which are perishable because if something is born then death is inevitable for that.

Karma Yoga – It is termed the path of action as well. The Lord explains that the truly powerful are those who follow Karma Yoga, engaging earnestly in fulfilling their external duties while maintaining inner detachment. Your duty is solely to act, not to concern yourself with its results. Don't make the consequences of your actions your primary focus. While explaining how one can attain God through their actions, the Lord says:

'tasmad asaktah satatyam
karyam karma samachara
asakto hyacharan karma
param apnoti purushah'

Bhagavad Gita: Chapter 3, verse 19

Relinquish attachment, and perform deeds as a matter of duty because by working without being engaged to the fruits, one attains the Supreme. The enlightened beings do not renounce their mundane duties, as it may create disharmony in the mind of mediocre beings who looks up to them for inspiration. They possess knowledge, having abandoned the fruits of their actions and being freed from the bonds of birth. Further, the Lord describes the attributes of a yogi: The individual whose mind remains steadfast in the face of challenges, devoid of desires, and unbound by attachment, fear, or anger, embodies the essence of a yogi or a wise sage.

Bhakti Yoga – This path is also recognized as the path of devotion. The Lord explains that absolute devotion, whether directed towards a specific form or the formless, leads to the attainment of the Supreme. Arjun inquires of the Lord, "Who excels, those who worship the formless aspect of God or those devoted to a particular form?" The Lord responds, "Both paths enable devotees to reach the Supreme. However, I consider those who are devoted to a certain form as great yogis." Lord Vasudeva adds ahead:

'mayy aveshya mano ye mam
nitya-yukta upasate shraddhaya
parayopetas te me yuktatama matah'

Bhagavad Gita: Chapter 12, verse 2

I regard as great yogis those who focus their minds on me and consistently practice devotion with unwavering faith. The Lord emphasizes Bhakti Yoga as the most convenient and highest among all yoga, as an individual can readily concentrate on a form without various distractions. The Lord proclaims that true devotion must be characterized by selflessness, with the devotee surrendering all to their cherished deity.

Each of these paths guides an individual toward self-realization and union with the Supreme Being through varied approaches. The quintessence of the Bhagavad Gita can be summarized as follows:

- The soul or the Aatma is eternal and cannot be destroyed by anyone or anything. Therefore, there is no need to grieve for the living or the dead.
- One ought to focus on accomplishing their duties without attachment to the outcomes. Every selfish action leads to karmic entanglement, while selfless actions pave the way to liberation.
- Although we have the right to act, we do not have control over the results of our actions.
- Our mind can be both our greatest ally and our most formidable enemy; it is imperative that we harness its power for our benefit.
- A true yogi remains equanimous in all circumstances and fulfills their duties without attachment.
- Recognizing the Divine's presence in all beings leads to enlightenment.

- God is the ultimate source of creation, permeating all existence.
- We are not the sole agents of our actions; they arise from the interplay of the three qualities of nature: Sattva, Rajas, and Tamas.
- Strive for moderation in all aspects of life, avoiding extremes, as it is the path to ultimate bliss.
- Offer every action to the Divine, surrendering the results with absolute devotion, to attain ultimate peace.

Overall, the Bhagavad Gita acts as a manual for leading a virtuous life, attaining spiritual satisfaction, and grasping profound insights into existence. Its timeless teachings extend beyond cultural and religious confines, offering universal wisdom.

If I were to endeavor to encapsulate the entirety of the Bhagavad Gita, countless volumes would fall short of capturing its essence. Thus, following the directive of the Divine, I have extracted only a fraction from its boundless reservoir of wisdom.

The Bhagavad Gita served as my initiation into the concept of yoga, which I had previously misunderstood as merely sophisticated physical exercises. Credit for this misconception often falls upon self-proclaimed yoga masters, who focus solely on the physical aspect of yoga. However, yoga encompasses far more—it signifies union with the Divine, a path through which one can perceive the true Self and the ultimate truth.

Initially, I encountered considerable difficulty in thoroughly comprehending certain verses within the Bhagavad Gita, as their deeper meanings often require contemplation. I revisited the text repeatedly, striving to grasp its essence accurately. Over time, I began to perceive myself as Arjun, engaged in a dialogue with Lord Vasudeva Krishna. It became evident to me that Lord Vasudeva

Krishna was imparting the wisdom of the Bhagavad Gita directly to my soul.

I devoted myself to its study daily, whenever I found a moment. Gradually, the inner turmoil of fear, distress, worry, irritation, agitation, and anger began to dissipate; a sense of serenity and composure enveloped me. Remarkably, my perspective on life and the world around me underwent a profound transformation. Previously, my thoughts, feelings, and actions were entirely self-centered, with myself as the focal point of the cosmos. However, upon attaining wisdom and embracing inclusivity, sorrow and agony dissipate from my life. I began to perceive the Divine's presence in all entities. As a result, the complexities, challenges, and crises that once plagued my life dissolved. I'm grateful for the wisdom imparted by this sacred scripture.

Ignorance serves as the fundamental source of human suffering, leading individuals to adopt a self-centered outlook. Through ignorance, one becomes isolated in nature. This encapsulates the primary teaching of the Bhagavad Gita. This scripture transcends its role as a religious text confined to ceremonial observance. Its verses, akin to precious gems, hold profound wisdom that surpasses any specific faith. Indeed, this sacred text belongs to all of humanity, irrespective of religious affiliation. I can assure you that through sincere study and reflection, whether you identify as a believer or not, Hindu or otherwise, the Bhagavad Gita has the potency to deeply impact your life. Its significance cannot be adequately expressed in words. For me personally, the Bhagavad Gita was the catalyst for a profound spiritual awakening; liberating me from the confines of worldly pursuits. Yet, this was just the beginning of my journey towards self-realization—an initial spark that ignited a spiritual transformation within me.

CHAPTER 2

GURUKUL AND THE QUEST FOR GURU

Before proceeding further, allow me to share an incredible tale that I once heard from a revered yogi several years back. It is said that there lived a devotee of Lord Narayana named Kashiraj. By God's grace, Kashiraj had all the amenities including a beautiful house, a great running corporation, farming land, a flourishing family, brothers, friends, and relatives. Kashiraj lived in a small town which was situated on the bank of the river Yamuna. As part of his daily routine, he would cleanse himself in the river and conduct his rituals every morning. Upon completing his prayers and beginning his journey back home, Kashiraj would often glance back and observe four footprints in the sand instead of the expected two. This occurrence consistently filled him with a sense of divine blessing and he used to utter it with a firm belief: Lord Narayana walks with me.

Several months later, one day, destiny dealt Kashiraj a severe blow. His colleagues betrayed his trust, resulting in significant losses in his business. Gradually, Kashiraj invested all his wealth to overcome the losses though, he got no aid. Despite navigating through the crisis, Kashiraj found himself deserted by his brothers, family, and other relatives, who withdrew their support during his time of adversity. Nonetheless, Kashiraj remained unperturbed by their abandonment, holding firm to his faith that Lord Narayana stood beside him. He held firm in the belief that whatever happened, the Lord would never abandon him.

One day, as Kashiraj journeyed home following his customary river rituals, he reflexively glanced back at the footprints. However, to his dismay, he found only two imprints in the sand, accompanied by a few thorns stained with blood. Witnessing this scene, his heart filled with sorrow. Following that, Kashiraj gazed at the sky and expressed with anguished spirit, "Despite my coworkers betraying me, I held my peace. I endured the loss of my business in silence. My loved ones turned away, yet I remained steadfast. But you, my Lord... you were my only hope, and even you have forsaken me!"

Kashiraj couldn't hold himself back and then tears rolled out from his eyes. In his dream that night, Lord Narayana appeared and gently inquired, "Why did you assume that I had abandoned you? How could you even entertain the notion that I would turn away from you?" The Lord continued, "Of course, as you walk, I walk alongside you, matching your steps. The additional footprints you used to observe on the sand were always mine. Today, as you made your way home, you didn't notice the thorns along the path. Before those thorns could pierce your feet, I lifted you into my embrace. The footprints you saw today were mine, and the blood on the thorns was also mine. Kashiraj, such doubts were never expected from you."

With those words, Lord Narayana vanished in the air. Kashiraj awoke abruptly, tears streaming down his face. Overwhelmed with remorse, he offered a heartfelt apology to Lord Narayana. From that moment on, Kashiraj lived his life in harmony.

Often, when we find ourselves isolated due to unwelcome circumstances, we tend to lose faith in God. Our human perspective on God is somewhat peculiar. We believe that if we are devout worshippers and offer sincere prayers, then surely, we should be spared from life's crises. Considering we supposedly reside under God's protective care, it's almost humorous to think that God must actively guard us. Isn't it ironic?

We ought to reflect on whether God truly requires our worship and prayers, or if God delights in it at all. In reality, God always grants us what is truly beneficial for our growth and well-being, rather than simply what we desire or believe we deserve. A poet once expressed: 'If things unfold as you desire, it's good; if not, it's even better.'

In the past, I too held the belief that our worship and rituals were merely to appease God, fearing that failure to do so would incur God's wrath. However, over time, these misconceptions dissipated, and I began to wholeheartedly adore God with love, rather than being driven by fear.

A few days later, we mutually decided to put a halt to our startup endeavor. I found no reason for regret in that choice, as I had adopted the perspective that all occurrences serve our greater good. In due course, I returned to Gurukul Kangri Vishwavidyalaya, a university in Haridwar where I was enrolled in a Microbiology undergraduate program. Taking advantage of my aunt's presence in Haridwar, I opted to stay at her place during my time there.

To be frank, I never felt like I was the chosen one, and I hadn't experienced anything supernatural in my life from the time I was born until I enrolled in Gurukul. However, a few months after being admitted to Gurukul, my mother, Shrimati Babita Saini, unexpectedly passed away. She was known for her gentle nature. Once, she recounted to me that shortly after my birth, they noticed some Sanskrit characters etched on my forehead, accompanied by a reddish mark.

Initially, no one in the household could decipher the exact letters inscribed. As I matured, however, those markings gradually faded into obscurity. Nevertheless, I never experienced any peculiarities or disruptions in my life due to that phenomenon. I grew up much like anyone else. Even my mother would jest that I wasn't the most well-behaved child; rather, I was quite mischievous. Whenever she reminisced about my playful antics from childhood, she never failed to bring them up. Despite the passage of several years, her absence leaves a palpable void in our family.

Upon my admission to Gurukul, I enthusiastically delved into the realm of fashion; perhaps you have encountered individuals who take pleasure in being well-dressed. Just picture a young man with slightly long black hair, neatly trimmed on the sides, a short beard, adorned with a thick silver chain around his neck, a copper coin ring adorning his right index finger, a heavy steel bangle in the wrist, attired in slim-fit outfits paired with high ankle sneakers, sporting a muscular physique.

These details might offer you a glimpse into my appearance during that time. The driving force behind my persona stemmed from the strict regulations of my previous school, where adherence to a set of stringent rules was mandatory. Our school principal, Dr. Shalu was a phenomenal lady—a staunch idealist, who prohibited male students from maintaining long hair, wearing slim-fit uniforms, jewelry, or even watches inside the campus premises. Hence, once the school period concluded, I relished the freedom to indulge in the sartorial expressions I had longed for since my boyhood.

Despite these inclinations, I remained diligent in my academics, consistently achieving pleasing grades. I remember, when the first-semester results were announced at the university, my professors were notably impressed by my academic performance. Initially, they may have perceived me as someone solely absorbed in his own world, perhaps even a bit rebellious, but over time, they had to reassess their initial judgments.

As the third year of my graduation commenced, the teachings of the Bhagavad Gita had a profound impact on me. Prior to my return to Haridwar, I underwent a significant transformation, both internally and externally. My demeanor, gestures, thought processes, and perspectives underwent considerable changes; I found myself adopting a more submissive demeanor than before. Unexpectedly, I chose to shave my head and discard all my jewelry. Instead, I started wearing a Rudraksha rosary around my neck and began adorning my forehead with round yellow sandalwood and red vermilion Tilak (a sort of religious mark), symbolizing auspiciousness.

The act of applying Tilak on the forehead carries diverse significance. Broadly, it represents auspiciousness and purity. The sandalwood Tilak is believed to help maintain a cool and focused mind. From a religious standpoint, Tilak serves as an emblem representing the lineage and beliefs of an individual. Within Hinduism, various lineages and sects have distinct patterns for applying Tilak. Vaishnavites, devotees of Lord Vishnu, often apply Tilak in a 'U' shape at the center of their foreheads. Followers of Lord Shiva and Goddess Shakti, such as Shaivites and Shaktas, typically adorn their foreheads with three horizontal lines of ashes, accompanied by a red dot positioned in the middle or between the eyebrows. Devotees of Lord Ganapati may apply Tilak in a crescent moon shape, while followers of Lord Hanuman commonly wear orange Tilak, each symbolizing their devotion to their respective deities.

In Tantric tradition, a Tilak represents certain mystical aspects such as the approach of worship or the spiritual attainments of a practitioner. If one encounters a practitioner from the Naga Sadhu or Aghora sects, it's customary to observe them adorning their foreheads with distinctive colors arranged in intricate patterns, each carrying profound significance reflective of their spiritual journey. An additional significance of Tilak in our yogic customs lies in its ability to catalyze the activation of the Agana

Chakra (energy center), positioned between the eyebrows. A proficient master or Guru possesses a precise understanding of the Agana Chakra's location on the disciple's forehead and applies Tilak accordingly, initiating the awakening of this particular chakra.

The Rudraksha is renowned for its potent healing properties, acting to balance the chakras within our bodies and safeguard practitioners from detrimental energies. Through personal experience, I have noticed Rudraksha beads resonate uniquely when exposed to such energies. Traditionally, devotees of Lord Shiva utilize these beads for mantra recitation.

Back then, I wasn't aware of the significance of Tilak and Rudraksha beads; I simply carried them to project a devout image. As the saying in my village goes, 'A brand-new priest recites the name of God loud.' My friends were all amazed to see me in that attire. I recall one close friend, Mayank Bharadwaj, teasing me about it once. On my birthday, he posted a photo of me in that getup on social media, captioned: 'A Very Happy Birthday to Shri-Shri 1008 Maha-mandleshwar Madhusudanand Ji Maharaj.' With that caption, he mocked me by declaring me a revered monk. That's just how friends are.

Once during a Microbiology lecture, the professor was elaborating on the structure of a Bacterial Cell when suddenly, a group of students barged into the classroom chanting slogans, 'Long Live Mohit Chauhan.' They then urged fellow students to join Mohit Chauhan's campaign for the Student Union President position. With the professor's consent, some students left the classroom with the group. Once they departed, the professor turned to the remaining students and inquired, "Does anyone understand the necessity of a group or clique?"

There was no response; silence enveloped the room. In a bold tone, the professor remarked, "The one who fears loneliness, who believes they cannot endure solitude, seeks companionship. A lion wanders alone, confident in its strength. Now, you must determine whether you are a lamb or lion, possess strength or fragility."

These words resonated deeply within me. Since that day, I resolved to steer clear of crowds. After classes, I would seek solitude, immersing myself in the teachings of the Bhagavad Gita, and began to listen to online discourses by monks and yogis.

As time passed, gradually I realized that several aspects of our self-perception are not entirely accurate. The things we believe belong to us are not truly ours, as our names and identities are assigned by others. The physical body we inhabit is not inherently ours; it is crafted from elements sourced from nature and thus it belongs to nature. As it is nature's possession, upon death, we must relinquish it back to nature. Even our breath is not our own, as we can manipulate its natural rhythm but cannot voluntarily halt breathing; it is governed by natural forces. Now the questions emerged: Is there anything I can genuinely claim as mine? Who truly am I? What defines my genuine identity? What represents the ultimate truth?

These inquiries filled my thoughts, and the more I attempted to uncover answers through introspection, the more entangled I became in perplexity. While seated in my room one evening, engrossed in browsing the internet, the words of that motivational speaker unexpectedly resurfaced in my mind. I pondered, 'Let's discover the key books that one should read at least once in their lifetime.' As I started surfing Google, a list of titles appeared on my mobile screen. Among them, a particular name grabbed my attention: 'Autobiography of a Yogi' by Paramahamsa Yogananda. The title of the book resonated with me, evoking both familiarity and fascination, particularly because the motivational speaker mentioned it in his talks. Without hesitation, I decided to purchase it online.

There is a common belief that when you first start reading, you begin with ordinary books before gradually advancing to more profound ones. However, my experience defied this notion; I was fortunate to start with exceptional work. It was as if I was blessed, starting my journey with the esoteric Bhagavad Gita and then immersing myself in the Autobiography of a Yogi.

Undoubtedly, this book needs no introduction as it stands among the globally acclaimed literary works. I must share this with you, everything I encountered within its pages mirrored what I had previously only witnessed on television. Truly, discovering that such phenomena exist in reality left me utterly dumbfounded. Within the pages of this book, I encountered astonishing tales of monks and yogis wielding supernatural powers. One yogi possessed the extraordinary ability to be present in two separate locations simultaneously. Another monk exhibited the power to hypnotize wild beasts, including lions and tigers. Additionally, there was a yogi who seemingly defied gravity, effortlessly levitating in the air.

Furthermore, the text speaks of a remarkable yogi who could transform into any form at Will and could also annihilate that form at any moment. This yogi remained eternally youthful, residing in a realm where the laws of time and space function differently than on Earth. Then, within the text, I came across a mystical ashram named Gayan Ganj, somewhere in the Himalayas that is inaccessible to ordinary mortals. It is said to be inhabited by profoundly enlightened beings, such as siddhas, sages, yogis, and masters, who have achieved the zenith of spiritual realization.

This eccentric book wielded a magnetic pull, propelling me forward on the journey of self-discovery. I thirsted for deeper knowledge about mystics and their otherworldly capabilities. Enthralled by the transformative journey of Swami Paramahamsa Yogananda, I resolved with unwavering determination to seek out a Guru, to guide me along this path of spiritual awakening.

When treading paths unknown, it is prudent to seek the wisdom of those who have journeyed before. Without a doubt, the presence of a Guru is indispensable in the pursuit of self-realization, as they offer the guidance crucial for navigating uncharted territories. However, in contemporary times, locating a truly knowledgeable Guru poses a formidable challenge. In all honesty, we often lack the ability to discover a suitable Guru for ourselves; instead, the Guru tends to find us. Rather than passively awaiting the Guru's arrival, one ought to continue to move ahead while engaging in foundational practices.

While it's advantageous to encounter an external Guru. If that doesn't happen, one can turn inward and invoke the inherent Guru present within; the divine essence residing within each being can serve as a guiding light along the journey. I contemplated the possibility that if I were fortunate, I might cross paths with a divine being, whom I would humbly ask to accept me as their disciple. With this aspiration in my heart, I embarked on my quest to find my living master.

Haridwar city is renowned as a stronghold of monks and saints, teeming with countless shrines and ashrams. Nestled in the foothills of the Himalayas and graced by the sacred river Ganga, it exudes a pious ambiance. The name 'Haridwar' translates to the 'Gateway to Lord Narayana,' signifying its significance as the starting point for pilgrimages to the revered Badrinath Temple, dedicated to Lord Narayana in the north. As I found myself in this sacred realm, surrounded by countless sages, I felt compelled to explore the shrines and ashrams of Haridwar individually; with the hopeful intention of conversing with the monks, pondering the chance that my Guru might be among them, awaiting our destined encounter.

Initially, I paid a visit to the Pilot Baba Ashram, renowned in Haridwar for its impressive architecture and intricate sculptures. Upon stepping inside the ashram, I was greeted by a multitude of idols, each bearing its unique colors and forms. These included representations of various deities such as Lord Vishnu, Lord Shiva, Lord Ramachandra, Goddess Shakti, Lord Ganapati, Lord Hanuman, Lord Dattatreya, Lord Vasudeva Krishna and Arjun in his chariot, Gautama Buddha meditating under a tree, as well as depictions of our ancient sages, freedom fighters, animals, birds, and humans.

The ashram seemed to be adorned with idols at every turn, creating a serene yet vibrant ambiance. Notably, positioned at the rear was a colossal statue of Lord Shiva in a seated posture, likely one of the largest idols in Haridwar. However, the most captivating sight was the miniature zoological garden within the premises, where ostriches, swans, ducks, white rabbits, and various other animals peacefully coexisted.

As I roamed the premises, my attention was drawn to a collection of luxury cars neatly parked in the ashram's private lot. Among them was a weathered saffron-colored vintage Mercedes Benz from the 1970s or 1980s. Adjacent to the cars, a sizable private pool caught my eye. Observing these opulent possessions, a sense of bewilderment overcame me, prompting an internal inquiry: What purpose do such lavish acquisitions serve in a monk's ashram?

At that time, my perception of monks, saints, yogis, and sages was shaped by the belief that they shun material comforts and embrace a life of simplicity and solitude. After thoroughly exploring the hermitage, I sought information about Pilot Baba, the ashram's founder, at the office. To my disappointment, I learned that Baba Ji resided overseas and only visited the ashram on specific occasions, making it unlikely for me to meet him. "No matter," I reasoned inwardly. "Haridwar abounds with ashrams and saints." With that thought, I continued on my journey.

Subsequently, I proceeded to the neighboring hermitage, Om Deendayal Ashram, located just a few steps beyond Pilot Baba Ashram. This ashram presented an intriguing atmosphere, as it exuded a profound tranquility. Upon arrival, I found the main entrance open, yet there was no one present to inquire about entry. After a brief hesitation, I ventured inside and stood in the lobby, taking in my surroundings with a whole 360-degree turn. The expansive grounds of the ashram stretched out before me, adorned with numerous closed rooms. Despite the spaciousness, not a single bird could be seen within the premises. Moments later, a man dressed in a light-colored kurta-pajama and a blue Sikh turban emerged from outside.

"What brings you here, young one?" the man inquired with humility.

"I have come to meet Maharaj Ji, the chief monk," I replied, extending my greeting.

"Oh! Have you made an appointment before arriving?" he inquired further.

I shook my head in mild surprise, unaware that meeting and greeting the saints required prior appointments. After observing me for a moment, he gestured toward a row of rooms. Expressing gratitude with a bow, I proceeded in that direction. My heart fluttered with excitement; it marked my first encounter with a saint. As I approached the row, a melodious chanting of hymns in praise of Goddess Lakshmi emanated from one of the rooms. Assuming it to be Maharaj Ji, I patiently waited outside until the hymns ceased. After a couple of minutes, the singing paused, prompting me to knock on the door. A slender middle-aged man dressed in a white dhoti greeted me as he opened the door.

"I have come to see you, Maharaj Ji," I greeted him with a bow and a smile.

"Okay," the man responded, returning the grin.

"Are you Maharaj Ji?" I inquired after a brief pause, noticing his silence.

"No, young man, I am just the cook here. Maharaj Ji is in that room," he chuckled, pointing towards a nearby door.

"You were singing hymns, so I thought you must be... anyway, thank you," I acknowledged with a nod before approaching the correct door and knocking.

"Come inside," came a voice from within. Entering, I found an elderly saint with long white hair, clad only in a saffron dhoti, reclining on the bed. As he noticed me, he sat up and swung his legs over the edge. I bowed respectfully, touching his feet before standing before him with folded hands and a smile.

"What's your name and occupation?" the saint inquired after a moment.

"My name is Madhusudan, a student at Gurukul, Maharaj Ji."

"Hmm, and what brings you here?" he questioned after a brief pause.

I pleaded, gazing at him with hope-filled eyes, "I want to know the ultimate truth, Maharaj Ji. Please guide me in the right direction."

After observing me top to bottom for a moment, the saint asked, "Have you ever attended our discourses?"

I shook my head, realizing I didn't even know his name. "Have you ever listened to Pilot Baba?" the saint inquired further.

"No, Maharaj Ji," I admitted. Then he remarked casually, "Go and attend the discourses first; then you may come to see me."

With those words, he dismissed me. Disheartened, I touched his feet once more before exiting. I hadn't expected the saint to turn me away empty-handed like this. On the following day, I sought out another monk who resided in a modest hut. I had glimpsed him several times during my visits to the Daksha Temple. As I approached, I found him leisurely strolling outside his humble dwelling. With deference, I bowed and reverently touched his feet before stepping aside with folded hands. This middle-aged monk was clad simply in a pale saffron dhoti, with a substantial rosary of Rudraksha beads draped around his neck.

"What brings you here boy?" the monk asked.

"Baba, I want to know the truth."

"What truth?" he asked in a perplexed tone.

"Truth about the Self, Baba. I want to know the absolute reality."

"What do you do?" the monk inquired ahead while inhaling deeply.

"I'm a student."

"You don't belong here; where are you from and what about your family background?"

"My father owns an area of agricultural land and I belong to a small village in the western region of Utter Pradesh."

After thinking for a while, the monk uttered, "You are still young and inexperienced, my boy. Focus on your studies and don't get caught up in such matters. Trust that everything will fall into place in due time, according to God's will."

With those words, the monk retreated into his hut, and I made my way back home. Once again, I left with nothing but a sense of despair. During that moment, I didn't give much credence to the monk's words, but unknowingly, he had foretold the events to come.

A few days later, I visited Maa Anandamayi Ashram after learning about her briefly from Swami Yogananda's book. Maa Anandamayi was a mystic from the West Bengal region; she was considered by many to be a saint and a living embodiment of the divine. Upon arrival at her ashram, I found a sizable gathering. Inside, some devotees, mainly elders, were earnestly worshipping a photograph of Maa Anandamayi in a shrine. All were wearing white robes and certain rosaries around their neck. Unable to find someone suitable to converse with, I left after exploring the entire premises.

In the following weeks, I continued my quest, visiting various other hermitages, yet failing to find the answers I sought. Through encounters with different monks and saints, one realization became increasingly apparent: Not every person resembling a monk is genuinely one, nor is every inhabitant of shrines and hermitages necessarily a saint. The presence of rosaries and saffron robes does not always denote spiritual attainment.

Gradually, my preconceived notions about monks and saints began to dissipate. Nevertheless, I refused to concede defeat; my quest persisted, fueled by the hope that remained alive in my heart. Then, one day, I encountered a monk who served as the administrator of a magnificent ashram.

CHAPTER 3

SHRI YANTRA MANDIR

During that period, visiting shrines and hermitages to commune with saints and monks had become routine for me. However, over time, I ceased posing inquiries because I couldn't encounter anyone capable of guiding me along the path I sought. Either my inquiries were too straightforward, or the individuals I approached were not equipped with the answers I sought. One day while wandering, I found myself at the imposing Shri Yantra Mandir. Interestingly, it wasn't my first encounter with this shrine. I had often glimpsed it from the roadside while passing by. However, it wasn't until now that I felt compelled to step inside.

Locals had mentioned that the shrine was built using fine Rosa marble imported from overseas, adding to its allure. Yet, what truly fascinated me about this shrine was its distinctive design. Crafted in a manner that resembled the 'Maha Meru Shri Yantra' when viewed from above, it presented a mesmerizing three-dimensional projection of the Shri Yantra.

As per the Tantric scriptures, a Shri Yantra is a geometrical diagram or structure associated with Goddess Lalita Tripura Sundari, who is part of the group of goddesses renowned as the 'Ten Mahavidyas'. The esteemed tradition of Goddess Lalita Tripura Sundari is famously known as Shri Vidya. Primarily, in the practice of Shri Vidya, this Yantra serves as a tool for invoking the deity or conducting worship.

As I stepped into the shrine's premises, I encountered its main door firmly shut. Curious, I decided to explore further. To my surprise, I soon realized that what I had entered was not just a shrine but a sprawling ashram of grand proportions, resembling the estate of a wealthy individual. Taking in the impressive infrastructure, I made my way towards the far end of the hermitage, where I discovered a beautifully appointed room. In the outskirts, there were four bamboo chairs along with a table, arranged with care. Standing back a bit, I scanned the area, hoping to catch sight of someone. Eventually, my patience was rewarded when I noticed an elderly monk emerging from the rear of the room. He had a bald pate, wore weathered saffron robes, and his feet were clad in white slippers. The monk adorned himself with a lengthy rosary of Quartz crystal and a peculiar Rudraksha bead rosary. I couldn't help but marvel at the unique texture of the Rudraksha beads, unlike any I had encountered before.

"Come over boy," the monk uttered while grabbing one of the chairs placed outside.

"Namaste, Maharaj Ji!" I greeted him by touching his feet humbly and then stood beside him.

"Where are you from?"

"I live a couple of miles away from here."

"Very well! Sit with me."

The monk graciously offered me a seat, and we engaged in a casual conversation about my studies and family. After some time, I expressed my curiosity and asked him to share something about himself. The monk started briefing: I am Narayana Das Kothari, entrusted with the administration of this ashram and shrine. I am a direct disciple of Mahamandleshwar Swami Shri Vishwadevanand Puri Ji, the esteemed founder of this hermitage.

Curious to learn more, I asked him gently, "How did you become a monk?"

"I was in my teens when I left my home and came to my Guru," the monk responded taking a deep breath.

"Why did you abandon your home, Maharaj Ji?"

"As a child, I was deeply drawn to devotion, much to the disapproval of my parents. While I lacked interest in conventional studies, I found pure joy in worship and singing hymns. Thus, feeling disconnected from the expectations at home, I eventually left. Back then, I resided in our ashram in Kashi along with my Guru."

The hermitages I had visited in recent days were all vast and splendid, equipped with every conceivable amenity. This led me to ponder: What level of wealth would be necessary to construct such magnificent establishments?

With little hesitation, I posed the question to the monk, "Roughly, what would have been the construction cost of this ashram?"

"You can't even fathom the cost, my boy," the monk chuckled. He added ahead, "And don't assume that these structures were all built solely through donations. Who could afford to donate such a colossal sum? Everything you see here is the result of my Guru's endeavors. It's all thanks to his remarkable spiritual attainments. My Guru Maharaj was an exceptionally skilled yogi." He continued, "You see, young man, when Guru Maharaj transcended into the Divine after leaving his physical form, we preserved all his belongings in his private chamber. Those artefacts are not ordinary; they possess tremendous power. Our Guru Maharaj employed them during his spiritual rituals."

Upon discovering more about his Guru, I became captivated. Fueled by curiosity, I queried the monk, "Why were those artefacts locked away in the room? Why doesn't anyone, including yourself, use them now?"

"Ah!" the monk replied with a knowing smile, "those artefacts hold power beyond our comprehension. Only our Guru Maharaj possessed the wisdom and skill to harness their true potential.

After contemplating briefly, I inquired, "Could you possibly give me a glimpse of those artefacts?"

His response came swiftly and unwaveringly, as he declared, "Access to Guru Maharaj's room is strictly prohibited for anyone."

Nearly an hour elapsed before I sought permission to depart. "It's nearing the time for the evening rituals," the monk advised. "The shrine doors will soon open. I suggest you go there first, seek the blessings of the divine mother, and then depart."

I acknowledged his suggestion with a nod, offering a bow before making my way towards the shrine. The shrine exuded magnificence both externally and internally. The gleaming white marble flooring surpassed even the most elegant mirrors in its radiance. The ceiling boasted intricate architectural designs, a testament to masterful craftsmanship.

In the sacred inner chamber, an extraordinary gold and silver idol portrayed the four-handed Goddess Lalita Tripura Sundari seated above the reclining figure of Lord Shiva. Typically, I had encountered idols and images depicting Goddess Kali with Lord Shiva reclining at her feet. On either side of the Goddess idol stood small idols of Goddess Lakshmi and Saraswati. Positioned at the Goddess's feet was a roughly one-foot-sized golden Shri Yantra. Additionally, outside the inner sanctum, there were idols of Lord Ganapati and Lord Hanuman.

At that time, a few devotees were present in the shrine, engaging in worship. A young priest sang a hymn dedicated to the Goddess while circling a brass lamp in the air before Her idol. Following the worship, I made my way back home. Darkness had nearly descended by the time I arrived. After having my meal, I retired to bed. While lying down, I reflected on the events of the day, feeling profoundly blessed. Eventually, after much wandering, I encountered someone who welcomed my presence and engaged in conversation with me.

For almost a fortnight, I maintained a routine of visiting the monk after my classes. Over this period, a genuine connection blossomed between us. We often sat down for tea, engaging in conversations that delved into various aspects of spirituality and the path of monkhood. During one of our conversations, the monk recounted an incident that occurred several years ago at the shrine. He shared with me how a group of bandits attempted to rob the shrine, specifically aiming to steal the Goddess idol and Shri Yantra. However, despite their efforts, none of them were able to move the Yantra even an inch from its place. Consequently, they were forced to leave the shrine empty-handed.

Meanwhile, the monk added, "The Shri Yantra holds the unworldly power of the mother goddess. Only those with pure intentions and unwavering faith in their hearts can easily lift it. However, if one harbors deceitful motives, the Yantra becomes immovable. In this hermitage, there are young devotees who effortlessly lift the Yantra for cleaning and return it to its rightful place."

I was both astonished and exhilarated upon hearing about that remarkable event. After a brief moment, I asked with curiosity, "Maharaj Ji, what are Siddhis?"

He explained softly, "When a sincere devotee, seeker, or practitioner establishes a profound connection with a deity and merges their consciousness with it, then it is said that the practitioner has attained that particular deity. The deity bestows the Darshan (vision) upon the practitioner and grants them extraordinary powers if they so desire. These extraordinary powers are known as Siddhis." He continued, "Merely glimpsing at something is not the true essence of the Darshan. Rather the Darshan entails capturing a specific form within one's mind. Continuously gaze at the form without blinking until its image becomes magnified and draws closer to you. Persist in gazing until tears well up in your eyes. Only then will you truly experience the Darshan. The next time you visit a shrine, gaze unwaveringly at the idol of the deity and open yourself to blessings."

On an ordinary day, upon my visit to the monk, I observed that he had visitors. After introducing me to them, we sat down together and enjoyed cups of tea. During our conversation, one of the visitors inquired about a fellow monk who had resided in the ashram a few months prior. Upon hearing the monk's name, the expression on the host monk's face changed abruptly. He suddenly became visibly enraged and proceeded to verbally abuse the absent monk in front of everyone. I was taken aback, amazed to hear such offensive language from his lips. How could a monk harbor such intense wrath and feelings of inferiority toward another monk? It was difficult for me to comprehend.

Although both offensive language and sacred hymns are merely words that can be found in any dictionary or vocabulary, the emotions and sentiments attached to them set them apart from each other. The true essence of being a monk or saint isn't defined by external symbols or practices, such as wearing saffron robes and rosaries, but rather by the inner transformation that occurs through the renunciation of emotions such as anger, envy, hatred, greed, lust, addictions, and the realization of God in all beings. Genuine monkhood entails detachment at the level of the mind, recognizing that while our physical bodies are dependent on the material world for sustenance, true liberation comes from mastering our sentiments. Without cultivating gentleness and compassion, any amount of outward penance is rendered meaningless. This brings to mind an illuminating anecdote, which seems apt to share at this juncture.

Once upon a time, in a distant realm, there ruled a monarch of great honor and virtue named Namami. His name echoed far and wide, revered for his noble deeds and righteous ways. One day, King Namami embarked on a hunting expedition into the depths of the forest, accompanied by his four trusted chiefs and a band of loyal soldiers. Amidst the ancient trees and winding paths, the king caught sight of a graceful antelope drinking from a serene pond. The king approached the antelope with great care, but as he drew near, the antelope sensed his presence and promptly began to run away. Determined to pursue, King Namami gave chase, his chiefs and soldiers following in quick succession. Alas, amidst the frenzy, they lost sight of their sovereign and the path they tread in the wilderness. In their plight, the chiefs devised a strategy to divide their group and search for their lost king. As they scoured the woods, the soldiers stumbled upon a humble abode, where a needy man sat with an empty bowl in his hands.

"Hey, beggar! Did you happen to see King Namami pass through here?" asked one of the soldiers, using a disrespectful tone.

"I am blind, Sire," the needy man responded in a gentle manner. "But I haven't heard anyone's footsteps coming this way."

"Useless!" muttered the soldiers disdainfully as they continued on their way.

A short while later, the chiefs arrived at the same spot. One of them addressed the blind man, "Excuse me, have you noticed King Namami passing by here?"

"I am sorry, Sire. I cannot see, but some people did pass through here a while ago. They were also asking about King Namami," the blind man replied.

The chiefs realized that the people the blind man mentioned were likely their soldiers. Seeking to demonstrate his superiority to his companions, one of the chiefs extracted a gold coin from his possession and dropped it into the blind man's bowl, remarking, "Here you go, my friend. I am offering you this gold coin out of generosity. However, it's unfortunate that you are unable to see both the gold and the one giving it."

With a collective chuckle, the chiefs proceeded on their way. After some time had passed since their departure, King Namami finally arrived at that spot; his throat dry and longing for relief. Spotting the humble dwelling, his eyes brightened with hope. With a respectful bow, the king approached the man and pleaded, "Honorable one! Could you please provide me with some water to quench my thirst? I have lost my way in the woods, and my throat is parched."

"I humbly bow to you, King Namami. The water is inside the hut. I deeply apologize, my king, for my inability to see. You will have to retrieve it yourself," the man replied with genuine regret.

The king was astonished by his words. With a puzzled expression, he inquired, "But how do you know that I am King Namami if you cannot see anything?"

The man chuckled and said, "My lord, earlier when some individuals approached me and inquired about you, they treated me disrespectfully. From their demeanor, I deduced they belonged to a lower class. Later, another group approached, their tone carrying an air of arrogance, suggesting they were of slightly higher status. However, upon your arrival, my king, you treated me with utmost honor. Instantly, I recognized you as the king, for only a monarch of noble character would behave so graciously."

The king was deeply impressed by his discernment and generosity, and in appreciation, he bestowed upon him his diamond ring before continuing on his journey.

Let me impart one essential insight, my dear friend: Your attire, physical appearance, wealth, lifestyle, social status, or online presence will never authenticate your status as an esteemed individual. I harbor no opposition to any of these, but it's your treatment towards others and the depth of your empathy that truly defines whether you belong to the notable figure or are just another in need. Therefore, prioritize humility and compassion in your dealings with others. Speak in such a way that the listener falls for you; I can assure you, it requires no expense at all.

After that incident, a deep sorrow settled within me. Since then, I ceased reaching out to monks and saints altogether. The yearning to meet and converse with them in person vanished from my mind. A week later, I found myself at the 'Adi Shakti Maha Kali Siddha Ashram' quite by chance. While passing through there, the enchanting atmosphere and tranquility of the location compelled me to pay it a visit. However, I didn't intend to see anyone there.

Nestled by the banks of the river Ganga, this ashram boasted a picturesque setting. At its heart stood a magnificent white marble shrine dedicated to Lord Shiva, with the gentle flow of the river Ganga as its backdrop. Unlike conventional shrines, this one had open sides, inviting the tranquil ambiance of nature. Only a modest entrance adorned the sanctum sanctorum. Drawn by the serene ambiance, I found myself returning to the ashram every evening. All was transpiring in accordance with the grand design of the cosmos.

I found solace in the shrine's solitude, accompanied only by the symphony of flowing water and the gentle caress of the river-kissed breeze. Rarely did I encounter any individual amidst my visits. At the heart of the sanctum lay a phenomenal four-faced Shivalinga. Its majestic visage was carved with masculine strength, each face converging to survey the world in all directions. Seated at the shrine's center, I would align myself, my gaze naturally drawn to the frontal aspect of the Shivalinga, as if in silent communion.

Since my boyhood, I have been devoted to Lord Shiva, inspired by my father's unwavering faith in Him. Witnessing his devout worship instilled a deep reverence within me. It was during my inaugural visit to the shrine that I embraced Lord Shiva as my spiritual guide, entreating

Him for direction until I encountered my true Guru. For an extended duration, I would fix my gaze upon the Shivalinga without blinking, unknowingly practicing Tratak, a form of one-pointed meditation. At that time, I was simply seeking the Darshan of the Lord, as elucidated by the monk of the Yantra Mandir.

Nearly a week later, an extraordinary event unfolded. One evening, while seated in the shrine, my gaze fixed steadfastly upon the Shivalinga, I gradually perceived a remarkable phenomenon, the Shivalinga seemed to be smiling at me. In response, I returned the smile and continued to gaze upon it without interruption. Soon thereafter, the size of the Shivalinga began to magnify swiftly, and tears welled up in my eyes uncontrollably. Unable to withstand the overwhelming spectacle for more than a few seconds, I closed my eyes and instantly found myself engulfed in a state of profound ecstasy. It was an unearthly experience. From that moment forward, I dedicated myself to meditating upon the Shivalinga.

Upon departing from the shrine every evening, I faithfully beseeched Lord Shiva: Grant me guidance, my Lord. Have mercy upon me and lead me to the refuge of a suitable Guru.

As time elapsed, my longing to meet the Guru intensified, and I kept on beseeching Lord Shiva for guidance. Certainly, I can attest from my own experience that earnest prayers never fail to receive a response. Roughly a month later, the Lord responded to my fervent appeals.

CHAPTER 4

ODYSSEY TO THE HOMELAND OF LORD KRISHNA

For a long time, I had been eager to visit the homeland of Lord Vasudeva Krishna—Mathura and Vrindavan with my fellow mates. Mathura is renowned as the birthplace of Lord Vasudeva Krishna, and the Lord spent much of His boyhood in Vrindavan. Thus, both places are significant pilgrimage sites for Hindus. We often talked about going there, but for various reasons, we kept postponing the trip. Eventually, we set a date and made a plan to go.

However, two days before our planned departure, everyone backed out. Some had urgent work, and others faced different obstacles. I decided to adhere to the plan, considering it might be a sign from the cosmos; perhaps my Guru was waiting for me there and preferred that I come alone. I sensed that undertaking this journey solo could be essential for my spiritual growth. Through contemplation, I realized that while the Guru would offer guidance, the path ahead was mine to traverse alone. Therefore, why delay the commencement of this journey?

As the anticipated date dawned, I embarked on a train journey from Haridwar to Mathura. Departing at 06:00 A.M., the voyage stretched over eight to nine hours. Seeking to save money, I opted for a ticket in the general coach. Coming from a middle-class upbringing, my family habitually traveled in general compartments owing to their affordability, and I was unaccustomed to reserved seating on trains.

Fortunately, I secured the window seat in train, an unexpected delight during a lengthy journey in the general compartment. Since childhood, I have cherished the allure of observing the passing world through the train window. The sight of trees, plants, and verdant landscapes racing by in the opposite direction always thrilled my mind.

From my vantage point inside the train, I observed a diverse array of fellow passengers: avid newspaper readers, food enthusiasts, chain smokers, gossiping groups, avid readers, music aficionados, unsolicited advisors, boastful individuals, daydreamers, students, corporate workers, and many others. It dawned on me that perhaps a train is the only place where one can witness such a wide range of human diversity all at once.

It was the time when Facebook was gaining prominence, marking the gradual evolution of social media. While scrolling through my Facebook feed, I unexpectedly came across the name of Mr. Gopal Sharma on my phone screen. I have known Gopal Sir since my school days. He was a scientist residing in Mumbai at that time, but his ancestral village was close to my school. Our school principal shared a close association with his family, therefore, whenever Gopal Sir visited his village, he would invariably pay a visit to our school, often delivering talks on philosophy and spirituality. His words had a certain enchantment that never failed to fascinate me. I connected with Gopal Sir on Facebook after school.

When I saw Gopal Sir's name on my screen, memories of his inspiring talks came rushing back. Without a moment's hesitation, I reached out to him, sharing my quest briefly. Within an hour, Gopal Sir responded, sharing his contact number, and asked to make a call. Following that, I called him; enquired about his well-being, and then summarized everything. Gopal Sir was pleased to learn that I had spiritual inquiries at such a young age.

"Sir, do you have a spiritual Guru?" I queried directly, after a pause.

"Yes, indeed," he affirmed.

"I seek guidance," I continued, "how can one find a true Guru?"

"We do not seek out our Guru," Gopal Sir explained, "for we lack the wisdom to discern their authenticity. There exists no litmus test for verifying a true Guru. Instead, when the moment is ripe, the Guru reveals themselves to you."

"What I'm supposed to do now?" I asked ahead in a tone of uncertainty.

"If you are open to it, I could give you the contact information for my Guru. He is a magnanimous saint, and it might be worthwhile for you to have a conversation with him. He might be able to offer some guidance."

Subsequently, Gopal Sir provided me with his Guru's contact information, which I promptly saved to my phone. Around 04:00 P.M., I arrived at the Mathura station. Stepping off the train, I was greeted by scenic artwork adorning the station walls—beautiful handcrafted paintings depicting themes associated with Lord Vasudeva Krishna. The sight immediately reaffirmed that I was indeed in the homeland of the Lord.

Overwhelmed with a sense of blessing, I began to imagine various scenarios in my mind—I would touch the soil where the Lord walked, stroll along the streets where He played, and dip my hands in the sacred water of the Yamuna River where He frolicked with His companions. These thoughts enveloped me in a euphoric sense of anticipation, akin to paradise within. However, I soon recollected that reality differed from our fantasies. Swiftly emerging from my daydream, I confronted the truth of the situation.

To begin with, I visited the Janam Bhoomi, the sacred site of Lord Krishna's birth. According to the scriptures, this site was once a prison where Mother Devaki gave birth to the infant Krishna. Nowadays, the entire area is transformed into a spacious shrine dedicated to Lord Krishna and His beloved Shri Radha Rani.

At the entrance, a sculpture of Lord Krishna with Arjun seated on a chariot greeted visitors. The police officers stationed there instructed me to leave all personal belongings outside, including my mobile phone, watch, wallet, and any other gadgets. Nearby, small stores were available for devotees to deposit their belongings. After storing my items, I joined the lengthy queue for entry. Strict security measures were in place within the Janam Bhoomi premises, with photography prohibited and no cameras allowed.

A short distance from the entrance, on the right-hand side, a few stairs led to a magnificent shrine dedicated to Lord Radha-Krishna. Upon entering, I noticed numerous devotees in line for the Darshan. Some were singing hymns, others chanting the Lord's name, and many patiently waiting their turn with offerings in hand. In the sanctum sanctorum, a beautiful idol of Lord Krishna and Radha Rani was enshrined. I took my time to enjoy the Darshan and receive their blessings. There were several other idols of deities around and carvings on the pillars. The ceiling of the shrine displayed a stunning handcrafted painting of the Lord dancing with His companions.

As I explored the shrine, I observed the walls adorned with copper sheets on which the entire Bhagavad Gita was inscribed. To fully appreciate the shrine's beauty, I sat on the floor for a while. Afterward, I moved on to see the particular spot where the Lord Vasudeva Krishna took birth.

During my boyhood, I watched many television shows about the incredible life of Lord Vasudeva Krishna, depicting how the wicked King Kansa imprisoned the Lord's parents and kept them in iron chains. However, I did not realize that the prison house had been transformed centuries ago. Upon entering, I looked around, expecting to see that chamber and iron chains, but there were no remnants of the prison to be found. It was just an empty place surrounded by reddish marble walls. Then I asked curiously a priest, "Where is the actual prison house of King Kansa in which the parents were imprisoned?"

"You are standing at the spot, boy," the priest replied passing a gentle smile.

"But it doesn't look like a prison," I uttered while gazing around. "I want to see that actual prison house where the Lord took birth."

The priest laughed and said, "Son, it was right here about 4000-5000 years back. How could one sustain anything for such a long period? You won't find any remnant belonging to that era here."

That was a sensible explanation. Following that, I moved out from that site. One thing that struck me as odd was the heavy security around the Janam Bhoomi premises. Several armed military personnel were stationed throughout the premises. Curious, I asked a soldier about it; he explained, "Every day, numerous devotees visit here from all over the country and even from overseas. This site is one of the prominent religious spots in our country, which increases the potential for chaos."

After thoroughly exploring the Janam Bhoomi area, I headed towards other sites. The sun was about to set; meanwhile, I booked a room in a nearby guest house before it got dark. After settling in and placing my backpack in the room, I lay down to rest for a while. Soon after, I remembered that Gopal Sir had given me his Guru's contact number and suggested I speak with him. Without hesitation, I dialed the contact number.

"Ram Ram Saa! Who am I speaking with?" came the response in the Rajasthani dialect.

"Namaste, Maharaj Ji! This is Madhusudan Saini. I received your contact details from Mr. Gopal Sharma," I replied dearly.

"Ah! Sharma Ji. I am listening attentively, please continue," the individual uttered politely.

I once heard a tale from Swami Vivekananda's early years, whenever he encountered a monk or saint, he would pose a direct question: Have you experienced God? Remarkably, only his Guru, Shri Ramakrishna, replied in the affirmative. Inspired by this, I too posed a similar question, following in Swami Vivekananda's footsteps. I harbored the belief that if this individual were a genuine saint, he too would answer in the affirmative.

"Maharaj Ji, I have a query in my mind."

"Feel free to ask," the man answered gently.

"Have you ever encountered God?"

"Yes, I have," he responded instantly.

Indeed, his immediate affirmation bolstered my confidence. It was akin to a thirsty person asking for water and being assured that someone knew where to find it. Honestly, I hadn't anticipated such a straightforward 'Yes' as his response.

"Can you help me realize God?" I asked ahead in a hopeful tone.

"Certainly!" he responded momentarily.

"What do I have to do for that?" I asked eagerly.

"You just have to come to me, dear. I live in Pali, Rajasthan."

"Thank you so much, Maharaj Ji. I will come to see you soon," I uttered and hung up.

Upon talking to the saint, a strong feeling arose within me that I must journey to Rajasthan to meet him someday. However, the specifics of when and how to make this happen remained uncertain at that moment.

Later, I had dinner and decided to visit the renowned bank of the River Yamuna, known as Vishram Ghat. However, I was unfamiliar with the exact route to the bank and found myself searching for someone to ask for directions. My puzzled expression made it evident to anyone that I was a stranger in the area. Observing my demeanor, a man around 45-50 years old came forward and uttered, "Welcome to the birthplace of Lord Krishna, young man."

From his Tilak and long hair tied in knots, he appeared to be a Vaishnava Brahmin. Smiling, I bowed to him with folded hands. "Where have you come from?" the Brahmin asked me gladly.

"From Haridwar, Maharaj Ji," I responded pleasantly.

"Oh, that's great! Heavenly land Haridwar. Do you have any companion with you?" he asked ahead showing great affection.

"No Maharaj, I'm alone."

"I am a local Brahmin and I can accompany you on a tour of the River Yamuna, showing you five other major shrines of Mathura, including the Dwarkadhish Mandir. In return, I would ask for a mere fifty-rupee fee for my services."

I began to reflect: Truly, this is God's grace. My Lord has sent a companion for me; now, I require no one else to seek guidance. He will lead the way.

Expressing gratitude in my heart for assistance I responded to him, "Certainly, let's seal the deal."

I could easily afford the fifty-rupee fee; I was rich enough. Initially, the Brahmin directed me to a store to purchase items for offering at the shrines. Then, he led me to another store to buy flowers and a lamp for the river. Everything appeared favorable until that point. Then, the Brahmin subsequently took me to a location where a woman, apparently known to him, was seated with a small idol of a Goddess. She accepted all the offerings, marked my forehead with a yellow Tilak, and requested that I bow down to the deity and make a donation in the name of the Goddess. Realizing the deceitful tactic, I found it quite challenging to decline her request. Hence, unwillingly I contributed donations within my financial capacity. Similarly, the Brahmin escorted me to several other small shrines and encouraged me to make donations there as well.

One cannot coerce or manipulate someone into donating; it is supposed to arise from personal conviction. I have witnessed in some shrines and spiritual retreats that they emphasize visitors and devotees to contribute in the name of God, faith, welfare, livelihood, and many others. Typically, they do not directly ask for donations but employ cunning methods to make refusal difficult. How can it be considered charity if someone is compelled to do it? When you give without a sense of charitable intent, it loses its value. It becomes meaningless. Therefore, always donate thoughtfully; ensure it reaches those truly in need. Have a sense of gratitude in your heart while giving, as you are serving as a conduit for the Divine. You may not possess the means to provide for others, so consider it a blessing to be able to contribute. And if you do not feel this sense of fulfillment, it's perfectly acceptable not to donate.

In no time, I ran out of cash. Eventually, we reached Vishram Ghat. The place was bustling with devotees—some bathing in the river, others performing rituals. Countless lamps in small leaf pots floated on the water reminding me of River Ganga. Upon arrival, the Brahmin instructed me to remove my shoes aside and stand in the water, which I did. He then lit the lamp in the leaf pot and directed me to offer it to the River Yamuna. Next, he asked me to cup some water in my palm and recite a prayer for the salvation of my ancestors, which I echoed after him. Following that, the Brahmin led me in a prayer for the liberation of my biological parents and urged me to pledge to feed Brahmins and cows as a vow.

"How many Brahmins and cows do you pledge to feed in the name of liberation of your parents?" the Brahmin inquired curiously.

Everything seemed acceptable until the point of donating to the shrine and making offerings, but now this? I realized I couldn't step back because he had tapped into my emotions about my parents. When it comes to the well-being of one's family, anyone would go to great lengths if requested.

"What would be the cost per head for the feeding?" I asked, a hint of concern in my voice.

"Only five hundred rupees for one cow and a Brahmin." He added ahead confidently, "It's a small amount considering the liberation of your parents. They will surely find peace in heaven after passing away. You are performing a noble act, so don't hesitate. They would be proud of you."

However, five hundred rupees wasn't 'only' for me at that moment; it was a significant amount. But I found myself entangled in sentimentality, unable to back out. Even though I didn't want to, I murmured, "Okay, I will feed one."

"Alright. Close your eyes and repeat after me," the Brahmin began chanting a prayer, and I echoed his words. With God in my thoughts, I couldn't help but question: What kind of assistance is this, my Lord? I believed it was your grace, but he is taking advantage of me effortlessly, and I'm powerless to intervene, despite being aware.

However, the story didn't conclude there; there was more excitement awaiting me. Something unexpected unfolded ahead, leaving me entirely stunned for a moment. Following the rituals, the Brahmin instructed me to put on my shoes, and together we started to proceed towards the Dwarkadhish Mandir. Along the way, I informed him of my depleted cash situation, prompting him to guide me to a nearby ATM. In the meantime, I stated casually, "I will withdraw some cash and give you five hundred and fifty rupees, and then you can drop me off at the guest house."

Hearing this, the Brahmin raised his eyebrows and stared at me. "What are you talking about, young man? You vowed to feed eleven Brahmins and cows. You owe me five thousand five hundred and fifty rupees," he declared, making my heart sink.

"What are you saying? I said one, not eleven," I responded in shock. "I think you misunderstood, Maharaj Ji. I don't have that much money to give."

Hearing this, the Brahmin grew agitated and began shouting at me, "This is unacceptable, boy. You ought to be ashamed of yourself for cheating in such a sacred matter. By not fulfilling your vow, you are condemning yourself to the inferno. There is deceit in your heart, and God will never forgive you for this."

The Brahmin continued to rage, spewing all sorts of accusations. His words provoked me, so I retorted, "I won't end up in the inferno, but you surely will. Here, in the Lord's land, you are committing such a nefarious act against an innocent devotee. You ought to be ashamed of yourself."

While arguing, we reached the ATM. I withdrew one thousand rupees from there and politely said to the Brahmin, "Take your five hundred and fifty rupees and let me go."

Despite this, the Brahmin continued attacking me with his harsh words, "Krishna is watching you. You are impious, and He will punish you. By engaging in such scandalous deeds, you will not gain the reward of visiting this pilgrimage. You will face the consequences of your sin. Mark my words, you will never find peace in life." The Brahmin cursed me.

"Absolutely, Maharaj! Krishna is indeed watching everything and knows who is truly cunning and impious. I will face my karma, and you will face yours. Take this money if you still want it; otherwise, I'm leaving," I declared boldly.

When you are innocent, courage comes naturally. However, when you do something unethical, you feel an inner fear and hesitation; you might pretend to be brave, but deep down, you know you have been deceitful. You can't fool yourself.

The cunning Brahmin refused to take the money. As we continued accusing each other, we reached the Dwarkadhish Mandir. Inside, I had the Darshan of Lord Dwarkadhish, another name for Lord Krishna as He is the king of Dwarka city. The shrine was pretty crowded, and security guards were ensuring no one lingered too long. When I stepped outside, I saw the Brahmin gathering locals and recounting the incident. Knowing it was his territory, I sensed it wasn't the time to be brave, so I quietly slipped away into the crowd.

That day, I learned an important lesson: Not everyone who offers help is genuinely there to assist you. People often have motives, and their actions could be either mutually beneficial or detrimental to you while benefiting them.

Always keep it in your head, not everyone who approaches you is sent by God. They might make you believe they are helping you, but they could be deceiving you, just like the Brahmin tried to deceive me in the name of liberation. Liberation is not granted, even by those who proclaim themselves as God's man and are willing to do so. Allow me to present a compelling narrative that serves to clarify my perspective.

In the distant past, there existed a charming town renowned as Devakashi, where residents from diverse backgrounds led lives filled with happiness. During that period, people had great faith in rituals. The Brahmins of Devakashi were known for their meticulous conduct of ceremonies aimed at promoting familial harmony, fostering prosperity, and facilitating the liberation of ancestors. One day, a yogi arrived in the town and noticed a Brahmin conducting sophisticated rituals with a family by the riverside. Fueled by curiosity, the yogi approached them and inquired gently, "What kind of rituals are you performing here? Please explain, I would love to know."

"We are conducting after-death rituals dedicated to securing liberation for the ancestors of this family," the Brahmin declared with assurance. "During their earthly existence, they were perceived as wicked and devoid of the virtuous acts necessary for the tranquility and salvation of the being. Through this ritual, we will certainly dissolve their entire karmic burden, ensuring their inevitable ascent to higher spiritual realms."

Upon hearing this, the yogi chuckled and continued on his path. After covering some distance, the yogi encountered some more similar situations. It became evident to him that the Brahmins were entangling the innocent townsfolk in the name of liberation. The yogi felt that he needed to intervene to halt this. After contemplating for a moment, an idea struck his head.

A couple of days later, the yogi arranged a banquet and extended invitations to all the townsfolk. Without exception, every family in the town accepted the invitation and participated in the feast. As they all gathered to partake in the meal, the yogi made an announcement, "I have prepared a miraculous dessert for each of you. What makes this dessert extraordinary is that if consumed in honor of a loved one, it will magically reach their stomach."

Upon hearing this, the ordinary townsfolk were filled with wonder and began exchanging astonished looks with each other. However, the Brahmins burst into laughter and ridicule.

"How could such a thing be possible? It's absurd!" the chief Brahmin exclaimed; his tone laced with offense. "The dessert can only reach someone's stomach if they eat it themselves. You are deceiving these humble people."

All gazes were fixed on the yogi, everyone eagerly awaiting his response. "If your alleged rituals hold such power to dissolve one's karma after death, then I can certainly craft a dessert capable of traversing from the stomach of one living person to another on its own," the yogi politely stated.

Upon hearing the yogi's statement, everyone became attentive to his words. The yogi continued, "The chief Brahmin is correct; the dessert must be eaten to reach one's stomach. Similarly, one must endeavor on their own for the dissolution of their karmic account. No one else can do that for them, regardless of how skilled the individual is. If there exists evidence demonstrating that these rituals can grant liberation, kindly provide it for examination before everyone."

Everyone stood silently there. The yogi added, "Simply carry out your duties selflessly, and only then will you be liberated from the consequences of your actions. This is the only way."

With a deep understanding of the yogi's message, everyone expressed their gratitude towards him.

Feeling disheartened by the unexpected turn of events, I found myself reflecting on the sacredness of the land of the Lord. Before arriving in Mathura, I had envisioned it as a place of immense blessing for its inhabitants. Yet, I chose to release those thoughts and returned to the guest house. There, I sought solace in reading a few verses from the Bhagavad Gita. As its wisdom calmed my mind, I drifted into a peaceful sleep. The coming day was anticipated to be remarkable, as I had an itinerary to explore Vrindavan.

CHAPTER 5
AN ENCHANTING IDOL

The following morning, I got dressed neatly, ready for my visit to the appealing city of Vrindavan. Upon checking out from the guest house, I hailed a shared auto-rickshaw, as the distance from Mathura to Vrindavan could be covered in merely fifteen to twenty minutes by any motor vehicle. Inside the auto-rikshaw, I found three other young devotees around my age, all donned in traditional attire of dhoti and kurta. However, it was apparent they were not natives of the region. Moments later, one of them inquired, "Are you alone, Prabhu Ji?"

Some devotees of Lord Krishna, specifically from the Gaudiya sect often address each other as 'Prabhu Ji' out of reverence and respect. By addressing each other in this way, devotees acknowledge the divine presence within each individual.

I responded with a smile and a nod. Then another guy asked, with a hint of curiosity, "Typically, people visit here with companions for enjoyment. How do you plan to have fun alone?"

"I'm not here for amusement, Prabhu Ji," I responded with a soft grin. "These sorts of pilgrimages are not meant for entertainment. I have come solely for the Darshan of my Lord, and I believe one doesn't necessarily need a company for that."

Hearing my response, they exchanged smiles among themselves, understanding my sentiment. Along the way, we passed by a few significant shrines, including the Pagal Baba Mandir, a renowned shrine in Vrindavan. Upon reaching there, the auto-rickshaw driver kindly dropped me off at the entrance to this notable shrine. I have come across a rather intriguing tale concerning the establishment of the Pagal Baba Mandir.

As the story goes, many years ago, there lived a needy man who found himself in a financial crisis. Desperate, he sought assistance from a local landlord, who agreed to lend him money on the condition that he would repay it gradually in installments. Despite diligently making his payments on time, the cunning landlord deceived him. When the man attempted to make his final installment, the landlord falsely claimed to have received none of the previous payments. Despite the man's efforts to remind him of their agreement, the landlord remained obstinate and eventually took legal action against him. Summoned to court, the man recounted the entire ordeal before the magistrate in great detail. After hearing him, the magistrate asked, "Do you have any witness who could testify about installments?"

The poor man paused briefly before answering him, "Certainly! I have completed all the installments in the presence of Lord Banke Bihari (another form of Lord Krishna). He will vouch for it."

The magistrate requested the address of the witness, to which the man provided the location of the Banke Bihari Mandir in Vrindavan. Subsequently, the court issued a summons in the name of Lord Banke Bihari to Vrindavan. On the day of the hearing, an elderly gentleman appeared before the court and testified regarding the installments. He attested that he had been present when the man made all the payments, providing specific dates and times. He urged the magistrate to cross-reference this information with the landlord's ledger. Upon inspection, the magistrate found detailed records of all installments, corroborating the witness's testimony.

Consequently, the magistrate dismissed all the allegations against the man and imposed a fine on the landlord. After everyone had departed from the court, the magistrate approached the needy man and inquired about the elderly witness. The man graciously responded, "He was the omnipresent Lord Banke Bihari, who always stands in support of those in need."

Upon learning about Lord Banke Bihari, the magistrate remained amazed and then he renounced all his worldly possessions and settled in Vrindavan. He devoted himself entirely to worshipping the Lord, becoming deeply enamored with him to the point of losing all sense of self in the divine love. Consequently, the locals of Vrindavan began referring to him as 'Pagal Baba' (the mad saint). Following his passing, the community erected a shrine in his honor.

The shrine comprised approximately six to seven floors, each adorned with idols of numerous Hindu deities. During my visit, I discovered a peculiar belief associated with the shrine: It is believed that if one inscribes their desires on the walls of the shrine, Pagal Baba would grant them certainly.

Upon entering the shrine, I observed that every inch of the wall space was covered with lengthy sentences expressing devotees' wishes. Some had penned entire paragraphs detailing their desires. As I attempted to read a few of them closely, I couldn't help but burst into laughter. While some wishes were eccentric, the majority revolved around aspirations for government jobs and romantic endeavors. Personally, I refrained from inscribing my desires on the walls. I believe that one ought to only ask those who are unaware of their wishes. Since God is omniscient, there is no need to articulate our desires to it.

After spending approximately an hour there, I proceeded towards the ISKCON Temple. Renowned as one of the eminent shrines in Vrindavan, it wouldn't be an exaggeration to deem it a gem of the city. Shri Shrila Prabhupada, the founder of the International Society of Krishna Consciousness (ISKCON), established this shrine. As I stood at a distance from the main entrance, I noticed a lengthy queue of devotees awaiting their turn to deposit their footwear on the periphery of the shrine. Following suit, I joined the queue and placed my footwear before entering the shrine premises.

Having visited several shrines in Haridwar and Rishikesh, none quite compared to the grandeur of the ISKCON. Unlike traditional shrines, ISKCON's architecture resembled that of a lavish palace. Intricate carvings adorned the doors, walls, and windows, while the courtyard floor boasted an elegant chessboard-like pattern in black and white marble. Despite the presence of more than a hundred devotees at that moment, the premises remained impeccably clean, devoid of any trace of dust or litter.

A considerable number of devotees from abroad had also gathered there. Never before had I witnessed such a diverse congregation of foreigners in any shrine. What struck me most was their attire; instead of Western clothing, they were all adorned in our traditional garments. The women wore sarees and ghagra-cholis, while the men donned dhotis and kurtas. It seemed to exemplify a unique aspect of Bharat; we embrace everyone with our cultural customs.

Among the attendees were several young monks who had shaved their heads, leaving only a thick tuft of hair tied called Shikha, a symbolic feature of Vaishnavas. Each of them sported a 'U' shaped off-white Tilak on their foreheads, starting from the bridge of their noses and ascending in two lines. These two lines were connected with a miniature leaf shape, extending downwards towards the noses. According to Gaudiya Vaishnavas tradition, these two lines represent Lord Vasudeva Krishna's lotus feet, while the leaf-shaped design symbolizes Tulsi. They believe that the human body serves as the dwelling place of Lord Vasudeva Krishna.

In the shrine's courtyard, some devotees were seated on the ground, engrossed in playing classical musical instruments such as the Harmonium, Mridanga, and Mangiras. Their melodious chanting of 'Hare Krishna Hare Krishna Krishna Krishna Hare Hare, Hare Ram Hare Ram Ram Ram Hare Hare' echoed through the air, a practice known as 'Hari Naam Sankirtan'—the devotional activity of glorifying the Lord through the repetition of His holy name.

The enchanting music beckoned me irresistibly, compelling me to join them. Taking my place among the group, I fervently chanted along, matching their rhythm. As we continued, our collective fervor intensified, and soon we were swaying in unison, carried away by the ecstasy of our chanting. After a while, I found myself completely immersed in the chant, my eyes closed as if enveloped in a cocoon of divine bliss. All worldly thoughts vanished from my mind, leaving me unaware of my surroundings or the passage of time. My sole focus was on chanting the Lord's name. Unbeknownst to me, I had penetrated a state of profound meditation.

Some individuals believe that meditation is a deliberate act, mastered through specific techniques. However, I must dispel this misconception. Meditation is not something one does; rather, it is a state one falls into and remains in the present. It transcends mere activity—it is a state of being. To enter into meditation, primarily one must let go of the struggle to achieve it. The moment an individual relinquishes this effort, he or she naturally slips into a meditative state.

Until that moment, I was only acquainted with the conventional technique of meditation: sitting upright with crossed legs and attempting to concentrate. However, I found this approach peculiar. All the devotees participating in the Sankirtan were in a state of meditation, whether consciously aware of it or not. It mattered not their posture, hand positions, or whether their eyes were open or closed—they were entirely in meditation.

Just as there are various routes to reach a destination, there are numerous methods of meditation, each suited to different individuals. Without a Guru, the only way to discover which method suits you is through trial. Just as we try on clothes to assess their fit, similarly, we must experiment with different meditation techniques to find the one that resonates with us. Regardless of the path chosen, the destination remains the same.

Upon emerging from that state, I realized that more than an hour had passed while I sat there. Gazing around, a graceful white lady dressed in an elegant ghagra-choli caught my attention. Her ghagra was floating in the air, resembling a blooming flower as she danced joyfully beside me; completely absorbed in her movements. Nearby, an elder monk, likely one of the senior members of the shrine, sat on a couch adorned with a magnificent garland of red and white roses around his neck. I noticed his unwavering gaze fixed upon me.

As the Sankirtan came to a close, the monk approached me, performing a gesture that surpassed my wildest imagination. With deliberate gentleness, he rose from his seat, removed his rose garland, and placed it around my neck. I was utterly astonished by this unexpected act of kindness and found myself momentarily unsure of how to respond. In a gesture of gratitude, I bowed to him. In return, the monk reciprocated the gesture with folded hands before departing.

At that moment, I felt as though I was on cloud nine, interpreting the gesture as Divine's grace. Overwhelmed with joy, I began to wander blissfully through the surroundings, adorned with the fragrant rose garland. Having spent a considerable amount of time there, I decided to explore other destinations and set my sights on the Banke Bihari Mandir.

Exiting the ISKCON temple, I had barely taken a few steps when I encountered an elderly woman in need. With hands folded in respect, I bowed to her, and without waiting for her to speak, I removed the rose garland from around my neck and gently placed it over hers. Meeting her eyes, brimming with tears that she struggled to contain, I could sense her gratitude and joy. A smile graced her lips as she bestowed upon me a blessing for a happy and fulfilling life.

To me, blessings are profound expressions of love and affection that emanate from the depths of one's heart. They carry a phenomenal energy, often serving as a protective shield against adversity. Hence, I believe it is essential to seek and receive blessings, for they hold genuine power.

Later on, I continued my journey and approached the vicinity of the Banke Bihari Mandir, one of the most revered shrines in Vrindavan. There is a popular saying that a visit to Vrindavan remains incomplete without seeking the Darshan of Lord Banke Bihari, akin to visiting Haridwar but not immersing oneself in the pious waters of the River Ganga.

'Banke Bihari' is an epithet for Lord Vasudeva Krishna, worshipped in the form of a playful child. The term 'Banke' refers to the Tribhanga posture, where the Lord's body gracefully curves at three distinct points: the neck, waist, and knee. 'Bihari' signifies the 'supreme enjoyer'. Legend has it that Swami Haridas, a revered saint and great devotee of Lord Krishna, worshipped the idol of Lord Banke Bihari. It's also believed that upon his fervent appeal, Lord Krishna and Shri Radha Rani merged and manifested themselves in the form of Lord Banke Bihari.

The line to enter the shrine stretched endlessly, with heads filling every available space. Amidst the sea of devotees, I couldn't fathom the reason behind such a massive turnout. What was it about this shrine that drew such fervent devotion? Eventually, after maneuvering my way through the crowd, I finally reached the entrance. Stepping inside, it took some time before I caught a glimpse of Lord Banke Bihari.

The moment I laid eyes on the Lord, I was spellbound. Standing before me was a small, pitch-black idol adorned with an array of jewels and ornaments. Despite its distance from where I stood, the idol's exquisite silver eyes sparkled with an otherworldly brilliance. It felt as if the Lord Himself was present in that sacred space.

For a brief moment, my senses were overwhelmed, leaving me in a state of awe and reverence. Almost instinctively, after a few minutes, I found myself raising my right hand as high as I could, seeking to capture the attention of the Lord. It was akin to how we raise our hand in a crowd to signal someone we know. At that moment, I raised my hand, silently imploring the Lord to acknowledge my presence amidst the throng. I couldn't quite explain the impulse behind this action, but I felt a strong sense of connection with that phenomenal idol. My gaze remained fixed on the idol, locked onto the beautiful eyes of the Lord without wavering, despite the crowd jostling around me.

As the crowd surged, pushing and pulling, I refused to divert my gaze even for an instant. However, when the priest drew the curtain before the Lord, our silent communion was abruptly interrupted. With a sense of reverence, I lowered my hand, bowed my head in acknowledgment, and exited the shrine.

Whether you choose to believe me or not, I can attest that I have never witnessed anything as enchanting with my own eyes before. It was more than just an ordinary idol; I felt the palpable presence of the Divine within it. Seeing Lord Banke Bihari, I realized that my visit to Vrindavan had truly been blessed.

Upon leaving the shrine, I began to comprehend why devotees from far and wide were drawn to the sanctuary of Lord Banke Bihari. Tears welled up in the eyes of several devotees upon beholding the Lord, a testament to its profound impact. This was no mere lifeless statue; there was an undeniable energy emanating from it that stirred intense emotions within all who beheld it. I experienced something indescribable at that moment, a connection that transcended words.

As the day progressed into its afternoon phase, there remained a few more destinations on my itinerary. Following a meal at a nearby restaurant, I proceeded to explore further. After a brief walk, I arrived at Nidhivan, where I discovered that it was closed for the afternoon and would reopen after 04:00 P.M. With time to spare, I decided to wait nearby. Adjacent to Nidhivan was the Shahji Temple, where I chose to pass the time along with other devotees also awaiting the reopening of Nidhivan.

Suddenly, a mischievous monkey leaped down and snatched a man's eyeglasses. Before the man could react, the monkey scampered up a nearby wall and settled there. The man, understandably upset, began shouting and gesturing at the monkey, attracting the attention of bystanders.

In a surprising turn of events, a bystander produced some Frooti drinks and tossed a Tetra pack toward the monkey. Seizing the opportunity, the monkey deftly caught the pack and promptly released the eyeglasses. It was evident that the monkeys in Vrindavan were quite adept at such interactions with humans, perhaps due to regular encounters like these. The bystander, who appeared to be accustomed to such situations, charged the man thirty rupees for a ten-rupee drink pack, effectively compensating for the returned eyeglasses.

Nidhivan is a compact and dense garden filled with unusual plants and trees that are short and twisted. Since boyhood, I have been fascinated by the tales surrounding Nidhivan. According to local lore, this site is shrouded in mystery. The community believes that even today, Lord

Vasudeva Krishna and His beloved Shri Radha Rani manifest there at night to partake in Rasaleela, a divine dance or play. But that is not the only marvel; rumors abound that the trees and plants of Nidhivan transform into Gopies, beautiful female companions of the Lord, to join in the Rasaleela. No one is permitted to remain there after sunset, and even animals and birds such as monkeys, crows, pigeons, parrots, etc. hastily depart as dusk falls. Locals warn that anyone brave enough to stay in Nidhivan overnight to unravel its mystery faces the risk of losing their eyesight, suffering mental instability, and encountering a grim fate by dawn. They abstain from even glancing at the Nidivan during the night. Some nearby residents claim to hear the haunting melodies of flutes and the tinkling of anklets during the nocturnal hours coming from the site.

The entire perimeter of Nidhivan is encircled by towering walls, ensuring no unauthorized entry. To this day, the enigma of Nidhivan remains unsolved. In the vicinity stands a stunning shrine dedicated to Lord Radha-Krishna, affectionately known as Rang Mahal. Here, the priests diligently prepare beds for the Lord and adorn the surroundings with an array of decorative items such as garments, bangles, jewels, colors, and more.

Additionally, they arrange a vessel brimming with water, along with offerings of Paan and desserts. Once all preparations are completed, the shrine is securely locked at night. Upon reopening the following morning, a peculiar view is seen: the meticulously arranged items are found lie scattered about, the edible offerings are found consumed, the water level in the vessel is found to be depleted, the bed appears messed up as though someone has slept in it, and the cosmetics are found used.

Intrigued by these inexplicable occurrences, I felt compelled to explore the mysteries of Nidhivan further. Around 05:30 P.M., the gates to Nidhivan were unlocked, and devotees began to stream in one after the other. A narrow pathway, flanked by bamboo sticks and delicate sheaths, led us through the garden to Rang Mahal. Bamboo barricades lined both sides of the path, guiding visitors along the designated route and preventing stray movements.

Despite the anticipation of witnessing something unusual, I found the atmosphere rather ordinary. However, what caught my attention were the trees and plants, rumored by locals to transform into Gopis at night. The vegetation within Nidhivan exhibited remarkable characteristics. The tree trunks appeared thoroughly dried, yet adorned with lush green leaves. Some trunks were hollow, yet they thrived. The tree's texture was peculiar—they didn't stand erect, nor were they particularly tall or robust. Instead, they sported long, twisted branches, seemingly reaching out to each other in an unusual embrace.

Remarkably, we were informed that these trees required no watering, yet they had stood for millennia in their peculiar state. As with a background in botany, I found myself in awe of the flora within Nidhivan, puzzled by their unconventional growth and texture.

Upon completing my exploration of the site, I proceeded towards my next destination—a marvelous shrine renowned for its remarkable architecture, considered among the most splendid in Vrindavan. Some of you may already be familiar with the shrine I'm referring to here—the Prem Mandir. It stands as a monumental tribute to Lord Radha-Krishna and Lord Sita-Ram, crafted entirely from white Italian marble. Founded by Shri Jagatguru Kripalu Ji Maharaj, Prem Mandir showcases exquisite craftsmanship with intricately carved marble adorning every facet of the structure.

The shrine's allure was further accentuated by meticulously landscaped gardens, ornate fountains, and movable idols scattered throughout the premises. Inside, the walls were adorned with vivid paintings depicting various divine plays of Lord Krishna. Upon entering, I was greeted by a resplendent chandelier suspended from the ceiling, casting a luminous glow throughout the shrine.

On the ground floor, a captivating sky-blue idol of Lord Vasudeva Krishna and His beloved Shri Radha Rani, adorned with vibrant attire and jewels, captivated the senses. Ascending to the second floor, I encountered a striking idol of Lord Ram along with His consort Goddess Sita, further adding to the grandeur of the shrine. Overwhelmed by the opulence and splendor of the Prem Mandir, I couldn't help but marvel at its magnificence.

After spending merely an hour exploring, I made the decision to find accommodation for the night. In the meantime, while wandering around, I happened to pass by the bus stand, where I heard a familiar sound: Jaipur... Jaipur... Rajasthan.

It was the assistant bus driver calling out to passengers bound for Jaipur, Rajasthan. The mention of Rajasthan immediately brought to mind the conversation I had with Gopal Sir and his Guru. Suddenly, a compelling thought surged through my mind: Board the bus before it departed. This is your moment, seize it. Your Guru awaits you. Do not hesitate, Madhu, this is the sign.

Without further deliberation, I hurriedly boarded the bus bound for Jaipur city in Rajasthan.

CHAPTER 6

A SAINT AS FAMILY MAN

Only the Supreme can unravel the mysteries of the divine play of the Supreme. The following day, I had to return to Haridwar, and now, without any prior planning or thought, I found myself traveling to Rajasthan. It was nearly 08:00 P.M. when the bus headed toward Jaipur. While searching for a suitable seat, I noticed a monk dressed in white robes sitting alone in a corner. I chose to sit near him. His Vaishnava affiliation was evident from his Tilak, shaved head, and long Shikha. I felt fortunate to be seated next to him, thinking I might have the opportunity to learn something from him.

After a while, my stomach reminded me that I had skipped dinner in my rush. Fortunately, I had some snacks in my backpack. I took out a pack of biscuits, unwrapped it, and offered some to the monk, thinking it would be a graceful way to begin a conversation. However, he immediately declined. I politely insisted, but he firmly refused and turned his face toward the window. I couldn't perceive why, but there was an unfamiliar stillness on his face that didn't seem like serenity at all. It felt as though he wasn't feeling pleased about leaving Vrindavan.

We sat in absolute silence for a long time because I couldn't figure out how to start the conversation. Eventually, I broke the ice and inquired humbly, "Where are you heading, Prabhu Ji?"

Without looking at me, the monk murmured, "Jaipur." Although his answer made it clear that he wasn't in the mood for conversation, I was a bit persistent and decided to strive once more.

I knew some Vaishnavas lived with their families, following all the religious principles. So I asked the monk politely, "Do you reside in Jaipur with your family or consort, Prabhu Ji?"

However, the monk took offense at my question and responded angrily, "What kind of question is that? Can't you see that I am a monk? We don't have families."

Hearing his words, I realized it was best to remain silent. Well, you can't force someone into a pleasant conversation. But this question lingered in my mind: What sorrow could a monk possibly have?

I refrained from asking anything further, put on my earphones, and played some music to amuse myself. Now I just wanted the bus to reach its destination as soon as possible.

Around 01:00 A.M., the bus arrived at the Jaipur bus stand. As the driver parked the bus in a lot, a swarm of auto-rickshaw drivers surrounded us, urging passengers to use their services. Among them, a boy younger than me approached and asked, "Where do you want to go, elder brother? Come with me."

I told him I was looking for a hotel or guest house to stay in for the night. "Certainly! Please come with me. I will show you a classy room in a nearby guest house which will be in an affordable range," the boy said passionately.

"Phew! Cool then, take me there," I said with a sigh of relief. Following that, the boy whistled loudly in a distinctive manner, and within seconds, an auto-rickshaw pulled up and stopped beside me.

"Please get inside, brother. Let us take you to the guest house," the boy uttered dearly.

"I need to return here in the morning, so take me to the nearest place," I instructed the driver as I settled inside.

"Don't worry, brother. The guest house is close by, and if you'd like, we can pick you up in the morning."

"I would appreciate that. By the way, is there any place to eat nearby? I skipped dinner and I'm starving."

"Certainly! Let's head to the eatery first."

The boys took me to an eatery where I had a regular Thali consisting of two rotis, some rice, and two vegetable dishes. After the meal, the auto-rickshaw boys dropped me off at a guest house where I booked a room for the night.

After washing up, I lay down on the bed and began to reflect on the day. I was equally amazed and grateful to witness the arrangements of the Divine. Alone in a strange city, far from home, and with no one knowing where I was, I encountered no obstacles. Things were unfolding smoothly on its own; I was moving with the flow of events, like water.

As I pondered over all that had happened, I became convinced that the saint I was going to meet would indeed be my Guru. The cosmos was swiftly orchestrating everything for our meeting. That night, I couldn't sleep soundly because I was overflowing with anticipation. In just a few hours, the greatest desire of my life was about to be fulfilled. Countless thoughts and questions raced through my mind about my Guru: What will he look like? What kind of attire will he wear? What will his meditation approaches be? What techniques and rituals will he use? What is his lineage? What will his ashram look like? and several others.

I had formed a particular figure of my Guru in my head by combining all the saints, holy men, and monks I had encountered and heard about so far. The next morning, I checked out of the guest house early, expecting the auto-rickshaw boys to be waiting for me outside. However, no one showed up. I have had a quirk since boyhood—I often struggle to remember routes. To be honest, it took me four days to memorize the route from my aunt's place to the university. Although I had a smartphone, Google Maps wasn't pretty advanced at the time—and arguably, it still isn't. So, I had to reach the bus stand by asking locals for directions along the way.

Upon reaching the bus stand, I found an eatery nearby and had some breakfast, knowing I might not get a chance to eat lunch. Afterward, I called the saint I was going to meet and informed him that I had arrived at the Jaipur bus stand and was on my way. I asked for directions, and the saint instructed me to take a bus straight to Pali. He explained that after a five to six-hour journey, I would reach a small town called Jaitaran, where I was supposed to drop off from the bus and ask for directions to the residence of the 'Ramsnehi'.

They referred to themselves as Ramsnehi, which means, one who is affectionate to Ram or God.

Following his instructions, I boarded a bus from Jaipur. After passing through Kishangarh and Ajmer, and enduring a six to seven-hour journey, I finally reached Jaitaran. Stepping off the bus, I stretched to ease the pain in my back from the long ride and the lack of rest the previous night. By then, it was late afternoon. I walked out of the bus stand, searching for someone who could help me with directions. I spotted a small blacksmith's shop nearby and approached the storekeeper for help. Before he could respond, a gentleman on a motorbike nearby spoke up, "Come with me. I am going in the same direction. I will drop you off—it's a bit far from here."

'What could be better than this?' I pondered silently, expressing gratitude to the Supreme for sending him to assist me. Then, I settled onto the back of his motorbike. About ten minutes later, the gentleman dropped me off in front of a massive hardware store. I thanked him profusely and bid farewell. However, I couldn't shake off the curiosity about why he chose to drop me there. It seemed odd since I didn't need anything from a hardware store. To find out, I decided to enter the store. As I stepped inside, I noticed three men engaged in a lively conversation in their local dialect. Upon seeing me, they paused their discussion momentarily.

"Namaste Ji! I was looking for Ramsnehi's residence, and someone dropped me here. Am I at the right place?" I asked politely.

They all glanced at me from head to toe simultaneously. "Please introduce yourself," one of them uttered humbly.

"My name is Madhusudan, and I'm from Haridwar."

"From Haridwar! That's quite a distance," the man exclaimed in amazement.

"What brings you here?" another one interrupted.

"I'm here to see the saint. He called for me."

"How did you find out about the saint?" he asked ahead curiously after a brief pause.

"Gopal Sharma Sir introduced me to him," I replied with a smile. "I'm his acquaintance."

"Oh! Sharma Ji from Delhi," he confirmed.

Gopal Sir seemed to be acquainted with almost everyone there. The man then took out his mobile phone and dialed a number. "Ram Ram, Guru Saa," he greeted in the local language before continuing, "an individual named Madhusudan Saini is here and wants to meet you."

All the disciples there exchanged greetings with "Ram Ram Saa," akin to the customary 'Namaste' in Hindi. After a pause, the man ended the call and remarked, "Walk with me, Guru Saa awaits you."

Leading me through a narrow passage from the store, we entered the compound of Ramsnehi.

Before we proceed further, allow me to share an intriguing anecdote that will provide you with context for the forthcoming events. Many centuries ago, there lived a king named Bhoomiputra, known far and wide for his prowess in battle and the prosperity he brought to his kingdom. His subjects held him in the highest regard, akin to celestial beings. Despite the prosperity and adoration, the king felt a deep void in his life. He longed for gratification and inner peace. In his quest for guidance, the king sought the counsel of various self-proclaimed saints and sages, yet none could offer him the solace he sought. One day, during a festival month, the king ventured out into the bustling city to observe his subjects. As he traversed the lively market in his chariot, children were joyfully playing with firecrackers. Amidst the commotion, a mischievous boy tossed a lit firecracker under the hoofs of the king's horses. Startled by the explosion, the horses panicked and bolted, causing chaos in the crowded market. The king jumped off the chariot immediately. Meanwhile, a resentful horse inadvertently kicked a merchant in the abdomen, near his navel, causing him to collapse in agony. Witnessing the merchant's suffering, the king swiftly headed to assist him.

"Are you alright?" the king asked the merchant worried while kneeling beside him.

"I, I a...m...blessed by God's grace...," the poor merchant murmured, his voice stuttering as he ignored his physical pain.

The king discerned from the merchant's tone that he was enduring unbearable agony, yet he expressed gratitude towards God. This revelation perplexed the king deeply. He pondered over the merchant's demeanor, questioning: As the sovereign of the Earth, I possess every conceivable luxury, yet my mind is fraught with turmoil, whereas this humble merchant, despite suffering a grievous injury, remains composed. How can this paradox exist?

This contemplation stirred a sense of agitation within the king, prompting him to inquire eagerly, "How come you find gratitude towards God? You have been gravely injured due to someone else's mistake. What reason is there to express gratitude?"

"My king, it's by the grace of God that I still draw breath. Had the horse's kick landed slightly higher, there is a strong chance it would have struck me directly in the heart. Conversely, had it landed slightly lower, it would have caused grave harm to my genital region. In either case, my encounter with the god of death would have been imminent. Thus, I am indebted to God for sparing my life," the merchant responded, smiling through the pain.

The king was stunned by the merchant's words, he implored with folded hands, "Please, share your wisdom with me, O great sage! Help me cultivate this mindset in my own life. Enlighten me, I beg you, take some pity on me."

"Your Majesty, please do not make me sinful by calling me that. I am but a speck of dust; the true greatness lies elsewhere. All credit belongs to him for guiding me."

"Who is this being? Where can I find him?" the king asked eagerly, a spark of hope in his eyes.

"He is my master, Chandrachooda, an enlightened being who resides in the woods on the other side of the river. You must visit him once, my king. He will certainly bestow wisdom upon you."

King Bhoomiputra promptly ordered his commander to take the injured merchant to the royal physician for treatment and then made preparations to journey into the woods. Without prior notice, the king set out with his men, but they were unable to find a ferryman to take them across the river. As a result, the king and his men had to wade through the river on their own to reach the other side. They ventured deep into the woods in search of the master but could not locate him. Eventually, they encountered a herdsman peacefully tending his cows. The king decided to ask the herdsman about the master, but before he could speak, the herdsman greeted them, "Welcome, Your Majesty! How is the merchant faring now?" the king and his men were taken aback by the herdsman's words.

"You weren't there when it happened, and this forest is far from the city. How do you know about that incident?" the king asked, astonished.

"Because I am the one you have come so far to find, my king," the herdsman replied, laughing heartily.

The king and his men were wide-eyed in disbelief, scrutinizing the herdsman from head to toe. They could hardly believe that this simple herdsman was the enlightened master they had been seeking despite their arduous journey.

"But you are a herdsman, and you don't even look like an enlightened being," the king said, eyeing him with suspicion.

"King Bhoomiputra, with all due respect, may I ask you a question?" the herdsman asked with a tender smile.

"Hmm, go ahead," the king replied.

"Are you the ruler of such a vast empire because you are competent and mighty, or merely because you dress like a ruler or look like one?"

The king remained silent; his eyes downcast. The herdsman added, "There is a vast difference between truly being enlightened and merely appearing so. Physical appearance is just an illusion; you ought to never judge someone based on how they look. Instead, focus on what they hold in their heart."

Hearing this, King Bhoomiputra fell at the herdsman's feet and pledged himself as his disciple.

Behind the hardware store lay the ashram of the Ramsnehi. As we entered, I began to take in the surroundings. Large trees cast wide, cooling shadows, and there were several living quarters built at a distance. To my right, an isolated section housed a large building that appeared to be off-limits to outsiders. On my left stood a massive two-story hall. Much of the area was open, reminiscent of a village setting. A white seven-seater SUV car was parked under one of the trees. The ground lacked green grass, cemented pathways, or marble. There were no signs of lavish decoration inside the ashram. Everything was quite modest, perhaps because it was situated in a rural part of Rajasthan. Unlike other ashrams I had visited, there was little hustle and bustle, giving the place a distinctly different atmosphere.

We approached a room with the word 'Ram' inscribed on the door, along with a sign indicating 'Women are prohibited from entering'. The man accompanying me instructed me to wait outside for a moment. He knocked on the door and entered. A few seconds later, he emerged and invited me inside. As I entered, I saw a tall, broad-shouldered man with neatly trimmed white hair, around 60-65 years old, dressed simply in a white kurta-pajama, sitting on the bed. At first glance, I couldn't believe this was the individual I had traveled so far to meet. The saint looked ordinary, with nothing peculiar about his appearance. His room was also very usual, furnished only with a basic bed and a wardrobe. Well, I bowed to the saint, touching his feet.

"Ahh! You have arrived. How was your journey?" the saint asked warmly while blessing me.

"It was long," I replied with a touch of humor.

"Go, have some food first. I will meet you in a while," saying this, the saint signaled to the individual to take me to the dining area.

I had met, read about, and heard of several yogis, sages, saints, seers, mystics, and monks. Based on that, I had anticipated that my Guru would look like a distinguished yogi—wearing saffron robes, with a long white beard and flowing locks. However, the saint resembled none of these. He didn't appear as a yogi, sage, monk, or even a spiritual practitioner. Apart from that, I was bewildered to learn that the saint was a family man, and the premises were not merely a hermitage but his residence. He lived there with his entire family, including his wife, children, and grandchildren. He was also the owner of the large hardware store outside. The man who had escorted me from the store was his elder son. At that moment, I felt like King Bhoomiputra, scratching my head and wondering how on earth such an individual could be a spiritual master.

The man led me to the cooking area located at the back of the ashram. There, I saw three women dressed in traditional Rajasthani attire, busy with preparations. He asked one of them to bring food for me and invited me to sit on a mat spread on the ground. After a while, a woman approached with a plate in hand. It contained two vegetable dishes and millet flour rotis. It was my firsthand experience with Rajasthani food, which was quite different from what I was used to. I was accustomed to soft wheat flour rotis, but these millet rotis were rough and thick in texture, making them difficult to chew.

Nearby, a roly-poly woman, around 50-55 years old, was seated on a wooden chowki (a small table used for sitting in the village).

"Where are you from, boy?" she asked in her thick native tongue.

"From Haridwar, mother," I replied while stopping chewing the food.

"Hmm, from quite far. But who told you about this place in Rajasthan?"

"He is familiar to Sharma Ji from Delhi," the man answered this query, and then everyone cast me a familiar glance with a smile.

She then offered me another roti, but I declined, as I was content with just two. It was later revealed to me that the woman was the saint's consort. Afterward, I returned to the saint's room. I witnessed several individuals dressed in Rajasthani attire, with turbans on their heads, seated on the ground at the feet of the saint. Upon seeing me, he instructed one of his men, "Call Narayan."

A man stood up instantly and exited through a narrow door in the room, leading to the hall. "Introduce yourself, young man," the saint uttered looking at me.

I briefed him about myself and how I know Gopal Sir. Meanwhile, a differently-abled individual approached us and said, "Ram Ram Guru Saa, did you summon me?"

"Yes, Narayan. Meet him, he is Madhusudan from Haridwar. He reached here an hour ago. Please lead him to the meditation hall and embark on the journey of transformation," the saint instructed him.

Afterward, we both paid our respects to the saint with a bow and then Narayan Ji guided me to the meditation hall.

CHAPTER 7

INITIATION INTO THE LINEAGE

Narayan Ji was a slender, brown-skinned man in his mid-forties with a physical disability. He had been affected by the polio virus since his boyhood, leaving both his legs twisted and nonfunctional. As a result, he relied on his hands for mobility, wearing wooden slippers on his hands instead of his feet.

Narayan Ji guided me from the saint's room into the meditation hall. As we entered, I observed that it was a massive hall with multiple entrances. At the front of the hall, a stage displayed a large banner hanging centrally on the wall. The banner prominently featured the name 'Ram' in bold red letters within a glowing sun, which was encircled by a sky-colored ring. Along the edges of the circle, 'Ram' was inscribed in small letters. The four corners of the banner depicted images of fire, earth, moon, and water.

On the right side of the wall was a portrait of an elderly saint kneeling, identified to me as 'Sadguru Sukhram Ji Maharaj,' a revered Guru in their lineage. On the left side, a poster illustrated the locations of various mystical realms within the physical body at certain points. The remaining walls and pillars of the hall were adorned with poetic lines exalting the glory of Lord Ram, akin to the Dohe (couplets) by Saint Kabir.

Several medium-sized wooden wardrobes were affixed to the walls of the hall for storing belongings, and fine meditation mats were spread out on the floor. Upon a thorough examination of the hall, it was apparent that these people were devout worshippers of Lord Ram. However, I was slightly puzzled because I didn't see any idol, portrait, or other symbols related to Lord Ram in the entire hall, aside from His name. Curious, I asked Narayan Ji about this, and he shared something fascinating with me.

"There is no idol of the Supreme here because it transcends any specific form. The Supreme exists beyond forms, shapes, sizes, and textures. Therefore, we simply worship His name, which is 'Ram'," Narayan Ji elaborated in a graceful tone.

I struggled to comprehend his notion of a formless God. He sensed my confusion and shortly remarked, "Ah! You must be thinking of Shri Ramchandra, the king of Ayodhya. However, that is not who I am referring to. It's ironic that most people spend their lives knowing only one Ram, King Ramchandra. However, Saint Kabir Das Ji Maharaj has spoken of four different Ram. Allow me to elucidate Kabir's perspective for you:

'Ek Ram Dashrath Ka Beta,

Ek Ram Ghat-Ghat Me Baitha,

Ek Ram Ka Sakal Pasara,

Ek Ram En Sabse Nyara'

The initial Ram is the renowned monarch, Shri Ramchandra, the eldest son of King Dashrath. The second Ram is the one residing within all beings as the soul. The third Ram is the one who has brought forth everything in this infinite cosmos, while the fourth Ram surpasses the other three, transcending narration, explanation, and comprehension. We are devoted to this fourth Ram."

Until then, I was unfamiliar with these four distinct facets of Lord Ram. Prior to that moment, my knowledge was limited to Shri Ramchandra alone. Following that, initially, Narayan Ji acquainted me with their lineage, Ramsnehi; highlighting Sadguru Sukhram Ji Maharaj and Shri Darayav Ji Maharaj as the prominent saints within it. Subsequently, he instructed me by pointing towards the portrait of Sadguru Sukhram Ji Maharaj, "Move forward and prostrate before Sadguru Sukhram Ji Maharaj."

I drew nearer to the portrait and humbly offered my reverence before it. Narayan Ji interjected, "This is the proper technique: Lay flat at Guru Maharaj's feet, then perform the prostration."

Following Narayan Ji's guidance, I positioned myself flat before the portrait and performed the prostration. Thereafter, he instructed me to sit upright on a meditation mat, as it was time for Diksha (initiation). At that juncture, I anticipated the saint's arrival for the initiation, but he didn't appear. I was perplexed as to why this individual was initiating me instead of the saint; is he my Guru?

These thoughts circulated in my mind as I sat there, reflecting. "Fold your hands and close your eyes," Narayan Ji instructed and without hesitation, I followed his guidance. Following that he added, "Now repeat after me: Hail Sadguru Sukhram Ji Maharaj! Oh, compassionate saint, I seek refuge in you. Shower your grace and guide my path. From this moment onward, I surrender completely at your divine feet. Please bestow your compassion upon me, Maharaj. I wholeheartedly acknowledge you as my Guru, and henceforth, I am yours. My entire being, with all its strengths and weaknesses, is entrusted to your care. I beseech you to accept me as your disciple and lead me on this journey."

I echoed every word that Narayan Ji recited with the utmost attention. Nevertheless, these words felt hollow, devoid of personal resonance. Uttering them mechanically was a response to instruction rather than a reflection of heartfelt conviction. To be honest, I wasn't ready to embrace their lineage, particularly after learning about their concept of a formless God.

Since childhood, I have been a devotee of Lord Shiva. How could I, in an instant, surrender myself before a portrait at someone else's behest? I lacked knowledge about their beliefs, so the idea of surrender felt as alien as a lotus blooming in the sand. Being a reader of the Bhagavad Gita, I steadfastly adhered to my own beliefs.

Absolute surrender signifies the highest form of devotion, where desires, expectations, doubts, questions, and other queries dissolve entirely. It involves surrendering one's intellect thoroughly, which can be challenging for an intellectual being or a logical mind. Expecting absolute surrender from someone deeply rooted in their notions and beliefs is akin to expecting a lamp to emit darkness.

Narayan Ji rested his hand on my head, applying gentle pressure to the center of my forehead with his thumb, while whispering something softly; his words were barely audible to me. Then, he offered a prayer to his Guru, seeking blessings for my success on this exceptional odyssey.

"Now, I am bestowing upon you the 'Ram Mantra'. With your eyes closed, chant it while forming a rosary with your breath." He added, "Watch me closely and learn to synchronize the chant with each incoming and outgoing breath. The name of Ram is the mantra itself," Narayan Ji instructed, as he began chanting, Ram...Ram...Ram...with each inhalation and exhalation.

Watching him, I tried to synchronize chanting the name of Ram with my breath, but I struggled to maintain consistency. Sometimes I missed the chant while inhaling, and other times while exhaling; Narayan Ji interrupted me whenever I lost the rhythm.

After several unsuccessful attempts, I humbly addressed Narayan Ji, "I'm struggling to perform it correctly. Could you please suggest an alternative approach so that I can maintain the chant without interruptions?"

Upon my request, Narayan Ji offered guidance, "Try this: Count the chant about twenty times while inhaling, and likewise twenty times while exhaling."

Following his guidance, I restarted the chanting; this time incorporating the counting. Gradually, after a few minutes of dedicated practice, I found myself establishing a steady rhythm.

"Now, focus your concentration while chanting, and describe whatever you perceive," Narayan Ji gave direction after a while.

Following his guidance, with closed eyes, I began to concentrate on my chant. Time elapsed in such a manner, and then Narayan Ji inquired, "What are you seeing?"

"Nothing, just darkness," I responded.

"Keep chanting. It will take some time," he reassured me kindly.

"I'm finding it difficult to sit comfortably. Can I lean against the wall for a moment? My back is starting to ache from sitting upright," I asked softly.

"Absolutely not. You ought to rely solely on Ram for support. Your mind ought to be focused solely on Ram. Forget about everything else," Narayan Ji replied firmly.

With some discomfort, I resumed the chant. A few minutes later, he asked again, "What are you seeing?"

"Only darkness," I replied, still uncomfortable.

Always remember this, if your Guru or mentor treats you with excessive leniency and caters to your convenience, mark my words, that Guru is not beneficial for your spiritual growth. A true Guru challenges you at every step to grow and evolve on the path.

"Keep going, stay firm, and chant a little loud," Narayan Ji commanded after observing my discomfort.

Despite the agony in my spine and legs from maintaining the posture for so long, there was no mercy shown by Narayan Ji. Instead, he persistently directed me to chant without pause.

After a few moments, Narayan ji repeated his question, and my answer stayed the same. I couldn't grasp what he aspired me to perceive. Nevertheless, I didn't ask any questions, nor did I stop chanting.

"Okay! Now take some rest," Narayan Ji instructed a few minutes later. "We will sit again after a while. You have traveled a lot today. Go outside, make yourself comfortable."

I stepped out of the meditation hall and sighed with relief. While strolling, I thought to explore the ashram, but there wasn't much to see; the place had a homely feel. A few steps away, I noticed a Neem tree with a cemented boundary around it, typically found around giant Banyan trees. I went and sat under the tree's shade. For a couple of minutes, I scrolled through my mobile phone. When I didn't find anything engaging, I retrieved the Bhagavad Gita from my backpack and started reading it.

A while later, Narayan Ji noticed me sitting under the shades and approached. "Ah! We have an avid reader. How interesting!" he commented, noticing my reading. "What are you reading, by the way?"

"This is the Bhagavad Gita. I read it regularly," I responded pleasantly, but his reaction was not as enthusiastic as I had expected.

"Have you ever read it?" I inquired after a pause.

"No, I have never read it. Well, we have certain notable texts brimming with wisdom, written by Sadguru Sukhram Ji Maharaj and Shri Darayav Ji Maharaj himself," Narayan Ji responded smiling. "We only read those and chant the name of Ram. Our people do not delve much into philosophies."

While we were discussing these things, a young lady approached us and said, "Please come for the meal."

I assumed it was a tea break since it was only 05:00 P.M. However, when we reached the cooking area and sat on the ground, she served me a plate with rice, millet roti, and curry—a proper meal, not just snacks. Narayan Ji later explained that they didn't eat anything after sunset.

After finishing the meal, we returned to the meditation hall. The twilight gradually gave way to darkness, and everyone in the ashram began assembling in the meditation hall one by one, as it was time for evening adoration. I expected the saint to join us, but he didn't appear. Moments later, the saint's wife entered the hall and lit a lamp before Sadguru Sukhram Ji Maharaj's portrait. Subsequently, everyone began singing hymns melodiously; though they were in their local language, which I couldn't understand. While they spoke to me in Hindi, they conversed with each other in their local tongue. They sang the hymns joyfully in unison, and I stood with folded hands and closed eyes in my place.

After the adoration, everyone went to the saint's room to receive his blessings. I joined them, bowing to the saint before standing aside. The saint spoke to and blessed everyone but he didn't say a word to me. A moment later, I returned to the hall and sat next to Narayan Ji.

There was no designated sleeping area for the inhabitants; everyone slept in the hall. One by one, they retrieved their mattresses from the back of the hall and set them up on the floor. The women arranged their mattresses on the right side, and the men on the left.

Narayan Ji asked me to place my mattress next to his. I picked up two mattresses and set them side by side, one for Narayan Ji and the other for myself. As I was about to lie at my place, Narayan Ji commanded, "Chant for a while and then go to sleep."

However, I didn't feel like chanting again. It had been a long day, and now I just wanted to lie down. Nonetheless, reluctantly, I took a meditation mat and placed it near Narayan Ji's mattress, then sat down to chant. As I sat on the mat, Narayan Ji interrupted and asked me to prostrate before Sukhram Ji Maharaj before commencing the chant. As instructed, I approached the portrait, prostrated myself at his feet, and then returned to my place to chant.

Upon chanting for a while, I opened my eyes and glanced around. It was only 09:00 P.M., and almost everyone had already fallen asleep. For me, this was too early; I was accustomed to sleeping around midnight or even later. So, I closed my eyes and lay down on my mattress. As I relaxed, questions that had been lingering in my mind since I arrived started to surface: Is this the right place for me? Is this saint truly my Guru? Will chanting really lead me to experience the Divine? Why didn't the saint appear during the evening adoration? and so on.

My mind was thoroughly crowded with doubts; everything felt uncertain at that moment. Contemplating all this, I eventually drifted off to sleep.

The following morning, everyone rose promptly at 4 o'clock. Narayan Ji roused me and asked me to freshen up quickly; it felt as though I had just closed my eyes to sleep. Gradually, I rubbed my eyes and rose to my feet. Stepping outside, I noticed that darkness still blanketed everything. Following directions, I found my way to the washrooms and returned to the hall after washing up.

It was time for the morning adoration, which commenced at 05:00 A.M., just as it had the previous evening. Initially, they sang hymns in praise of Sukhram Ji Maharaj, followed by others honoring Lord Ram. After the adoration, we all had breakfast accompanied by milk. In the meantime, the saint emerged from his room and settled on a bamboo couch nearby. We gathered around him on the floor as he conversed with other disciples. In the midst of this, a question arose in my mind, so I asked, "How did you embark on your spiritual journey, Maharaj?"

"My ancestors followed this path, and my father was also initiated in the lineage of Sukhram Ji Maharaj. It is through their blessings that I find myself here today," the saint responded. He added, "Since childhood, I have been chanting the name of Ram like my father. As I grew older, I became disinterested in worldly matters and retreated into the solitude of the woods. There, I fervently chanted day and night for an extended period. Then one day, Sadguru Sukhram Ji Maharaj, out of compassion, blessed me with his divine presence.

The saint continued after a brief pause, "This body serves as a means to connect with the supreme energy, much like your mobile phone connects you with anyone on this planet. Similarly, this physical body can link you with the entire cosmos and its creator. Everything resides within you. Chant the name of Ram with love, my child. The more you chant with devotion, the sooner you will experience it. May Sadguru Sukhram Ji Maharaj bless you. Now, move to the meditation hall and chant."

I bowed at the saint's feet and made my way to the meditation hall. Narayan Ji followed, taking a seat beside me. Just as we were about to begin, my phone started ringing. It was Gopal Sir calling.

"Hello, dear Madhusudan! How's everything going? Gopal Sir inquired with enthusiasm.

"Namaste Sir! The chanting has been ongoing since yesterday," I responded.

"Guru Maharaj called me yesterday and informed me about you. I was pleased to hear that you reached there without delay," he said warmly. "Now, I am certain that you possess the dedication needed to walk this path. I admire your spirit, my boy."

Then he continued, "Don't mistake Guru Maharaj for an ordinary individual. He possesses divine grace, speaking from my own experience. Having visited numerous saints and spiritual masters in the past, I can attest that what I experienced in his presence is beyond description. I felt the presence of divine energy, and by his grace, I even had a vision of my inspiration, the great Gautam Buddha."

"That's wonderful, Sir! I will do my best and follow the instructions sincerely," I assured him.

"Show your genuine devotion at the feet of Guru Maharaj. He will surely guide your path. Prostrate before him with absolute devotion whenever you pass by him," Gopal Sir advised before hanging up.

Although Gopal Sir offered his advice earnestly, I remained unconvinced. My convictions were steadfast, and my intellect resisted the notion of surrendering to a mere unfamiliar mortal. Following that, Narayan Ji instructed, "Prostrate before Sadguru Sukhram Ji Maharaj and implore him to guide your path."

As per his guidance, I began chanting. After a few minutes, he posed the same question hopefully, yet once again, I refrained from uttering the words he longed to hear. Persistently, I continued chanting aloud, until out of the blue, I felt a sensation of constriction in my throat, as if something were choking me from within. My breath caught for a moment, and I began to struggle for air.

Narayan Ji observed keenly, placing his fingers on my throat and encouraging me to persist with the chant. "Some malevolent forces are obstructing your path. They will test you and endeavor to divert you from your journey. But do not fret; keep chanting. Ram Ji will protect you; the saints will shield you," Narayan Ji reassured, placing his warm hand on my shoulder.

After a moment, I experienced some relief, and my breathing returned to normal. Narayan Ji mentioned that such occurrences were common with certain individuals, but he assured me not to worry, as Sadguru Sukhram Ji Maharaj would shield me.

He then suggested taking a break, and we began discussing our everyday lives. I shared details about my family, studies, interests, and my visit to Vrindavan. In turn, I inquired about his story and how he came to meet the saint.

Narayan Ji recounted that when he was a teenager, the saint visited his village for a discourse. It was then that he first laid eyes on the saint and listened to his teachings. From that day forward, he began chanting the name of Ram. Several years later, when the saint revisited the village, he recognized his devotion to Lord Ram at first sight. Pleased with his dedication, the saint brought him to the ashram. Since then, Narayan Ji has resided there, nurtured by the saint as if he were the saint's own child.

Narayan Ji shared some of his life experiences with me, and upon hearing his story, I felt he was a truly compassionate soul. Despite his disability, he never harbored resentment towards God; he found peace in acceptance of his circumstances.

During lunch, the saint served the meal with his own hands, and everyone received the food offerings as blessings. Their unwavering devotion to their Guru was palpable. After lunch, I returned to the meditation hall with Narayan Ji and resumed chanting. As I chanted ceaselessly for a few minutes, I suddenly felt a strong jolt, causing my entire body to tremble uncontrollably.

In no time, Narayan Ji placed his hand on my head and his thumb on my forehead, between my eyelids. Then, he instructed me to repeat after him, "Glory to Sadguru Sukhram Ji Maharaj! Oh, compassionate divine soul! Shower your grace upon me and ward off all malevolent forces. I beseech you to protect me and guide my path. Bestow your grace upon me."

I echoed each word after him, and immediately, my body returned to its normal state. Following that incident, I felt deeply troubled. I had no understanding of what was occurring within me or why. Narayan Ji advised me to continue chanting. Meanwhile, the saint called him into his room. So, he stepped out.

Narayan Ji informed the saint about the episode that occurred while I was chanting and relayed the information, I had shared with him, including my reading of the Bhagavad Gita. After a while, the saint summoned me to his room. I entered his room and prostrated myself before him, as Gopal Sir had instructed me.

"How are you faring, my son?' the saint asked in a gentle tone.

"I can't pretend that everything is going well," I replied without hesitation, meeting his gaze.

"Listen, Madhu," the saint said, looking directly into my eyes. "I want to pave your path, but your mind is already loaded with several stuff. There is no room for anything new. Though it's praiseworthy that you engage with the Bhagavad Gita, if you are here with me, it's essential to be fully immersed—mind, heart, and soul. You need to empty your mind and heart to receive what I have to offer. Just as one cannot pour water into a pot that is already filled to the brim, you must release all your preconceived beliefs and knowledge. These are the obstacles on your path. Your intellect is limiting you, my son. Do not get caught up in mere words, receive something that is beyond words and talks. Open yourself to receive by dissolving the barriers of the mind."

I bowed before him and quietly exited the room. As I sat beneath the tree, I pondered the saint's words. There was undeniable weight in his words; deep down, I knew he was right. Yet, I hesitated to admit it.

It's not easy to let go of deeply ingrained beliefs accumulated over a lifetime. Over time, these beliefs become intertwined with our identity, making them difficult to relinquish. To abandon them feels like losing a part of ourselves. Therefore, we cling to them tightly. However, if an individual possesses the strength to let go of all assumptions and beliefs and transcend them, their life can undergo miraculous transformations.

Something akin to this occurred when I relinquished my beliefs and notions. And from that moment onward, something extraordinary began to unfold—something I had never imagined possible.

CHAPTER 8

A VISION OF DIVINE ENTITIES

After deep introspection, I turned to Lord Shiva in prayer: My Lord, I have devoted myself to you since boyhood. I firmly believe that if you have brought me here, there is a meaningful purpose behind it. At this moment, I'm uncertain of what is right or wrong, but I'm confident of one thing—you will not let me lose my way. If anything goes wrong, please guide me and make it right.

Having spoken these words to Lord Shiva, I reached a pivotal decision to relinquish all that I had accumulated in my mind—be it the knowledge from texts, scriptures, the wisdom imparted by yogis and monks, or even my deeply ingrained beliefs. Thereafter, like a fledgling bird eager to explore the vast expanse of the sky, I embraced a sense of profound freedom.

Following a relentless internal battle of conflicting thoughts and ideas, I cleared my mind, embracing the belief that I was devoid of wisdom, utterly ignorant, and knew nothing about the Supreme, creation, and the reality of Self.

Thus, I geared up myself to receive fresh insights.

Shortly thereafter, I made my way to the meditation hall and humbly implored Narayan Ji to guide me once more, starting afresh from the very beginning. He directed me to bow before Sadguru Sukhram Ji Maharaj. Approaching Sadguru Sukhram Ji Maharaj, I offered my sincere obeisance. At that moment, I acknowledged the saint as my Guru and earnestly pleaded with him to accept me as his disciple. With utmost devotion, I extolled the glory of Sadguru Sukhram Ji Maharaj, earnestly entreating him to illuminate my path on this spiritual journey.

Thereafter, I seated myself on the meditation mat, closed my eyes, and commenced chanting with mindful focus. My entire concentration was fixed on the profound dark inner space observed with closed eyes, known as Chidakasha in yogic terms. I firmly resolved to adhere strictly to the instructions, without allowing any modification or intellectual interference.

After a few minutes had passed, Narayan Ji asked with evident delight, "Is the darkness still lingering, or do you perceive any signs of light?"

From his words, it appeared that he already knew I had surmounted all the obstacles in my path. Almost immediately upon his inquiry, a beam of light emerged, dispelling the darkness of the Chidakasha.

"Yes! There is light," I replied, marveling at the sight.

"Excellent! Can you determine if it's white light?" Narayan Ji inquired ahead.

"No, it appears to be a faint golden hue," I responded.

"Keep chanting, and let me know when it transitions into white," Narayan Ji advised tenderly.

I was astonished and somewhat delighted to see that glow because it hinted at a forthcoming change in my experience. It was a sign of progress in my spiritual journey. The chanting continued deeply, and in a fleeting moment, the golden hue evolved into a sublime white radiance. "What do you see now?" Narayan Ji inquired patiently.

"A radiant white light," I responded, smiling.

The light seemed to permeate everything around me, instilling a sense of tranquility. "Excellent! Now we will begin with the throat, as it is the source of the chanting sound," Narayan Ji instructed attentively. "As Guru Saa explained to you, this physical body serves as a vessel or instrument, containing everything within. You will now journey through this body, exploring the mysterious realms and dimensions of the cosmos. Every point in our body is directly connected to the cosmos, functioning as a gateway to other worlds and dimensions. Focus your attention on your throat; here lies the gateway to the realm of Goddess Saraswati. Invoke Her presence and beseech Her to bless you, clearing away all obstacles from your path so that you may progress smoothly."

Adhering to the instructions, I began to invoke Mother Saraswati with a prayer: Hail to Mother Saraswati! Oh, the embodiment of wisdom and bestower of speech, please grace me with your blessings and guide my path. I invoke you, Goddess of Art. Please bestow your blessings upon me.

With that, I started chanting while focusing on my throat. After a long while, I began to perceive apparitions of Goddess Saraswati, resembling the idols I had seen in various shrines. "Has She appeared?" A moment later, Narayan Ji inquired.

"Yes!" my tone was cheerful. "I'm beholding Her beautiful idols."

"No," he insisted. "Entreat Her to manifest in Her true form before you. Express your desire to witness Her true essence, not just the idols. You already have encountered various representations of the Goddess thus far, but now it's time to witness Her living presence."

I followed Narayan Ji's instructions precisely, but the Goddess did not manifest in Her true form. Only Her idols appeared to be revolving around the Chidakasha. When Narayan Ji asked again, I informed him that I could only see a lovely idol of Mother Saraswati. Undeterred, he advised me to continue chanting with unwavering faith that the Goddess would reveal Herself.

After a few minutes, Narayan Ji posed his question once more, yet my response did not meet his expectations. Then, with affectionate encouragement, he suggested, "Invoke Her once again with love. Pour your heart into your words. The Goddess is infinitely compassionate; She will surely answer your call."

I recited the prayer once more with deep affection, and then after a while, my inner space was filled with a radiant light, from which emerged a resplendent Goddess seated atop a magnificent white swan. Witnessing Her presence, every fiber of my being tingled with excitement. Narayan Ji, while noticing the expression on my face, understood that the Goddess had revealed Herself.

"Has She appeared?" he asked curiously.

"Yes! She has indeed appeared," I responded in an enthusiastic tone.

"Bow down to Her lotus feet and seek Her blessings."

I bowed earnestly before the Goddess, and She responded with a smile. Upon Narayan Ji's request to describe Her appearance, I began to detail Her majestic presence: She sits gracefully upon a lavishly adorned, massive white swan adorned with a silver pearl necklace around its elegant neck. Adorning Her head is an impressive crown adorned with glistening gems. Her long, flowing black hair cascades freely down Her back. Between Her wide eyebrows lies a crimson dot, and an intricate design of white sandalwood paste adorns Her forehead. Her eyes, large and captivating, are accentuated by dark kohl, resembling the darkness of a moonless night. A captivating long nose ring, adorned with a sparkling gemstone, graces Her nose. Her face emanates a divine radiance. Adorning Her slender neck are exquisite jewels, each embedded with an array of precious gems. Golden earrings, adorned with intricate designs, dangle from Her ears. Her wrists are adorned with dazzling bangles, and She wears elegant white robes adorned with golden motifs, complemented by an ornate golden waist chain. On one hand, She holds a sacred codex, while on the other, She holds a quartz rosary. Resting in Her lap is a Veena, a musical instrument. She appears resplendent, exuding a divine glow that envelops Her entire being.

Never before had I encountered such a graceful woman in all my years. Not even a hundred moons combined could rival Her beauty. "Marvelous! Now, implore Her for blessings to guide your path forward," Narayan Ji directed cheerfully.

I earnestly sought the Goddess's blessings, but She continued to smile at me, and I found myself simply gazing at Her enchanting form with delight. After a few minutes, Narayan Ji inquired, "Has She blessed you?"

"No, not yet," I responded pleasantly, "She is merely smiling at me."

"That's good, but ask Her for blessings," he insisted.

Following his instruction, I appealed to the Goddess once more for blessings to proceed, yet She remained unresponsive, continuing to smile at me pleasantly.

"She isn't responding to my plea, Narayan Ji," I informed him gently.

"Fine! Ask Her if She is pleased with you or not," he suggested ahead.

I asked the Goddess if She was pleased with me, to which She nodded. I briefed about this to Narayan Ji.

"Now, inform Her that you will persist in beseeching until She bestows her blessings upon you," Narayan Ji suggested.

I followed his advice and continued my entreaties. Amidst it all, the chanting intensified. After a few moments, the Goddess raised Her hand in a gesture of blessing, and then She vanished.

"The Goddess extended Her hand in a blessing gesture before disappearing into the light," I recounted to Narayan Ji, elated.

"Excellent! Now, proceed forward and shift your focus from your throat to your heart. Here lies the gateway to the abode of Lord Shiva. Invoke Him fervently, my son," he instructed politely.

With the departure of the Goddess, darkness once again enveloped the Chidakasha. Since that moment, something had shifted within me. I now experienced an unusual sense of euphoria, a distinct transformation coursing through my entire being.

Following that, I began to invoke Lord Shiva while concentrating on my heart. After a couple of minutes, Narayan Ji inquired, "What do you see now?"

"Just darkness," I whispered softly while continuing my chanting.

"Keep chanting mindfully," he directed.

When nothing appeared in the field of Chidakasha for a long time, Narayan Ji then directed me to join him in reciting a prayer: Hail to Lord Shiva! Oh, God of gods, the formidable destroyer, the supreme yogi, and the bestower of blessings, I invoke you. Please bestow your grace upon me and guide my path.

I joined him in reciting the prayer earnestly, my heart filled with the unwavering belief that Lord Shiva would manifest before me; since childhood, I have remained steadfast in my devotion to Him. I continued my chanting without pause, imploring the Lord repeatedly for His blessings.

Suddenly, a blue dot materialized before me, rapidly evolving into a brilliant blue light that engulfed the darkness of the Chidakasha. And then, right before my eyes, emerged a magnificent figure—it was none other than Lord Shiva Himself, accompanied by His divine consort, Mother Parvati. Drenched in the divine presence, I felt as if I, akin to a blind being, had at last glimpsed the radiant sun.

"What's occurring?" Narayan Ji asked with curiosity.

"Lord Shiva has arrived! He is here!" I exclaimed eagerly in joy.

Before me sat a towering, mighty, and captivating figure with a long knot of hair on His head. The knot was secured with a gold ornament depicting a hooded serpent and a clear crescent moon. The rest of His well-groomed, dense dark hair flowed over His broad shoulders and down His back. His complexion was as fair as the snow on the Himalayas. He bore a large Tripund, three horizontal gleaming lines adorning both His forehead and His bulging biceps. His ocean-blue eyes exuded an otherworldly aura, while a giant black hooded serpent as a necklace adorned His neck, contrasting against His fair skin. Large, circular gold earrings adorned His ears, and His broad chest was adorned with various Rudraksha rosaries of varying textures and lengths. Black beads and Rudraksha adorned His biceps and wrists. In His right hand, He held a colossal golden Trident, with a giant Damru (two-sided drum) bound to it. He wore only a thick tiger skin around His waist, with a metal bangle adorning His right ankle. His bewitching presence captivated all who beheld Him, leaving them entranced by His unparalleled charm.

Truly, there is none like Him in all three worlds. This specific manifestation of Lord Shiva is also revered as Shankar Nath or Suyambhu/Shambhu Nath. Beside Him stood Goddess Parvati, the sovereign of all creation, bedecked in a resplendent golden crown and adorned with countless precious ornaments. Her luxuriant, slightly curled hair cascaded freely down Her back, reminiscent of a peacock displaying its feathers. A prominent red dot adorned the center of Her eyebrows. Clad in robes of red and white, She exuded a remarkable grace and elegance. A captivating aura surrounded the form of the Goddess.

"Is He solitary?" Narayan Ji inquired.

"No, Mother Parvati is accompanying Him," I responded with delight.

"Show respect to both of them by bowing down, and inquire if they are pleased with you," he directed further.

With utmost reverence, I bowed before Lord Shiva and Mother Parvati, expressing my gratitude, and uttered, "My Lord, I'm honored by your presence. I wish to know, are you pleased with me?"

In response, Lord Shiva smiled and nodded. His enchanting grin enveloped me in a comforting embrace.

"Did He acknowledge you?" Narayan Ji inquired.

"Yes! The Lord is pleased with me."

"Did He communicate with you?"

"No, He simply nodded."

"Alright! Now seek their blessings," Narayan Ji instructed ahead.

I beseeched the Lord and the Goddess to bless me and guide my journey forward. Then, Lord Shiva exceptionally communicated with me; though He was smiling and remained silent, His voice echoed loudly and distinctly in my head: Ram awaits you, my son. Proceed onward, for my blessings will forever accompany you.

With His profound, resonant voice, the Lord uttered these words before they both disappeared, smiling. At that moment, the profound voice of Lord Shiva became etched in my subconscious, and His warm words remain vivid in my memory, even today.

Well, certain experiences surpass the boundaries of language, making them challenging to convey and describe entirely. Nonetheless, I will make every effort to express each nuanced detail as accurately as possible.

Following that, I informed Narayan Ji that Lord Shiva and Mother Parvati had vanished after blessing me. He then advised me to take some rest and stepped outside. Upon opening my eyes, I was amazed to realize that I had been sitting there chanting for more than a couple of hours.

Surprisingly, I felt neither tired nor uncomfortable. While chanting, my mind had been devoid of any thoughts. However, upon reflecting on the events afterward, I couldn't help but feel a bit skeptical: Was everything I had witnessed and experienced thus far real? Did my Lord truly speak to me? Is this all happening for real, or am I hallucinating? and countless other questions raced through my mind, leaving me mystified.

I longed to convince myself that everything was real, yet I couldn't shake off the feeling of uncertainty. Despite the smooth flow of events, it almost felt as if I were caught in a daydream. Truth be told, I felt a mixture of delight and mild perplexity, questioning whether all of this was my own fantasy or perhaps a delusion.

Now it was mealtime, and we congregated outside the cooking area. While everyone enjoyed their meals at a leisurely pace, my thoughts continued to linger on the events that had transpired. Later, all the devotees assembled in the meditation hall for the evening rituals. Narayan Ji handed me a book containing hymns written in Hindi. As I read from the book, I recited the hymns along with everyone else in the hall. Following the worship, we returned to our seats to resume chanting. At that moment, a yearning emerged within me for more of such mystical experiences.

"Now, close your eyes and begin chanting while focusing on your navel. Here lies the gateway to the realm of Lord Lakshmi-Narayana. My son, it's time to invoke them and seek their blessings," Narayan Ji directed concisely.

Following his guidance, I commenced invoking Lord Narayana while concentrating on my navel area. After a few minutes, as my concentration and chanting intensified, I witnessed a golden glow. In no time, I found myself engulfed by golden water. As far as my eyes could discern, there was nothing but water, with towering waves rising endlessly, resembling an eternal ocean.

"What do you perceive, Madhu?" Narayan Ji inquired gently.

"I see the golden ocean all around me. What is this place?" I asked, feeling bewildered.

"You have entered the realm of Lord Narayana, and the ocean you are witnessing is known as Sheer Sagar," he explained dearly.

I beseeched Lord Narayana to manifest and bestow His blessings upon me. After a while, the ocean became serene and a massive, multi-hooded golden serpent appeared out of it, coiled around a bed upon which Lord Narayana lay, with Goddess Lakshmi seated at His feet, attending to Him.

The Lord was deeply immersed in His Yoga Nidra (a super-conscious state), with one hand placed beneath His head. He had a majestic presence, adorned with a regal golden crown embellished with rare gemstones. His long, curly brown hair cascaded over His shoulders, and a distinct white and red Tilak adorned His forehead in a 'U' shape. His closed eyes resembled lotus petals and His skin emanated a subtle bluish glow. His stature appeared tall and lean, and His enchanting smile and captivating face seemed to hypnotize me. Strands of precious pearls adorned His neck, while small, fiery gems adorned His golden earrings. Delicate gold bracelets and armlets, encrusted with valuable, multi-colored gems, adorned His wrists and biceps. The Lord wore a vibrant yellow dhoti, fastened with a golden waist belt embedded with diamonds. A radiant Chakra spun gracefully on the first finger of His left hand, while His right hand held an exceptional white conch adorned with exquisite pearls.

Beside Him lay a spacious golden mace adorned with rubies.

The Goddess seated at His feet radiated the aura of an empress of the cosmos. A magnificent golden crown, embedded with glittering, colorful precious stones, graced Her head. Her long, curly, shiny black hair flowed freely. Her wide eyebrows were adorned with intricate designs of red and white Kumkum, and a round red and yellow dot adorned Her forehead. Her eyes, graceful and captivating, shone like a lightning lamp, and Her beauty was truly mesmerizing. She wore a large round Nath (nose pin) on Her nose, and heavy gold earrings dangled just above Her shoulders. Her neck and arms were adorned with exquisitely designed jewels that perfectly complemented Her red and yellow robes. Her face shone with a radiant glow as if the sun itself had drawn its brilliance from Her.

"Did Lord Narayana appear with Mother Lakshmi?" Narayan Ji eagerly inquired.

"Yes! I'm gazing at their divine forms. They look utterly entrancing, Narayan Ji," I replied in a seductive tone.

Narayan Ji chuckled, then instructed me to bow at their feet and seek their blessings. I bowed with dedication and implored them to bless me. However, I received no response.

"Did they respond?" Narayan Ji asked after a while.

"No, the Lord is lying with His eyes closed, and Mother Lakshmi is just smiling at me."

"No problem! Ask the Goddess for help. She will awaken the Lord," he suggested.

Then I implored the Mother for help, and after a moment, She closed Her eyes and reopened them alongside Lord Narayana. The Lord gazed at me and smiled. I bowed to them once more, and they raised their hands together to bless me. Instantly, all the visions vanished, and darkness surrounded me again. I relayed this to Narayan Ji, who then provided further instructions pleasantly.

"Now move ahead. It's time to visit the abode of Brahma Ji. Focus on your genital organ and sincerely chant the name of Ram," Narayan Ji instructed me warmly.

I began concentrating on my genital organ while chanting fervently. After a few minutes, the darkness within me was dispelled by a sudden, intense illumination, as if a thousand suns had risen in the sky simultaneously.

"What do you see now?" Narayan Ji asked.

"It's a place filled with intense luminosity!" I replied delightfully.

"Hmm...Lovingly invoke Lord Brahma," Narayan Ji instructed next.

As I began invoking Brahma Ji, a few minutes later, a huge four-faced figure emerged from the radiant light before me. He was seated on a giant pink lotus in Lalitasana mudra, His eyes closed. Though His long curly hair and beard glinted with silver, He appeared ageless. His face shone with a marvelous glint, and He looked exceptional. Each of His four heads was crowned with long, spectacular crowns, and a beautiful Tilak resembling a Tripund adorned the middle of His forehead. Magnificent gem rosaries hung around His neck, and thin golden armlets encircled His biceps. Heavy antique bracelets studded with deflagration stones adorned His arms. In His four hands, He held manuscripts, a rosary of white pearls, a large golden pot, and a fresh, bright pink lotus. He wore a pink fabric draped over His shoulder and a white dhoti tied at His waist, secured with a thick golden waist belt featuring a large round buckle.

I bowed to Brahma Ji with devotion and requested His blessings. Leisurely, He opened His eyes and, with a lovely grin, raised His hand. "Proceed, my son. My blessings are with you," His voice echoed in my head, and then He vanished.

Narayan Ji was elated when I told him about it. "Wonderful! Now focus on your rectum; it's the portal that will lead you to the abode of Lord Ganesh. Continue chanting with affection," Narayan Ji commanded.

I began to invoke Lord Ganesh, chanting while concentrating on my rectum. Soon, I had a vision of an immense figure seated on a grand, spacious throne. His appearance was otherworldly, with a majestic crown atop His large head and a well-rounded body adorned with valuable ornaments. Large, round gold earrings hung from His wide ears. His forehead bore a white Tripund with a red, glinting dot in the center. A long, wide red fabric was wrapped around His left wrist, covering both His shoulders and back. He wore a pink dhoti with a heavy gold waist belt embedded with numerous gems. Pots filled with diamonds and jewels surrounded His feet. In His left hand, He held a plate of Laddoos (sweets).

Despite having a limb resembling an elephant's trunk on His face, the lord did not appear like an entity with an elephant's face. His appearance was bizarre yet phenomenal.

"What do you see?" Narayan Ji inquired.

"I'm witnessing the presence of Lord Ganesh. He is seated on His throne, surrounded by numerous gems and jewels placed at His feet," I responded.

"Hehehe...Bow down at His feet and seek His blessings," he chuckled, giving instructions.

I paid my respects to Lord Ganesh and humbly requested His blessings to guide my path. You wouldn't believe it, but He bestowed upon me a Laddoo as His blessing before disappearing. Gratefully, I accepted it, honoring His gesture by touching it to my forehead.

"Why the big smile? What's happening there?" Narayan Ji asked curiously.

"Narayan Ji, Ganesh Ji blessed me with a Laddoo," I replied, filled with bliss.

"Marvelous! I have never before witnessed a deity offering their own possessions as blessings to the devotees.

Truly incredible!" he uttered in wonder. "Now, you ought to take some rest. We will continue our journey tomorrow. I can sense your excitement, but patience is key. There is still much to do. Tomorrow, you will encounter more mystical entities, including four infernos and twenty-one heavens."

After paying my respects to Sukhram Ji Maharaj, I took a stroll down the corridor. The words of Lord Shiva continued to resonate in my mind.

Typically, when something miraculous happens unexpectedly, it's difficult to keep it to oneself for long. We feel a surge of excitement and an intense urge to share it with our close ones. Likewise, I was overwhelmed with the desire to confide in someone about my uncanny experiences.

Without much thought about her potential reaction, I dialed Priyanshi, my close friend residing in New Delhi. I shared a brief overview of everything with her. However, she didn't believe me, which was evident from her response. Understanding her skepticism, I assured her that I would visit her soon and provide evidence to support my claims.

Returning to the hall, I laid down on my bed, contemplating the events Narayan Ji had mentioned. However, I couldn't recall when I eventually drifted off to deep sleep.

CHAPTER 9

MYSTERIOUS REALM IN THE COSMOS

The next morning, I woke up early feeling remarkably energized, as if decades of fatigue had lifted. Quickly, I tidied my bed and headed to attend to my morning rituals of bathing and relieving myself. Only a few individuals attended the morning prayers that day. Following the prayers, we enjoyed our delicious breakfast.

Guru Maharaj (the saint) was also present there, basking in the sun from a chair a short distance away. After finishing my meal, I approached him and respectfully paid my obeisance.

"What's the mood today, young one?" Guru Maharaj glanced at me, a playful twinkle in his eye.

"It's all thanks to your grace, Guru Maharaj," I responded with a respectful nod.

Guru Maharaj had long been aware of my doubts about him and his approaches. However, he left it to the Divine to address this.

"Keep chanting the name of Ram with sincerity, my son. May Lord Ram and Sukhram Ji Maharaj bestow their blessings upon you," he blessed me before heading back to his room.

After a while, I returned to the meditation hall with Narayan Ji. My mind brimmed with anticipation for the events ahead. Following his guidance, I paid my respects to Sadguru Sukhram Ji Maharaj and took my seat for chanting. True to routine, I started to chant mindfully as instructed.

After a few minutes, Narayan Ji offered further guidance, "Now, we will journey through your spine and explore other dimensions." He added ahead, "Focus your concentration at the base of your spine. We will progress from the bottom to the apex step by step."

I acknowledged his instructions and focused on the base of my spine while continuing to chant the name of Ram. Moments passed, and abruptly I found myself in a world engulfed in evil darkness, with red-hot magma surging through vast breaches in the land. Everywhere I looked, trees were ablaze, and there was no sign of life. Then, a horrifying sight unfolded before me: countless beings crawled on the ground, succumbing to the searing heat of the magma. Some, in unbearable agony, plunged into the fiery chasms. Their anguished howl pierced my ears, yet my mind remained serene as I observed everything with calm detachment.

I informed Narayan Ji of what I had witnessed, and he elucidated, "That is the first netherworld. All these beings are experiencing the consequences of their sins." He continued, "Do not let yourself be swayed by these sights. Press on and continue chanting."

Continuing my conscious chanting, I soon found myself in another netherworld. Despite the sun being in the sky, its rays were obscured by extensive, dark clouds. The land below was barren and desolate, where an array of beings were bound naked to towering stone pillars. Weird insects and creatures roamed freely, feasting on their flesh. Some creatures gouged out the eyes of those helpless beings, while others gnawed at their toes. Bloodsuckers drained their life force, and yet more creatures tore at their intestines. The air was filled with the agonized screams of the tortured, while many lay unconscious, their bodies ravaged and oozing dark, blackened blood. The experience was undeniably horrific and repugnant.

Continuing forward, I encountered the third netherworld where thousands of demonic creatures subjected beings to torment. They ruthlessly severed limbs by binding them to red-hot pillars, stands, and guillotines. Some beings endured constant beatings with sharp weapons, while others were subjected to skin-scratching by creatures with fangs and claws. Helpless and defenseless, the beings writhed in agony, their anguished cries echoing from all directions. I relayed what I witnessed to Narayan Ji, who instructed me to persist in chanting without allowing myself to be disturbed by these terrifying sights.

Later on, moving ahead suddenly I encountered something strikingly different from any other things I had previously seen in the three netherworlds. A formidable dark castle stood beneath a massive blood-red full moon in the sky. Menacing clouds rumbled ominously, casting a quite dread-inducing atmosphere over the weather.

"Where do you find yourself now?" Narayan Ji inquired after a while.

"I'm not certain. I see a dark castle ahead."

"Ah! I know where you are. You have reached the domain of Lord Kaalbhairav, the fierce sovereign of the netherworlds," Narayan Ji explained. "Proceed forward and enter the castle. There you will encounter Lord Kaalbhairav; seek His blessings."

As I drew nearer to the castle, the sound of thundering laughter and chaotic screams filled the air. Slowly, I ventured through a colossal metal gate, guarded by two towering, armed beings with dog-like heads. Despite passing by them, it seemed they remained oblivious to my presence, showing no change in their vigilant stance. Inside, I witnessed numerous undressed beings seated in rows on the ground, while dog-headed figures stood nearby, fastening heavy metal chains around them. The bodies of all these beings looked utterly worn down as if their vitality had been drained away.

At the forefront of the castle, a fearsome, dark-hued entity sat upon a massive throne crafted from skulls and bones. His hair, some locks tied atop His head while others hung wildly, framed a visage with a forehead smeared in red, adorned with a white Tripund marking. His big eyes blazed as if smoldering embers rested within them. A long black mustache graced His face, while a garland of human skulls draped His neck. Rudraksha beads adorned His robust biceps and wrists, and besides the hide of a wild beast, He wore no garments. Glowing golden bangles adorned His ankles. In His right hand, He wielded a whip embedded with blades, spinning it menacingly through the air and striking the beings like a tyrannical ruler upon His throne.

After a while, Narayan Ji spoke up, "Keep narrating whatever you witness."

So, I began recounting every detail, following his instructions to approach Lord Kaalbhairav and seek His blessings. As I drew near, the Lord looked upon me with a horrifying laugh. I bowed at His feet, and He graciously offered me a seat.

"You need not fear, great being," Lord Kaalbhairav's words echoed in my head with a sinister chuckle.

Thereafter, I explained my purpose for coming and implored His blessings. The Lord smiled and then raised His hand in a gesture of blessing. Later, Narayan Ji informed me that Lord Kaalbhairav punishes Tantrics, occult practitioners, necromancers, and exorcists who misuse their spiritual powers or Siddhi for evil deeds.

Those punished by Lord Kaalbhairav were Tantra practitioners who had tortured innocent beings and squandered their spiritual achievements by becoming entangled in the material world.

After a brief pause, Narayan Ji uttered, "Remember, whatever the human mind can conceive or imagine, it exists somewhere in this cosmos. We cannot conceive of things that do not exist."

Saying that he advised me to take a break. I opened my eyes, bowed to Sadguru Sukhram Ji Maharaj, and left the hall. My mind was burdened with thoughts of the beings in the netherworld. I had listened to numerous tales of heaven and hell from the elders, yet I had dismissed them as mere fabrications—how could such things possibly be real? However, that day, I witnessed those soul-stirring phenomena firsthand. My goodness! No one ought to ever have to endure such experiences, not even in the afterlife.

Then I was summoned for the midday meal, which I consumed swiftly before returning alone to the meditation hall. My eagerness to delve deeper into metaphysical experiences drove me to proceed without waiting for Narayan Ji. After bowing at the feet of Sadguru Sukhram Ji Maharaj, I settled into my spot and began chanting.

A few minutes later, I focused my attention on the middle segment of my spine, as of now I have grasped the process to some extent. As time passed, what unfolded before me was thoroughly unprecedented, surpassing the bounds of my perception.

The moment I focused intently on a specific point in the middle of my spine, I suddenly found myself entering the realm of celestial beings. Above the white clouds, I beheld ethereal creatures with expansive wings gracefully soaring. Their foreheads emanated a golden radiance, causing their rapid descent from the heavens to resemble stars falling from the sky. A luminous spherical object hovered above, casting an abundance of light that illuminated the world, though it bore no resemblance to the sun. This illumination imbued the sky with a subtle golden-yellow hue.

My senses were ensnared by the breathtaking sight of countless towering structures ascending majestically into the sky, surrounded by breathtaking lush green mountains of peculiar texture, where several rainbows cascaded like waterfalls. Towering trees loaded with leaves of varying colors adorned the landscape, while vast expanses of land were blanketed in red and mandarin vegetation.

Subsequently, I ventured forward and encountered another captivating realm where colossal planetary bodies filled the sky, replacing the familiar sun, moon, and stars. The inhabitants of this world were immensely advanced in every aspect compared to humans. Clad in suits crafted from peculiar luminous fiber, their technological prowess was astounding. A unique and powerful energy source infused vitality into every aspect, making everything operational. This energy seemed the driving force behind the seamless functioning of all systems, imbuing them with life and efficiency. It was as though this singular source orchestrated a symphony of motion and activity, ensuring everything worked in perfect harmony.

Moving further, I penetrated a realm overflowing with opulence. Fountains spouted forth colorful gems and precious stones alongside water, while large vessels brimmed with an array of diamonds, pearls, rubies, emeralds, sapphires, amethysts, and other treasures. Crystal-clear streams flowed; their banks adorned with glittering pearls akin to sand. In one corner of this world, I beheld mountains laden with gold, quartz, and moonstone.

As I beheld these wonders, a poignant realization dawned on me: While humans spend their lives yearning for such treasures, here they were mere grains of sand.

Satiated with these sights, I then entered a peculiar realm where every aspect, animate or inanimate, gleamed in pristine white. From the beings themselves, clothed head to toe in white, to their palace and the surrounding vegetation, all seemed to have emerged from the snow.

As I journeyed through that realm, a few minutes later, I found myself in a land where fairy-like entities flourished. These entities were extraordinarily entrancing, their appearances mesmerizing and enchanting, exuding an otherworldly allure that left me in awe. Their ethereal beauty and graceful presence made the entire landscape seem like a scene from a dream, vivid and surreal.

Moving on, I encountered a world devoid of land, where clouds served as the floating foundation for plants, trees, and creatures alike. In another dimension, a heavenly realm existed where trees, plants, stones, water, and mountains could communicate, all imbued with life. Furthermore, I encountered several enigmatic phenomena in other realms defying verbal description, such as an inverted world where the sky lay below. I find it challenging to fully describe these experiences in words.

Altogether, I was reaching the zenith of delight as I beheld these extraordinary visions. Suddenly, Narayan Ji interjected, "You are performing this alone?"

I opened my eyes and affectionately replied, "Yes, Narayan Ji and you won't believe what I have witnessed."

I proceeded to share with him the remarkable visuals I had encountered. Narayan Ji listened intently, a grin spreading across his face, clearly amused by the mind-bending experiences I was narrating.

"You must exercise patience, my dear. Rushing ahead isn't the way. You ought to progress along the path gradually, following the guidance step by step," Narayan Ji advised dearly. "Having traversed through all the heavens, it's now time to approach Dharmaraj. Keep chanting and focus on the crown of your spine. From there, you will penetrate the realm of Dharmaraj."

Meanwhile, Narayan Ji briefed me that Dharmaraj meticulously maintained the karmic records of every individual, tallying their actions over a lifetime, and then directed them to their appropriate destinations to reap the consequences of their deeds. Following his guidance, I began focusing on the crown of my spine. After a short while, I witnessed a phenomenal palace surrounded by countless beings queued outside. A while later, Narayan Ji inquired, "What do you see?"

"There is a palace," I responded, "outside of which countless beings are standing in a long queue.

He then directed me to move ahead and approach Dharmaraj to seek his blessings. Entering the palace, I beheld towering statues of deities on the pillars and numerous armed celestial beings standing guard, facing each other. Dharmaraj sat on a grand throne adorned with a giant crown and various ornaments, holding a massive mace in his hand. His forehead bore a red and white Tripund, and he possessed a slightly dusky complexion with a large curved mustache. An assistant seated beside him held a lengthy booklet.

Upon noticing my arrival, Dharmaraj rose from his throne and greeted me with folded hands. I bowed in return, and he graciously offered me a seat beside him.

"Dharmaraj welcomed me with folded hands and offered me a seat," I gladly informed Narayan Ji.

"What else is happening there?" he inquired further.

"I observe that several beings are queuing up and approaching Dharmaraj's assistant one by one. It appears he is verifying their karmic accounts in his booklet," I responded leisurely.

"Did you pay your respects to Dharmaraj?" Narayan Ji further asked.

"Certainly! And he reciprocated the gesture," I replied pleasantly.

"Engage in conversation with him. If you have any questions, you can ask Dharmaraj," Narayan Ji suggested.

However, before I could speak something, Dharmaraj initiated the conversation, inquiring about Guru Maharaj. I assured him that Guru Maharaj was doing well.

"Your Guru is truly an extraordinary saint. It's by the grace of the Almighty that you have such a Guru. You are supposed to consider yourself blessed," Dharmaraj remarked with a smile. In response to it, I nodded, feeling immensely blessed.

"Inquire about me," Narayan Ji urged after a moment. "I have been dealing with some health issues lately, and I am curious about what lies ahead."

So, I queried Dharmaraj about Narayan Ji's health. Dharmaraj revealed that Narayan Ji didn't have much time remaining on Earth and would experience increasing head pain as the time for departing the physical body drew near. When I relayed Dharmaraj's words to him, he became noticeably more subdued. Yet, there was a usual tranquility in his voice.

"Please inquire about the specific duration," Narayan Ji urged again after a pause.

"Not much," Dharmaraj responded with a faint smile.

Thereafter, Narayan Ji directed me to inquire about my own karmic account from Dharmaraj. I nodded and posed the query about myself.

"O great soul!" Dharmaraj responded gently. "As a result of your intense chanting in the name of Ram, all your karmic bondage has been dissolved. You are now liberated from all the consequences of both your righteous and sinful deeds."

Delighted, I relayed this information to Narayan Ji. "Thanks to the grace of Guru Maharaj." Narayan Ji continued, "Now on, you have the authority to command Dharmaraj to absolve all the sinful deeds of these beings only if you wish."

"Is that feasible?" I asked, astonished.

Narayan Ji then advised me to firmly command Dharmaraj. However, I hesitated to give such a directive, considering his stature as Dharmaraj. Instead, I politely appealed to him, "Could you please absolve the sins of all these beings so that they may reincarnate on Earth and dedicate their lives to the devotion of Lord Ram?"

With a gentle gaze, Dharmaraj responded, "Once in a million years, such compassionate saints descend to Earth. Oh, divine soul! If you wish for me to do so, I will certainly comply."

I relayed Dharmaraj's words to Narayan Ji, who was impressed upon hearing them. Subsequently, Narayan Ji instructed me to bid farewell to Dharmaraj and continue my journey. Following the instructions, I bowed to Dharmaraj and he reciprocated the gesture. As I exited the palace, everything vanished.

"Now, focus straight between your eyebrows," Narayan Ji continued, "This is where the waters of three sacred rivers converge."

Obeying his guidance, I centered my concentration at the point between my eyebrows. After a while, I witnessed three distinctively colored bodies of water merging at a single point. I informed Narayan Ji that I could perceive the presence of the three rivers.

"You are witnessing the convergence of the three sacred rivers: the Ganga, Yamuna, and Saraswati, he explained. "Now, immerse yourself in the confluence of these three rivers."

Upon his instruction, I found myself immersed in the water. Taking a dip into the confluence, I felt a revitalizing surge coursing through my entire body.

"Now, focus your concentration above your head," he directed, gently touching the center of my head.

Following his guidance, I concentrated on the point where his fingertip had made contact, all while the chanting continued fervently. A while later, Narayan Ji asked, "What do you see?"

"Just complete darkness, nothing more," I responded resolutely.

"Keep concentrating and chanting intensely. The blessings of all Gurus are with you. You can do this, Madhu," Narayan Ji encouraged.

However, our session was interrupted as it was time for the evening meal. "We will resume after the worship. Until then, feel free to do as you please, whether it's walking around or any other activity," Narayan Ji said before departing.

After having my meal, I took a stroll along the corridor for a short while and then returned to the meditation hall. We reconvened after the evening rituals. Narayan Ji instructed me to concentrate on the center of my head again. With the chanting of Lord Ram's name, I began to focus on that spot.

"Did you perceive anything?" he asked tenderly, but in response, I shook my head.

"Keep chanting, my dear, and maintain faith in Lord Ram," Narayan Ji murmured.

I continued chanting, but for a prolonged period, I saw nothing. So I inquired, "What will I encounter here?"

"A portal will manifest directly above your crown, and upon transcending all physical limitations, you will enter the realm of Siddhas," Narayan Ji explained. "Here is what you ought to do—sincerely beseech Guru Maharaj for assistance. He will undoubtedly bestow his grace upon you."

I fervently implored Guru Maharaj for assistance, and shortly after, a resplendent, massive lotus with thousands of petals appeared above my head.

"Have you witnessed the lotus?" Narayan Ji asked eagerly, a hint of bliss in his tone.

"Yes! There is a peculiar pink lotus," I confirmed jubilantly.

"Describe it to me in detail," he requested zealously.

"It's an immense lotus, fully blossomed with countless glittering petals, rotating over my head at a steady pace," I explained with overwhelming enthusiasm.

"Incredible! This is not an ordinary lotus, it's divine, known as Sahasradal Kamal," Narayan Ji exclaimed delightedly.

Instantly, I felt a sweet liquid dripping drop by drop into my mouth spreading a sense of ecstasy throughout my body. "Now, the nectar will descend directly from this divine lotus into your mouth. You must swallow it, as it is the key," Narayan Ji directed affectionately.

Following his instructions, I began to engulf the sweet liquid leisurely, and in no time, I found myself swiftly traversing the core of the divine lotus and entering an unbelievable realm.

CHAPTER 10

A CELESTIAL CEREMONY

As I traversed the sacred Sahasradal Kamal, I experienced a profound sensation of airiness. It dawned on me that a noticeable separation had occurred between my essence, the mind, and the body, giving me the sensation of levitation.

Out of the blue, the five greatest Siddhas of all time appeared before me, seated in lotus posture on black, volumetric rocks. They were meditating in a providential forest, each adorned in radiant robes with a beam of light emanating from their hearts. Ahh...! Witnessing them meditating, my heart overflowed with exhilaration.

"Have you beheld the presence of the Siddhas?" Narayan Ji asked humbly.

"Yes! I'm beholding the five great Siddhas seated on a rock in meditation," I replied, experiencing serenity.

"Wondrous! If you can identify them, speak their names," he instructed ahead.

"I can see Saint Kabir Das, Guru Nanak Dev, Gautam Buddha, Sadguru Sukhram Ji Maharaj, and Lord Mahavir."

I not only named them but also provided descriptions of their appearances. It took me no more than a moment to recognize them.

"This realm is known as Siddha Sheela," Narayan Ji remarked. He added, "Now, repeat my words with utmost sincerity: O great Siddhas! I bow at your lotus feet. Kindly shower your blessings upon me so that I may enter the 'realm of the immortals'."

I meticulously echoed every word, and soon, all the Siddhas leisurely opened their eyes. They cast their gaze upon me, nodding gently while extending their hands in a gesture of blessing, accompanied by their tender smiles. After a brief pause, Narayan Ji inquired, "Were you blessed by the Siddhas?"

"Yes, indeed! Each of them bestowed their blessings upon me," I replied with a sense of gratitude.

"Excellent! Maintain your chanting; you are now poised to step into the realm of the immortals," Narayan Ji remarked, visibly pleased with my advancement.

Within a matter of minutes, I found myself in an extraordinary world that defied description. The architecture of this realm was so captivating that it left me in awe. The inhabitants there appeared incredibly youthful, emitting a pure white glow from their bodies. Clad in luminous white garments, they exuded an aura of serenity. Some were gathered in clusters, sharing laughter and camaraderie, while others wandered about in a state of blissful joy. Some were engrossed in the workings of mysterious contraptions, while others sat in peaceful contemplation as if visualizing something profound. Rather than walking, these beings seemed to glide effortlessly as if traversing a pool of clouds.

Narayan Ji explained that this was the domain inhabited by revered sages, where only those who have attained divine enlightenment during their earthly existence transition upon shedding their physical form; these entities retain eternal youth and immortality. These beings possessed the ability to reincarnate at will and return to their realm upon fulfilling their purpose on Earth and other planets in other dimensions. These immortal entities were dedicated to preserving balance within creation.

"Eventually, the long-awaited moment has arrived, signaling the culmination of your astral voyage," Narayan Ji uttered tenderly. "Now, it's time to invoke Guru Maharaj, as he will lead you forth to the illustrious city of Ram."

I was electrified to catch sight of the city of Ram. It marked the pinnacle of my odyssey, the ultimate destination I had journeyed so far to reach.

In the dimensions of metaphysical existence, time unfolded in a manner distinct from the physical world. What may have been just minutes in the earthly realm stretched into hours within those ethereal dimensions.

As I began to invoke Guru Maharaj through chanting, a short while later, I was granted a vision of him adorned in a crimson Rajasthani turban and pristine white kurta-pajama; something different from his usual appearance. His presence exuded an ethereal glow akin to that of immortal beings.

Excitedly, I relayed the vision of Guru Maharaj to Narayan Ji; he instructed me to humbly prostrate myself before him and earnestly implore him to escort me to the city of Ram. Following Narayan Ji's guidance, I beseeched Guru Maharaj as instructed. With a gentle smile, Guru Maharaj grasped my hand, and together we ascended into the sky. Our journey was marked by encounters with myriad celestial phenomena, planetary bodies, and fantastical elements scattered throughout the cosmos, painting our voyage with wonder and awe.

At times, we progressed swiftly, akin to the pace of the mind, while at other times, we proceeded leisurely. At times, the vast expanse was shrouded in darkness punctuated only by the shimmering stars, while at others, I beheld the mesmerizing spectacle of nebulas, asteroids, and an array of vivid cosmic entities. Throughout the journey, I diligently narrated my observations to Narayan Ji.

After a considerable passage of time, we arrived at a spot encircled by towering white mountain peaks, with a milky lake nestled at its heart. Upon sharing this sight with Narayan Ji, he elucidated that this sublime lake was none other than the Manasarovar Lake. Until then, my knowledge was limited to the understanding that somewhere on Earth, beneath the great Mount Kailash, lay a sacred lake named Manasarovar. However, the scene before me transcended earthly bounds; we were no longer within the confines of Earth but in an entirely new realm. Subsequently, I learned that within this vast expanse, there exist countless manifestations of Mount Kailash and Manasarovar Lake.

Reflecting upon my experiences, I assert that the entirety of existence resembles an eternal dune, with us as mere ephemeral specks within its boundless sands.

"Please, share some details about the lake," Narayan Ji urged with keen interest.

"The lake is ensconced by mystical mountains, and its water is white, emitting ethereal vapors," I responded gazing towards the water.

"Fascinating! You must now immerse yourself in this miraculous water alongside Guru Maharaj." He continued, "Upon emerging from the lake, both of you will transform into resplendent grooms. As you are about to forge a union with Ram, it is imperative that you both appear immaculate."

Subsequently, Guru Maharaj and I alighted beside the lake and immersed ourselves in the waters of Manasarovar. True to Narayan Ji's prediction, both of us transformed into resplendent grooms. I glanced at Guru Maharaj; he was attired regally, resembling a ruler. His Rajasthani turban had metamorphosed into a majestic headdress embellished with diamonds and adorned with exquisite feathers. Strings of colorful pearls adorned his neck, and his white kurta-pajama had been replaced with robes of white and maroon hues.

Turning my gaze towards myself, I found that I too was bedecked in opulent jewels adorning my neck and arms. A delicate light-pink dhoti was fastened around my waist with an ornate golden belt. One aspect that particularly astonished me was the newfound radiance emanating from my own body, mirroring that of Guru Maharaj.

Narayan Ji's joy knew no bounds upon hearing the account, and he directed me further, saying, "Now, beseech Guru Maharaj to summon a chariot that will transport both of you to the city of Ram."

Following his guidance, I respectfully implored Guru Maharaj for the chariot. Soon after, a marvelous chariot drawn by seven white horses descended from the sky before us. Boarding the chariot, we set off swiftly into the heavens. Enraptured by the mystical sights unfolding in the cosmos, I felt as though I was bestowing blessings upon my eyes with each passing moment.

"After an extended interval, Narayan Ji inquired, "Do you perceive any sounds?"

"What kind of sounds do you mean?" I asked.

"As you draw nearer to the city of Ram, you will begin to discern the melodies of musical instruments," he explained.

I acknowledged his words and resumed my chanting. Moments later, he posed the question once more, and I began to discern a faint strain of music.

"Yes! There is a faint musical resonance emanating from somewhere," I eagerly informed Narayan Ji.

"That signifies your proximity to the city of Ram. The melodies originate from the location where the ceremony of your union is taking place." He added ahead with elation, "Upon your arrival, some celestial beings will extend a grand welcome to both of you."

After a long while, the chariot descended to an enigmatic realm, halting before a colossal golden portal.

"What do you observe?" Narayan Ji inquired cautiously.

"We find ourselves facing a massive golden portal," I responded, my gaze fixed upon the majestic structure.

"What does it look like?" he further inquired.

"It's magnificent. Adorning both sides are depictions of two suns, each inscribed with the name of Ram," I replied, filled with awe.

At that moment, the harmonious strains of musical instruments resonated clearly in my ears. When the portal finally swung open, my eyes widened in astonishment, and I stood transfixed, gaping at the scene unfolding before me. Inside the city, a divine ceremony was underway, attended by a multitude of exquisitely adorned beings. Everywhere I looked, the city was adorned with magnificent blooms and radiant lamps, enhancing its splendor. The entire atmosphere pulsated with festivity and celebration.

Moments later, a group of celestial beings, exuding joy and grace, approached us in a dance, bearing garlands of exotic flowers and baskets brimming with richly colored blossoms. With reverence, they bowed before us, applying Tilak to our foreheads before adorning us with garlands and showering us with petals, leading us inside.

As we followed them, we beheld the presence of numerous heavenly beings. A gathering of Gandharvas, the celestial musicians, immersed themselves in playing a variety of instruments including the flute, Rudra veena, Saraswati veena, sitar, mridang, shanka, shehnai, and various drums. Meanwhile, exceptionally beautiful Apsaras, the celestial dancers, graced the courtyard with their mesmerizing performances.

Among the celestial assembly, we also encountered groups of other beings such as Yakshas and Yakshinis (guardians of treasures), Siddhas, Saints, Seers, Dikpalas (guardians of directions), Suras (deities of heavenly abodes), and various other celestial entities.

The city of Ram boasted remarkable infrastructure crafted from distinct stones, featuring multiple expansive corridors, courtyards, sprawling lawns, and other magnificent edifices. Atop the towering domes, vibrant deep-yellow flags fluttered proudly, each bearing the name of Ram. Stone pillars adorned the courtyards, bearing finely carved idols depicting various ethereal entities in reverent poses.

Positioned at a distinguished location were venerable saints, whom Narayan Ji asked me to recognize. While some names seemed familiar, others were unknown to me. Narayan Ji specifically directed me to identify Shri Darayav Ji Maharaj among them by noting certain facial features, such as residual marks resembling those left by chickenpox. With his guidance, I located Shri Darayav Ji Maharaj, sitting leisurely among the group of saints.

Every aspect of the city exuded opulence, surpassing even the grandest of my imaginings. It was difficult to fathom that such lavish preparations were made in my honor. In the right-hand direction of the courtyard, a designated area was adorned with decorations, housing a sacred fire ablaze with sanctity.

Eventually, the eagerly anticipated moment arrived, the culmination of my fervent anticipation, as Guru Maharaj, myself, and the assembled beings awaited. A figure of unparalleled elegance and nobility entered the ceremony accompanied by attendants. Every entity in attendance rose from their seats, gazing upon Him with longing eyes. 'Hail to Lord Ram!' echoed through the assembly in unison. He was Lord Ram itself; He was my Ram...

How does one begin to describe His presence? Words seem inadequate to capture the essence of the Divine. Indeed, any attempt to depict Him here would pale in comparison, akin to a single grain amidst a vast wheat field. Truly, I had never encountered such a being in both the earthly and metaphysical realms. His countenance was bewitching, radiant as if illuminated by countless moons. Long, shiny, slightly curly brown locks cascaded from His illustrious crown down His back. A golden sun adorned the center of His forehead, while His earrings gleamed with what appeared to be fragments of the moon. An otherworldly garland adorned around His neck, accompanied by intricately designed ornaments. The Lord was dressed in brilliant white robes and His entire form exuded a divine golden aura, portraying Him as the sovereign of the cosmos. Only the ruler of creation could possess such resplendence.

I found myself enraptured by the breathtaking form of Lord Ram. And what occurred next was nothing short of extremely overwhelming. Lord Ram drew near, and in an instant, I found myself prostrating at His feet. As my hands made contact with His lotus feet, my chanting ceased spontaneously, and my eyes overflowed with tears, unable to contain the vast emotions within. 'Oh, my Ram!' were the only words on my lips as I surrendered to the ocean of ecstasy enveloping me. Witnessing my state, Narayan Ji repeatedly inquired about the unfolding scene, but I remained unresponsive. Lost in a trance-like state, I continued to repeat: 'Oh, my Ram!' in an unbroken stream of devotion.

Lord Ram tenderly lifted me from His feet and enveloped me in His embrace. Instantly, a profound vibration coursed through my entire being, evoking a sense of profound unity and completeness.

Such experiences defy verbal expression; they are beyond the limitations of words. They can only be lived, not articulated. All I can convey is that it transcended all boundaries of comprehension.

Lord Ram gently lifted my chin with His thumb and forefinger, casting upon me a captivating smile. I found myself utterly entranced by His enchanting visage. Soon after, Guru Maharaj joined us, delicately placing my hand into the Lord's. Together, we proceeded towards the sacred fire, surrounded by the jubilant chants of Lord Ram's name and the shower of flowers from the celestial beings.

In the presence of Guru Maharaj, we circumambulated the sacred fire, and at that moment, the sky began to rain gems and gold coins followed by flowers.

After an extended period, I regained my composure and recounted everything to Narayan Ji. Upon hearing everything, he bestowed his verbal blessings upon me and then proceeded with his instructions, "Now, request the Lord to escort you to His chamber."

Following his guidance, I implored Lord Ram to lead me inside. With a gentle grip on my hand, the Lord guided me to His regal chamber, where opulence and comfort abounded in abundance. We have arrived at the chamber, Narayan Ji," I exclaimed while experiencing ecstasy.

"Very well! Now request Lord Ram to instruct His attendants to prepare fifty-six food offerings for you," he instructed ahead.

However, I was thoroughly overcome with such profound contentment, akin to a weary traveler finding solace after decades of wandering. My mind was enveloped in a transcendent tranquility, devoid of any lingering desires.

"I desire nothing now, Narayan Ji. There is nothing left to attain, nothing left to discover. My mind is devoid of questions, queries, desires, or concerns. I have found my Ram; I require nothing else. I am immersed in absolute fulfillment within myself. Let me remain in this state of bliss," I expressed blissfully.

Nevertheless, he persisted in urging me to request the food offerings. As he had guided me throughout the process, I felt compelled to comply with his directive. I made the request to Lord Ram. He graciously smiled at me and subtly signaled to His attendants with a glance.

Within moments, they arrived bearing an array of delicacies presented in gold and silver vessels. Upon observing the lavish spread, I informed Narayan Ji of its abundance.

In response, Narayan Ji directed, "Now, ask Lord Ram to personally feed you, and enjoy the feast from His hand."

"But how can I make such a request?" I protested immediately. "He is the Lord; there is no need for such gestures. I'm absolutely content."

"You share a profound bond with Lord Ram now. He is your consort; you may ask anything of Him," Narayan Ji explained affectionately.

"But I have no such longing..."

"Do it, Madhusudan," he urged once more.

With folded hands, I politely requested Lord Ram to feed me by hand. The Lord looked at me affectionately and began to feed me lovingly. Lost in the bliss of sharing a meal with my beloved Lord Ram, I was interrupted by Narayan Ji, "Now, express your desire to partake of the 'Immortal Fruit'," he interjected.

"But I have no desire for any fruit, Narayan Ji. I'm truly content," I politely responded.

Nevertheless, Narayan Ji persisted with his firm instructions. Subsequently, Lord Ram gestured to His attendant, who promptly brought forth a radiant yellow, mango-shaped fruit. I informed Narayan Ji that the fruit was now in my sight.

"How does the fruit appear?" Narayan Ji inquired eagerly.

"It's exceptional! Slightly resembling a lush mango."

"Incredible! Go ahead consume it," he directed ahead.

As I took a bite, I became momentarily lost in its delicious flavor. It was a delightful symphony of tastes that left my taste buds thoroughly captivated. Truly, I had never tasted such a delicious fruit in my entire life.

"What about the flavor?" Narayan Ji inquired.

"Mmm... It's delicious! Narayan Ji," I responded, my tone filled with pleasure.

He chuckled heartily, then after a brief pause, instructed me to request permission to depart from the Lord. Upon hearing that, a sense of disappointment tinged my emotions.

"I have no desire to return to the mortal world, my Ram. Please allow me to remain here with you for eternity," I pleaded, holding onto the Lord's feet.

"My love, you have been with me since the beginning. You are not separate from me; you are an integral part of me. You can see me whenever you wish," Lord Ram reassured me in His ethereal voice that echoed in my head, placing His warm palm on my cheek.

Following that, I bid farewell to the Lord with a kiss on His feet. Abruptly, everything vanished, and the Chidakasha dissolved into emptiness. I opened my eyes slowly to find all the devotees seated around me, their hands folded in reverence. They bowed to me, and in return, I bowed to them. Finally, I turned to Narayan Ji and rested my head at his feet.

You are a guiding star amidst a sky filled with gratitude, Narayan Ji," I expressed sincerely in an emotional tone. "It's through your guidance that I was able to meet my Ram. I'm indebted to you."

"You are supposed to direct your gratitude towards Guru Maharaj, not me," Narayan Ji replied with a smile.

"To me, you are a true Guru because you led me through this journey," I insisted, holding his hand.

"Please, do not burden me with such words. It was all due to the grace of Guru Maharaj. I was merely a medium," Narayan Ji humbly responded.

"Now, we ought to go to meet Guru Maharaj," I suggested cheerfully.

"Certainly! He must be awaiting your presence," Narayan Ji said, placing his hand on my head.

I wiped my face and hurried towards Guru Maharaj's room, finding him seated on his bed. I clasped his feet and rested my head upon them. With a giggle, Guru Maharaj softly uttered, "Ram Hee Ram." In response, I echoed his words, "Ram Hee Ram," signifying the omnipresence of Lord Ram in everything.

Guru Maharaj gently placed his hand on my head and remarked, "This is the fruit of your penance from past lives. There are countless devotees associated with me, some striving for years to attain such a state." He added, "Continue chanting the name of Ram whenever you can. From now on, you need not bow to any other deity. You belong to Ram."

As his words sank in, a question surfaced in my mind. "Maharaj, I have a query," I ventured.

"Ask freely, my child," Guru Maharaj encouraged.

"Since my boyhood, I have been a devout follower of Lord Shiva. Now, you instruct me not to bow to any other deity. What if Lord Shiva takes offense?" I questioned.

"You ought to pose this question to Shiva Himself. Return to the meditation hall, commence your chanting, and invoke Shiva. He will provide you with the answer," Guru Maharaj replied humbly.

I paid my respects to him and made my way back to the meditation hall. Upon my return, I noticed the arrival of some new devotees, unfamiliar faces to me. Among them was a family from Hyderabad, consisting of an elderly couple and their married daughter. Additionally, another couple joined them in their chanting at the back of the hall. They seemed to be guided by a man, much like how I had been guided by Narayan Ji.

Suddenly, the daughter began to scream loudly and erratically. Without hesitation, the man placed his hand on her head and commenced commanding an unseen force to leave her body. It appeared as though the girl was experiencing some form of possession. I observed the scene intently from my position in the hall. After a brief moment, the girl returned to her usual state.

Shortly after, a young man of my age entered the hall and immediately prostrated himself at the feet of the man, crying uncontrollably like a child. I couldn't comprehend the dynamics of the situation. The man gently lifted him up and comforted him with a warm embrace. Eventually, the young man paid his respects to the individual and exited the hall after placing his belongings. I found myself pondering the entire scene: Who is this individual, and why did the young man break down upon seeing him?

Meanwhile, someone acquainted the newcomers with my presence, prompting the man to gesture for me to join them. Approaching him, I paid my respects before settling among the group. We began by introducing ourselves briefly. The man introduced himself as Champak Das, revealing that both he and his wife were government teachers from a small town in Rajasthan. Mr. Champak Das mentioned his acquaintance with Gopal Sir, indicating that he, like Narayan Ji, was one of Guru Maharaj's prominent disciples.

Mr. Champak Das then proceeded to share a condensed version of his journey and how he came to know Guru Maharaj. He explained that he had been a devout Vaishnava and a sincere devotee of Lord Hanuman until he encountered Guru Maharaj many years ago. He recounted attending one of Guru Maharaj's discourses in his village with his family, during which he became deeply absorbed in Guru Maharaj's teachings, losing track of time as six hours passed by unnoticed. Subsequently, he surrendered himself at Guru Maharaj's feet and received initiation from him. Mr. Champak Das also mentioned seeking permission from his beloved deity, Lord Hanuman, before making this spiritual commitment.

As we conversed, we also shared and discussed some of our own metaphysical experiences. During our conversation, Mr. Champak Das brought up a location in the Himalayas renowned for the penance practiced by yogis and mystics over millennia. He recounted having a vision of this place, describing mystic yogis with astonishingly long dreads and beards deeply engaged in meditation—some were even levitating, their beards touching the ground. According to him, these yogis did not age conventionally; rather, their age progressed over time. Some were reported to be 400 years old, while others surpassed 500 years. His account reminded me of Gyan Ganj Ashram, referenced in the book Autobiography of a Yogi. His narrative solidified my belief that places like Gyan Ganj were not mere legends but tangible realities.

Following our discussion, I confided in him about my dilemma, and he echoed the suggestion that I ought to seek guidance from Lord Shiva on this matter. With that, I bid him farewell and returned to my place for meditation.

Following Guru Maharaj's advice, I began to invoke Lord Shiva, focusing my concentration on my heart. After a few moments, the presence of the Lord manifested before me.

With deep reverence, I bowed before Him and expressed, "You guided me to Guru Maharaj, and now he advises me not to worship any deity other than Lord Ram. My heart struggles to accept this directive. What course of action should I take? Please illuminate me on this matter, Lord."

Upon hearing my apprehension, Lord Shiva responded with a gentle smile, "My dear, both of us are devotees of Lord Ram. How could one devotee take offense at another?" Lord Shiva continued, "Do not concern yourself with what others may say. With Ram residing in your heart, He will guide you through every aspect of your life. Therefore, always trust your inner voice and feel free."

With those reassuring words, the Lord vanished. With clarity, I understood what I needed to do. After that night, Guru Maharaj gave me the title of 'Saint' and everyone started honoring me. The next morning, the family from Hyderabad approached me to seek blessings. But I inhibited them humbly saying: This is all the grace of Guru Maharaj. You are supposed to seek his blessings only.

"With just a few days of effort, you have attained a state I have been striving for years to achieve. I have yet to reach the Sahasradal Kamal." The man continued with folded hands, "My daughter has also been distressed for nearly a year. Therefore, I have brought her with me to seek the Guru's blessings. As you are now recognized as a saint, through your grace, I believe happiness and peace will return to my family."

"Have faith in Ram, Sir. He will undoubtedly bestow His grace upon you. Continue chanting His name," I offered consolation with folded hands.

In truth, their gestures were not directed towards me, nor did they seek my blessings; they were bowing to the Divine, seeking the Divine's blessings through me. I held no authority to bless them. With this realization, I felt it was time to seek permission from Guru Maharaj for my departure.

The following morning, after the morning prayers and rituals, I approached Guru Maharaj and requested permission to depart. Although he wished for me to stay a few more days, I explained that I had classes to attend. Understanding my situation, Guru Maharaj granted me permission to leave.

As I prepared to depart, Guru Maharaj advised me to chant the name of Ram regularly, both in the morning and evening. He cautioned me against visiting any shrines or partaking in the Prasad or offerings of any deity, emphasizing that doing so could diminish the intensity of my chanting and my spiritual progress. Furthermore, he instructed me to maintain a life as a family man and continue living an ordinary existence.

If truth be told, I felt dissatisfied with the limitations imposed by Guru Maharaj. In my mind, I found myself replaying the words of Lord Shiva. But I was perplexed: Why did Lord Shiva suggest that? Why didn't He advise me to follow my Guru?

After bidding farewell to Guru Maharaj, I proceeded to the hall to take leave of Narayan Ji and the others. I embraced Narayan Ji and sought his blessings by touching his feet. Observing that the young man who had been in tears earlier, under the care of Mr. Champak Das, owned a motorbike, I asked him if he could drop me off at the bus stand. He kindly agreed, and we set off towards the bus stand together.

During our journey, he briefly shared his story with me. He revealed that he had reached a point in his life where suicide seemed like the only escape. It was Guru Maharaj who rescued him from that crisis and granted him a fresh start. Reflecting on my presence there, he remarked, "You are not an ordinary individual. No one approaches Guru Maharaj without a purpose. Only those who have had a connection with great saints in their past lives can find their way to this place. You must have had ties with the saints in your previous existence."

Although I didn't offer much of a response, I recalled fragments of my past lives while chanting, where I found myself in the company of saints. The guy left me at the bus stand, bidding farewell with a respectful 'Ram Ram Saa' bowing his head as he departed. I returned the gesture, reciprocating with 'Ram Ram Saa'. Shortly after, a bus arrived, and I boarded it, bound for Jaipur city.

As I sat on the bus, memories of my time in the ashram flooded my mind. One aspect that stood out to me was the absence of a donation box throughout the entire ashram. Guru Maharaj never requested any money from anyone.

Even if someone offered a donation, Guru Maharaj would supplement it with his own funds before returning it to the individual. Truly, he embodied benevolence.

Now, I needed to make my way to New Delhi as quickly as possible; someone awaited my arrival there.

CHAPTER 11

UNVEILING OF MYSTICAL POWERS

At approximately 2 o'clock in the afternoon, I was dropped off at the Jaipur bus stand by the bus. From there, I made my way to the railway station and asked about the train heading to New Delhi. I was informed that a train bound for New Delhi would leave in approximately an hour. During that time, I bought a ticket for the train's general compartment and enjoyed my lunch. At nearly 3 o'clock, the train arrived, and I observed that all the general compartments were overcrowded. Even though I hadn't foreseen such a crowd in all the general compartments, I found myself with no alternative at that moment. Hence, I managed to board the train somehow.

As for seating, there was barely enough space to stand comfortably on one foot, let alone both. I endured standing in such cramped conditions for nearly two hours. It was a chaotic scene; someone's luggage was resting on my head, another individual's arm kept hitting my face, someone pushed me from behind, and another stood on my shoes. I was entirely engulfed in the crowd, unable to see anything beyond the heads of my fellow passengers.

Gradually, my feet began to ache from the weight of the hefty backpack on my shoulders. I bore the discomfort for a while, but when it became too much to bear, I closed my eyes and silently prayed to Lord Ram for relief.

Sitting beside me was a newlywed couple. A moment later, the husband tapped my arm and kindly informed me that they were about to disembark, offering me their seats. I nodded appreciatively, mustering a grateful smile. At that moment, I felt grateful for two things at once: the swift response to my prayer and the opportunity to finally sit down.

Following a lengthy journey, I arrived at the New Delhi railway station around 9 o'clock in the evening. From there, I booked a cab to take me to the residence of my friend Priyanshi.

In reality, I harbored no inclination to flaunt my metaphysical experiences; I had no aspiration to be regarded as extraordinary. Nonetheless, my motive for sharing with others was to promote devotion to Lord Ram, with the hope that others too might receive the Divine's blessing. I aimed for them to realize that the material world isn't the ultimate truth; there exists something beyond it. My desire was for all to encounter that state of euphoria. Moreover, I had committed to Priyanshi that I would visit her, thus my intention in meeting her was to recount some remarkable events.

Upon arriving at Priyanshi's place, I hastily freshened up before enjoying a delightful meal together. Subsequently, I recounted the entire story to her, though her facial expressions suggested she found it akin to entertaining fiction rather than reality. It was evident from her nodding and demeanor that she wasn't convinced by my account and was merely pretending to believe my story.

To be fair, it wasn't her fault. I completely comprehend that it might be hard to swallow for someone who hasn't had experiences beyond the physical and mental realms to believe in such otherworldly phenomena. However, it was unacceptable to me for anyone to dismiss me as a mere fabricator of tales under any circumstances. I aimed to instill in her a belief in the existence of phenomena beyond the confines of the physical world; entities that transcend our usual dimensions.

Yet, in today's skeptical climate, trust often demands tangible evidence. Recognizing the need to lend credibility to my words, I felt compelled to demonstrate a small sample of spiritual power to Priyanshi, as I couldn't find an alternative means of validation at that moment.

"You believe I have fabricated fantastical tales in my mind and am now presenting them to you in an organized manner. How about I show you something genuine instead?" I inquired Priyanshi firmly. "What if I make you experience something beyond what you have encountered thus far?"

"Well, that sounds ecstatic. Go ahead," she chuckled.

"Alright! If that's what you desire. Please sit properly in a meditative posture," I instructed her firmly gazing deeply into her eyes. "I'm going to demonstrate to you a glimpse of the mystical powers I have attained by the grace of my Guru."

"Certainly!" she uttered comically while sitting swiftly before me folding her feet inside. Until that point, Priyanshi had been under the impression that I was planning some sort of prank on her. Following that, I instructed her to close her eyes and refrain from opening them until I gave her permission. With a smile, she complied, closing her eyes. Then I sat in the lotus posture and closing my eyes began chanting the name of Ram.

As I intensified my chanting, I tenderly touched Priyanshi's Anahata Chakra (heart chakra) with my palm. Immediately, her pulse started to rise in an unusual rhythm, mirroring her breath. Her body began to sway forward, almost as if she might lose consciousness. Concerned, I ceased the chanting and withdrew my hand. Gradually, we both opened our eyes and looked at each other. She seemed deeply affected by the encounter. "Are you convinced now?" I asked Priyanshi smiling.

For a few moments, she remained silent, merely nodding her head slightly. It took her some time to regain her composure and return to her normal state. Then I inquired curiously, "What did you realize?"

"As soon as you touched me, I sensed a powerful energy emanating from your palm, permeating my body with an intense vibrancy. It caused my heartbeat to accelerate rapidly and I felt overwhelmed by the surge of energy. It was as if I might lose consciousness and fall from the bed. Just as I began to feel this way, you withdrew your hand," Priyanshi narrated, exhaling a sigh of relief.

Allow me to confess; what I did was a terrible blunder. It was reckless and potentially dangerous because this action could have had serious consequences for Priyanshi. Neither she nor her body was prepared for such an experience. However, I was unaware of this at the time; it was only later, when I encountered a yogi named Om Swami, that I realized my error.

This underscores the importance of having a mentor in the life of a seeker. A Guru or mentor is someone who not only guides a disciple but also protects them from harming themselves and others. I'm grateful to Lord Ram for preventing any harm to both of us. I harbored no ill intentions, which is why the Divine protected me. However, following that experience, Priyanshi became eager to witness more unearthly occurrences. I then advised her to chant the name of Ram with faith.

The following morning, I departed for my village to visit my family. My village was about four to five hours away from New Delhi, and Haridwar was approximately two to three hours from my home. I decided it would be convenient to head to Haridwar after spending time with everyone in the village. Interestingly, none of my family members had any idea of my whereabouts for over a week.

I reached home comfortably before evening. After dinner that night, I sat with my father and openly shared with him everything that had transpired in the past few days. I recounted my experiences in Vrindavan, my conversation with Gopal Sir, my journey through Rajasthan, encounters with Guru Maharaj, various metaphysical experiences, and my union with Lord Ram. Although my father listened attentively, he remained largely silent in response to these events. It was clear to me that he, too, found it difficult to believe what I was saying.

As I concluded, I politely informed him, "From now on, my life is devoted to Lord Ram. So please do not compel me into marriage or other worldly matters."

This statement sparked a strong reaction from my father. Well, such is the nature of typical fathers. Back in the village, I had a close friend named Bhojraj Panwar. He was older than me, so I respectfully addressed him as Bhaiya (big brother). Like me, he was a dedicated seeker, which strengthened our bond. It brings to mind a quote by Amy Lee: 'Your vibe attracts your tribe'. Whenever I visited the village, we frequently met to discuss not only mundane matters but also our spiritual knowledge, experiences, and learnings.

The next day, I had a conversation with him over the phone and urged him to meet me as soon as possible. I felt he deserved to know about these profound experiences more than anyone else. Bhaiya agreed to meet me in the evening. I knew he was the perfect individual with whom I could share anything without hesitation.

In the evening, Bhaiya arrived at my home to meet me. After exchanging greetings, I began the conversation by saying, "I want to tell you about something that I have experienced, witnessed, and attained in the past few days."

"Go ahead, I am all ears," Bhaiya uttered smiling.

I began narrating the story to him from its very beginning. Though he listened with attention, his responses were minimal, and his expression remained devoid of enthusiasm. I had anticipated that Bhaiya, being familiar with such supernatural occurrences from our shared readings in spiritual texts, would be intrigued by the events. We both embarked on our spiritual journey influenced by the wisdom of enlightened individuals who had encountered such phenomena throughout history. However, his silence hinted that my account did not resonate with him. Nonetheless, Bhaiya chose not to express his skepticism at that moment. An hour later, he bid me farewell and extended his best wishes for my future.

The next morning, I journeyed back to Haridwar and resumed my academic pursuits. Whenever I found a spare moment, I would sit down and chant the name of Ram, regardless of my surroundings or the presence of others. Gradually, I began to sense the Divine presence permeating everything around me.

As we draw nearer to the Supreme, we naturally become more attuned to its presence in our surroundings. We begin to discern and understand the cosmic signs that manifest around us. I became so engrossed in devotion to Lord Ram that every morning, I awakened with His name on my lips, and each night, I drifted into sleep chanting His name. I dedicated all my actions and deeds to Lord Ram, resulting in a constant state of bliss. Whether something auspicious or ominous occurred, I accepted it gracefully as Lord Ram's Will.

Consequently, every small event around me seemed to be imbued with the grace of Lord Ram. My desires were fulfilled effortlessly, and whenever a question arose in my mind, the answers and solutions seemed to come from within, as if someone were speaking to me internally. Additionally,

I began to experience some extrasensory perceptions. While numerous folks might perceive all these as miracles, for me, they were expressions of God's grace.

Some weeks passed alike, and then the Diwali festival holidays commenced at the university, prompting my return to the village. One day, a friend of my father from a nearby village, Vikram Panwar, paid us a casual visit. Unbeknownst to me, Uncle Vikram was a devout devotee of Goddess Kali. My father may have recently mentioned me to him, prompting his specific visit to see me that day. Upon his arrival, my father called for me and notified me that there was a visitor who had come to see me.

As my father and Uncle Vikram sat in the guest room, I approached them with cups of tea. After exchanging greetings, I stood aside, placing the cups on the table. Uncle Vikram glanced at me briefly before turning to my father with a smile.

"Your son," he remarked, "is transparently blessed by a divine entity. The radiance on his face is a testament to the immense mercy of the divine being."

While I appreciated Uncle Vikram's words, I couldn't help but smile somewhat shyly. My father then proceeded to recount some of my experiences to him. Upon hearing them, Uncle Vikram began sharing his own uncanny encounters with us. He mentioned that he, too, occasionally experienced extrasensory perceptions through the grace of the Goddess, but he never sought any supernatural powers or Siddhi from Her.

Uncle Vikram explained that he had made a pact with the Goddess, promising not to ask for anything from Her nor to reject anything that She Herself wished to bestow upon him. Therefore, he just followed whatever the Goddess allowed him to perceive and experience, using his abilities to assist those who sought his help. Continuing his counsel, Uncle Vikram advised me dearly: Stay steadfast on your path, my son. Your father and others may attempt to sway you or divert your attention to worldly matters but remain focused. They will never grasp the depth of your spiritual connection with the Supreme Being. Therefore, pay them no mind and feel no obligation to justify yourself to anyone. Simply persist in your sacred practice, and trust that the Divine will take care of everything else."

I listened attentively to Uncle Vikram's words, while my father chuckled heartily at his advice. After a brief exchange, Uncle Vikram bid us farewell. I offered him a respectful bow with a gentle smile, and he reciprocated the gesture as he departed.

A few days later, an incident occurred that drew the attention of my family members to me. My father has a soft spot for animals and creatures such as cows, buffalos, dogs, horses, rabbits, turtles, and fish. At that time, we had a lovely green turtle residing in our cemented water tank at home, typically used for watering cattle in villages. One day, my father took the turtle out of the tank to let it roam around a bit on land. However, he became preoccupied with other tasks and forgot to return the turtle to the water. When my father remembered after a while, the turtle was nowhere to be found. Both my father and my younger brother Vishwa searched the entire place but could not locate it. In the evening, they briefed me about the turtle.

"Don't worry," I assured them, "I will find it in no time. My supernatural abilities will guide me to its hiding spot."

Despite their skepticism, I retreated to my room and began chanting. I implored Lord Ram to guide me to the whereabouts of the little turtle. After a short while, I emerged and directed my brother to the precise location where the turtle was hiding. As he searched there, he indeed found the turtle. Word of this incident quickly spread among our nearby relatives, as such occurrences tend to do. Soon, my family began to acknowledge that I possessed certain extraordinary abilities.

In addition to my spiritual practices, I was immersing myself in various spiritual texts to expand my understanding. One day, I stumbled upon a captivating book by Om Swami titled 'If Truth Be Told'. This memoir chronicles Om Swami's spiritual journey, detailing his transformation from a successful entrepreneur running a million-dollar company in Australia to a monk in search of the ultimate truth. Despite his material success and lavish lifestyle, Om Swami felt a deep-seated awareness that true gratification lay beyond material possessions. Thus, he made the momentous decision to renounce everything and return to Bharat in pursuit of spiritual enlightenment. Embracing monkhood in his youth, Om Swami ventured into the Himalayas to undergo rigorous penance. Through years of unwavering dedication and spiritual practice, Swami ultimately attained self-realization.

This beautiful book served as a profound source of inspiration, enlightening me about the lives of the Himalayan yogis, deep devotion, intense penance, and the journey of monkhood. Encouraged by its wisdom, I began immersing myself in Om Swami's discourses, driven by a longing to expand my knowledge and deepen my understanding of spiritual principles. His words reflected true authenticity.

During a discourse on spiritual powers and Siddhis, Om Swami underscored the importance of not employing one's spiritual abilities solely for gaining attention or impressing others. He advocated for using these powers to advance spiritually instead. Swami warned that becoming too reliant on such powers could lead a seeker astray, trapping them in the pursuit of transient pleasures. He likened spiritual attainments to a savings account, urging practitioners to utilize them wisely and with discernment.

Swami's words resonated deeply with me, prompting me to make a conscious decision not to exercise these powers unnecessarily. From that moment onward, I devoted myself to only chanting the name of Ram and immersing myself in spiritual literature and discourses to deepen my understanding. In one of his discourses, Swami advised: Choose one form of God and remain steadfast in devotion to it. When you visit a shrine, perceive your chosen deity in every idol placed there. After all, it is the same divine energy dwelling in all.

Following his guidance, I began to perceive every deity as my beloved Lord Ram, whether it was Lord Shiva, Goddess Durga, Lord Krishna, or any other deity. By seeing the divine presence of Ram in all entities, I honored my Guru's instructions without compromise.

I have delved into nearly all of Om Swami's books and gleaned invaluable wisdom from them. In his book 'A Million Thoughts', I grasped the quintessence of meditation and discovered several unconventional approaches to ease into meditative states. It was through Swami's teachings that I first encountered the concept of 'Kundalini'. Intrigued, I sought further understanding by immersing myself in his book 'Kundalini: An Untold Story'.

Over time, I acquainted myself with the principles of Tantra, Mantra, and Yantra. In my exploration of 'The Ancient Science of Mantras' by Om Swami, I gained insights into the true essence of Mantras, their diverse types, origins, and their immense potency. This enlightening journey unveiled the significance of chanting and how the vibrations emitted during Mantra repetition resonate within our beings and surroundings. As I delved deeper into the text, I gained insight into how my recitation of the name of Ram was not just a verbal act but a manifestation of energy, fostering a connection to realms beyond our ordinary perception through its resonant vibrations.

With each revelation, one truth became clear: what I knew was just a speck in a vast dune of wisdom still to be discovered. As my spiritual understanding deepened by the day, my attachment to worldly matters began to wane. The pursuit of a mundane existence, engrossed in ordinary tasks, began to feel meaningless. Often, I sensed a profound disconnection, as if the call of the Himalayas echoed within me. Slowly but surely, an irresistible urge to renounce all and embrace monkhood began to take hold.

During that period, I reunited with Bhojraj Bhaiya and confided in him about my inner yearnings. I expressed my desire to dedicate my entire life to serving Lord Ram, and thus, I wished to renounce all worldly attachments and seek solitude elsewhere. After pausing for a moment, Bhaiya uttered, "Listen attentively to what I am about to say." I nodded, and he continued, "I don't know whether your experiences are genuine or not. While I respect your Guru and acknowledge the importance of having a spiritual guide, I urge you not to blindly follow anyone or anything. You don't have to accept everything as truth. It's possible that what you have witnessed is a product of your imagination, illusion, or some other mental phenomenon. I cannot say for certain, but I can tell you this: whatever you have experienced is not the ultimate reality. You have not yet reached that stage. One cannot reach it by following another's path. You are still far from the end, Madhu."

"No, Bhaiya...!" I responded firmly in my disagreement. "I'm certain about what I have experienced. Ram cannot merely be a figment of my imagination. It was not an illusion; I distinctly felt His presence."

Bhaiya gazed into my eyes, then spoke after a brief pause, "There is a thin line between devotion and blind devotion. Consider that," he advised. "Do you not think that you have discarded your old notions and beliefs only to adopt new ones?"

His words gave me pause, and I fell silent for a moment, contemplating his perspective. Bhaiya added ahead, "Becoming a monk may seem like a simple decision, but truly embracing the monk's way of life is a profound undertaking. It demands thorough preparation; otherwise, you will fall apart."

Following his remark, Bhaiya introduced the concept of

Vipassana meditation and advocated for my participation in a ten-day Vipassana Meditation course. Although he had mentioned Vipassana once before, I hadn't paid it much heed at the time.

"I don't feel the need to explore any other meditation techniques; I find fulfillment in my chanting practice," I promptly declined his suggestion.

"I am not suggesting you give up your current practices or swap chanting for something else. I am merely inviting you to embark on a new approach and explore more in the realm of spirituality, one that may unveil new facets of yourself. The course is free of charge; all you need to invest in ten days of your time. After that, you are free to pursue whatever path you choose. I can assure you that these ten days have the potential to shatter many illusions of the mind. I sincerely hope you will consider this opportunity," Bhaiya concluded before taking his leave.

His words prompted me to engage in deep reflection, and after pondering for quite some time, I came to the realization that he had a point—I had let go of my previous beliefs only to cling to new ones. In truth, I was unwilling to envision anything beyond Ram; I couldn't bear the thought of losing Him. I had convinced myself that my experiences constituted the ultimate truth, but I was mistaken—it was merely the beginning.

Bhaiya's insight was correct; I cannot attain the ultimate truth by merely following in someone else's footsteps. As time passed, I grasped that this wasn't the final destination; rather, it marked a significant waypoint on my spiritual journey. There was still a wealth of knowledge, insight, learning, and discovery ahead of me. A clear intuition emerged, guiding me toward the decision to undertake the Vipassana course. Recalling the teachings of Lord Shiva, I opted to heed the guidance of my inner intuition. It became apparent that the cosmos held other plans for me. Hence, the speck moved ahead in the quest of the dune.

CHAPTER 12

VIPASSANA: AN APPROACH TO NIRVANA

Vipassana is a venerable meditation approach practiced by Siddhartha Gautama, the primordial Buddha roughly 2,500 years back. It is recognized as one of the most ancient meditation methods originating in Bharat, with mentions in various old scriptures. Even Lord Vasudev Krishna refers to this approach in the Bhagavad Gita.

The term Vipassana means ‘seeing things in their true form’. Most individuals have heard about Gautama Buddha and his wise teachings from a young age. However, only a few truly are familiar with the meditation approach that led him to Nirvana. I was also unaware of Vipassana meditation until a few years ago. It was Bhojraj Bhaiya who first introduced me to Vipassana, and later, I read about it briefly in Om Swami’s book.

Bhaiya, along with his wife, had participated in a ten-day Vipassana course a few months prior, and he shared numerous fascinating experiences from their time there. One evening,

I called him and expressed my interest in attending the ten-day Vipassana meditation course. Bhaiya began providing me with essential details about the course, such as how to apply for it online, the location of the nearest Vipassana Centre, what to bring and what to leave behind, the rules and regulations, and the best time to attend. He informed me that at Vipassana Centre, all forms of entertainment and communication, including gadgets, mobile phones, music, books, newspapers, and even blank paper and pen, would be prohibited. All sources of distraction would be restricted, and I would have to remain thoroughly isolated from the outside world for ten days, focusing solely on meditating, eating, and sleeping.

All this sounded quite engrossing because it promised a new and unique experience for me; I had never been in such an ambience before. Additionally, I felt exhilarated at the thought of living like a monk for ten days. Bhaiya specifically recommended attending the course during the winter months to avoid the nuisance of mosquitoes, which, as humorous as it may sound, can indeed cause significant distraction while meditating in the summer. He also advised me to apply a month in advance to secure a spot, given the high demand and limited availability. Consequently, I applied in December and chose the nearest Vipassana Centre to my location.

Fortunately, by the end of the month, I received a confirmation email. The course was scheduled to begin in the last week of January. Luckily, my semester exams concluded by the third week of January, and winter vacations had started. As the start date approached, I informed my father about the course and sought his permission to leave for Vipassana Centre.

Upon hearing this, my father started asking me a series of questions: Why do you need to go there? You possessed the grace of Lord Ram and ample spiritual amenities, despite this, what is the point of learning something new?

He continued, "You said Ram is everything to you, so what are you still searching? I believe you ought to concentrate on your academics now to secure a good job."

"Father, this is not a futile endeavor that I wish to undertake. Rather, through this approach, I will have the opportunity to delve deeper into myself and explore other dimensions of the spiritual realm. I aim to make the most of my vacation period by acquiring more knowledge that will enrich my spiritual understanding and motivate me to lead a righteous life." I added ahead affectionately, "Please trust me, Father. I'm not embarking on any misadventure."

Eventually, I managed to persuade my father by discussing several noble and worthwhile aspects of Vipassana meditation. Every parent's primary concern is that their children ought not to embark on paths from which it would be arduous to return. They never want their children to stray onto illegitimate paths and face hardships. Thus, our parents always strive to protect us, often by discouraging such exploration, risk-taking, and unconventional thinking. However, by the grace of the Almighty, I'm blessed with the best father in the world, and I pray that everyone receives such a gentle father. My father never outright forbade me from anything; instead, he always respected my perspectives. Although he shared the same concerns for me, he never encouraged me to conform to societal norms and take only calculated risks in life.

As advised by Bhaiya, I gathered all the necessary stuff into my backpack and notified my family that my mobile phone would be turned off for the next ten days, ensuring them not to be concerned if I didn't make contact.

The management team of Vipassana Centre instructed us to arrive a day in advance. Therefore, one day earlier, I set off on my Royal Enfield towards the Centre situated in a small village named Neval in the Kernal district of Haryana. After roughly two and a half hours of riding, I arrived at the 'Dhamma Karunika Vipassana Centre'. Situated amidst agricultural land, the Centre was distanced from any habitation, offering a serene and secluded environment.

A dirt road branching off from the main road led through fields and barns to the Centre. Upon reaching the entrance, a security guard inquired about my arrival before allowing me to enter. I parked my motorbike in an open parking area and proceeded further, taking in the surroundings. The premises occupied a vast expanse of land, and I learned that this entire property had been generously donated to Vipassana Meditation Centre by a retired civil servant.

Inside, there wasn't much commotion. As I neared the building complex, I noticed two boys around my age exiting one of the blocks. Making my way towards them, I reached the document verification room. Upon entering, I found it quite crowded. Some individuals were sorting through their luggage and backpacks, while others stood engaged with papers and documents in hand.

At the forefront, several members of the management team were seated at desks. I approached the first desk, where a man was organizing documents, a printer, and a laptop. After confirming my name on the list, he requested photocopies of my documents along with the confirmation document that I had downloaded from their registration site. After providing him with the necessary documents, he handed me a form to fill out. This form required me to provide basic details and answer various general questions, such as whether I had attended a Vipassana course before, if I practiced any other meditation techniques, if I was taking any medications, if I had any health issues or ailments, if I was a drug addict, and how I had learned about the Vipassana course, among others. I took a seat on a wooden bench and began filling out the form.

Participants of various ages, ranging from eighteen to approximately sixty years old, had gathered to attend the course. Among them were some participants from overseas. After a few minutes, a tall, fair-skinned individual entered the room. Upon submitting his documents, he took a seat beside me with his form. I assisted him in filling out the details, and as a result, we struck up a conversation and became acquainted. The guy introduced himself as Rishabh Kukreja, mentioning that he was an engineering student.

After some time, a staff member from the management team called out my name, and I approached his desk. He reviewed my form and directed me to the final desk, where I had to surrender my belongings such as my motorbike key, mobile phone, and wallet. In my backpack, I only had some warm clothes, hair oil, a comb, toothpaste, a toothbrush, bathing and washing soap, and my slippers. The staff member collected all these items and placed them in a small transparent zip bag, sealing it securely. Then, he attached a tag with my name and a specific number to the bag. Handing me a badge with the number B-13, he said, "This number will be your identity for the next ten days."

I tucked the badge into my pocket and relaxed back onto the bench. Once everyone received their badge, the management team instructed us to proceed to our assigned rooms based on these numbers. A short distance away, there were blocks labelled Block A, Block B, Block C, and Block D. Each block comprised seven to eight small rooms, accompanied by a small courtyard and a communal washroom area. Following my badge number, I made my way to Block B and located the room marked with the number 13. Opening the door, I peered inside.

The room measured hardly five feet in width and eight feet in length—compact yet ample for a single occupant. In addition to a compact bed, the room featured an unbarred cemented wardrobe embedded in the wall, along with a ceiling fan and a light fixture. After stowing my backpack in the wardrobe, I ventured outside to explore the surroundings. Rishabh was also lingering outside his block. Spotting me, he came over, and we engaged in conversation, discussing our college experiences and academic pursuits. In the course of our discussion, Rishabh inquired with curiosity, "What is your purpose for attending this ten-day course?"

"I'm on my journey of self-discovery," I responded warmly. "Despite meditating for a year, I'm eager to delve deeper into the realm of spirituality. So, I decided to spend my vacation exploring here."

I then turned the question back to him, asking, "Now, I'm curious to hear your story. What inspired you to come here?"

"I am not particularly devoted to spirituality; rather, my aim is to enhance the concentration power of my mind," he explained. "I aspire to excel in my academic endeavors and achieve impressive grades in exams. Someone in my known suggested that attending the ten-day Vipassana meditation course could aid in sharpening my mind."

"Fascinating! I hope this proves beneficial for you," I remarked with a smile.

As we conversed, we began to stroll around the area. In front of our blocks, there stretched a spacious lawn where several individuals sat engaged in conversation. As we walked, our attention was drawn to a large board displaying the daily schedule from morning to night. Reading it from top to bottom, I learned that we would be engaged in ten hours of meditation each day.

Throughout the premises, numerous smaller boards were positioned, each bearing a simple instruction: Please Maintain Noble Silence. Towards the rear of the premises lay an impressive meditation hall. The female participants were allocated separate blocks in an isolated section inaccessible to the male participants, with a dividing wall separating the two areas. I presumed similar arrangements were in place there.

As the sun dipped below the horizon, casting the sky into darkness, everyone congregated in the dining hall for dinner. We retrieved plates and bowls from the cabinets, lining up one by one to collect our food. The dining hall resembled a college canteen, with numerous tables and chairs scattered throughout the space. Large steel containers on the tables held lentils, a dry vegetable dish, rice, and rotis. A coordinator served the meal, and we filled our utensils before finding seats wherever we pleased.

Following dinner, the head coordinator addressed the group. He began by extending a warm welcome to all participants and then introduced us to Shri S.N. Goenka Ji, a prominent lay teacher of Vipassana meditation in our era. Additionally, he acquainted us with the essential rules and regulations of the Vipassana Center, which were obligatory for all participants to adhere to:

- For the following ten days, it's imperative that you maintain noble silence, meaning no communication whatsoever. Avoid any gestures with your hands, lips, or eyes. If you encounter any issues, you may approach the coordinators and convey them using minimal words.
- All attendees must adhere to punctuality. Each morning at 4 o'clock, a sacred bell will be rung by the coordinator. Upon hearing it, you are required to rise from your beds and prepare yourselves within half an hour, ensuring arrival at the meditation hall before 04:30 A.M.
- Within the meditation hall, seating arrangements will be organized according to your assigned badge numbers for ease of identification. You will locate your designated seat smoothly, eliminating any confusion. Upon entering, silently take your seat.
- Honorable S.N. Goenka will provide guidance throughout the meditation session. Mindfully listen to his audio and video recordings, and diligently follow his instructions step by step.
- A Vipassana meditation instructor will be available in the meditation hall to assist you. Should you have any questions about your meditation practice, you

may seek individual guidance from them after the session.

- If you engage in any other meditation practices or religious rituals in your daily routine, kindly refrain from them for the next ten days and fully dedicate yourself to Vipassana. This focused approach is essential to achieve the desired results of Vipassana meditation.
- If you have any prayer beads or similar items that you use during your daily spiritual practices, please hand them over to the coordinator. It is important to eliminate any objects that may distract your mind during the meditation.
- During this period, it is essential to maintain purity, so please refrain from consuming any intoxicating substances. If you have any such substances, kindly surrender them to the coordinator. Additionally, abstain from engaging in any sexual activity.
- Do not cause harm to any living creature nearby. Refrain from theft or any such activities that may distract your mind or compromise the sanctity of your practice.
- Avoid engaging in activities on the lawn that may attract the attention of others such as yoga, exercise, running, etc.
- The vegetarian food will be served in its pure Sattvik form, and we request that you do not waste it. Please take only what you need. After finishing your meal, wash your dishes and return them to their designated places. Please ensure to keep your surroundings clean and tidy.
- If you need any essential items such as medicine or other daily necessities, please write them down in the notebook located outside the dining hall. Include the name of the item along with your badge number, and

we will do our best to provide it for you if feasible.

- Men are forbidden from entering the women's area, and likewise, women are prohibited from entering the men's area, regardless of whether their spouse is present. You will only be able to meet your partners after the ten-day period.
- Practice diligently and adhere strictly to the rules and regulations. Any sort of breach of these guidelines will compromise the purity of your practice. Please bear this in mind.
- Should anyone among you find these regulations untenable or anticipate difficulty in complying with them throughout the course, you are welcome to depart early tomorrow morning without any inconvenience. Yet, once this choice is made, you must remain within the premises for the entirety of the ten-day period, whether you like it or not.

Following that, the head coordinator instructed all of us to proceed to our rooms while observing noble silence. Before retiring to bed, I spent some time chanting and then offered a prayer to Lord Ram, expressing gratitude for guiding me to this unique opportunity to learn an exceptional approach and embrace a different lifestyle. However, I reassured my devotion, affirming that for the next ten days, I would serve the Lord through Vipassana meditation. I sought the Lord's blessings to help me assimilate this meditation practice while adhering to all the prescribed rules and regulations.

The following morning, I was roused from slumber by the resonant toll of the sacred bell. Despite the lingering heaviness in my eyelids, I recognized the challenge of leaving the warmth of my bed on a wintry morning. Nonetheless, I mustered my resolve and proceeded to the washroom, rubbing my eyes to dispel drowsiness. Though the lights illuminated the surroundings, the external world remained shrouded in darkness and chill. A dense mist descended from the obscure sky. I hastily refreshed myself with warm water before making my way to the nearby meditation hall. Placing my slippers in the designated stand outside, I entered the hall.

The interior of the meditation hall was truly magnificent. Impeccably designed, it exuded a sense of serenity and tranquility. The floor was adorned with pristine white fabric, upon which rows of square-shaped meditation cushions, draped in soothing sky blue, were meticulously arranged. Each cushion bore a distinctive badge number, ensuring order and organization within the hall.

At the center of the front wall loomed a massive white screen flanked by speakers on either side, while a sophisticated projector hung from the ceiling. In addition to the lighting and fans, the walls were equipped with multiple air conditioners for comfort. The hall boasted considerable space, accommodating thousands of meditators comfortably. Some chairs were positioned at the rear to accommodate individuals with spinal concerns who couldn't sit on the floor.

The meditation hall had two entrances, one from the men's section and the other from the women's section. Moreover, it was divided into two sections, with female meditators seated on the right and male meditators on the left. At the forefront, a Vipassana instructor, appearing slightly advanced in age, was seated. Everything was meticulously arranged, and I admired their efficient management.

Slowly, all the meditators settled into their seats. Glancing around, I estimated there must have been nearly one hundred to one hundred and fifty meditators occupying the entire hall. Each individual's gaze wandered aimlessly; I too observed other meditators without directly meeting their eyes. The entire hall was enveloped in complete silence, with coordinators exchanging hushed words among themselves. Then, precisely at 04:30 A.M., all the bright lights abruptly dimmed, leaving only a faint, muted glow in the hall.

Following that, the voice of Shri S.N. Goenka Ji resonated in our ears. He commenced by reciting some Suttas in the Pali language. Given that Pali was among the oldest languages globally, it served as the language for numerous Buddhist canonical scriptures. Following this, Goenka Ji directed us to close our eyes and assume a comfortable posture with our spines erect. He recommended adopting a meditative posture conducive to prolonged sitting. "Now, strive to focus on your breath. Mindfully observe each inhalation and exhalation," Goenka Ji further instructed.

This marked the initial and foundational stage of Vipassana meditation, also known as Anapana, which involves observing the natural breath. With my eyes closed, I began the practice of observing my breath as it flowed in and out. After a brief pause, Goenka Ji remarked, "Your attention will drift repeatedly as the mind seeks to wander again and again. Yet, it's essential to be gentle with your mind and politely guide it back to the natural breath."

Initially, I assumed that focusing on breathing would be effortless because it's a continuous process within our bodies. Unlike chanting, where you must consciously articulate words, breathing occurs naturally from birth. However, as smooth as it appeared, it proved to be equally sophisticated. As Goenka Ji had cautioned, I encountered the same challenge, likely because I was accustomed to concentrating on chanting the name of Ram, whereas here, I had to remain in stillness as a mere observer.

While practicing Anapana, my mind often wandered from one thought to another, and within moments, I would lose track of my focus. I found myself drifting along with the thoughts swirling in my mind, forgetting to attend to my breathing. Every five to ten minutes, Goenka Ji would gently remind us to remain attentive and observe our breath. Despite his reminders, I found myself slipping back into my thoughts shortly after refocusing on my breath. I struggled to maintain awareness of my breath, unaware of when my mind would veer off track.

At times, thoughts about my family, career, future, spiritual journey, and the allure of the Himalayas occupied my mind, while at other times, reflections on Guru Maharaj and his teachings dominated my thoughts. This pattern persisted until 06:30 A.M. when Goenka Ji began reciting Buddhist Suttas, and the hall lights brightened. Afterward, the coordinator instructed us to leave the hall one by one and make our way to the dining area for breakfast.

As the sun ascended in the sky, the mist began to dissipate slowly. Some people headed directly to the dining hall, others took leisurely strolls in the garden, and the remainder returned to their rooms. I was among those who went straight to the dining hall. Breakfast options included milk, tea, idli, poha, biscuits, and bananas neatly arranged on the tables. Cozily, I selected items according to my appetite, noticing that badge numbers were also designated on the dining tables, indicating assigned seating.

By chance, Rishabh and I found ourselves seated at the same table, yet we avoided making eye contact. A silence enveloped the hall, punctuated only by the clinking of utensils. Observing the subdued atmosphere, I couldn't help but feel a sense of strangeness, a sentiment that I suspected was shared by others experiencing this environment for the first time. With the next meditation session scheduled for 08:00 A.M., I took advantage of the hour-long break to return to my room and indulge in a brief nap.

Promptly at 07:50 A.M., the coordinator signaled the start of the next session by ringing the sacred bell, prompting everyone to reconvene in the meditation hall. There, Goenka Ji resumed his guidance, urging us once more to focus on our breath. Despite my efforts to attentively observe my breath, I found my mind wandering incessantly.

Each time, I diligently redirected my focus, only to find myself ensnared once again by wandering thoughts. This internal struggle persisted throughout the three-hour session, leaving me grappling with my own unruly mind.

After the session concluded, we proceeded to the dining hall for lunch.

During lunch, we were served flavorful lentils and a mixed vegetable dish accompanied by rotis and white rice. Following the meal, I wandered out to the lawn where fellow meditators were basking in the sun or taking leisurely strolls. An hour later, the bell's chime signaled our return to the meditation hall, prompting us to gather once more.

The practice of observing the breath resumed. After a few minutes, Goenka Ji guided us to observe attentively which nostril was active during inhalation and exhalation. I followed his instructions, focusing on the functioning of my nostrils. Initially, it held my interest, but before long, I found myself lost in thought while monitoring the airflow through my nostrils.

After a prolonged period, I became aware that I had lost focus on my breath. Immediately, I redirected my attention to my breathing. However, moments later, I realized that my mind was engaged in a continuous stream of thoughts, meandering through various topics without interruption. Whenever I attempted to disengage from this mental chatter, it urged me to open my eyes and glance at the clock to gauge how much longer I had to remain seated. This cycle persisted for two hours. Then, upon Goenka Ji's instruction for a ten-minute break, I felt a sense of relief and exited the hall.

Our minds are conditioned to seek instant pleasure, craving experiences that offer immediate gratification and a sense of novelty. We may find joy in dancing in the first rain of the season, but lose interest if the rain continues for days. The sight of snow-covered mountains may initially captivate us, but lose its charm upon repeated viewing. Similarly, there was no thrill or excitement in sitting in the hall and observing the breath repeatedly. Consequently, my mind wandered from one thought to another, behaving much like a mischievous monkey.

Following the break, I resumed my Anapana practice in the hall, grappling with maintaining my focus. This session concluded at 05:00 P.M., signaling a tea break. I indulged in a cup of tea accompanied by some biscuits and snagged an orange to savor while lounging on the lawn. Settling into a quiet corner, I observed my fellow meditators scattered about. Despite everyone being in their own space, a few individuals were sharing laughter and exchanging glances with their acquaintances from afar.

A few fellows reclined on the grass, shielding their faces from the sunlight. Another man traced his fingers through the grass as though searching for something hidden. Nearby, a young boy sat, repeatedly inscribing and erasing something in the soil. Meanwhile, those who exchanged laughter and smiles likely believed they were discreet in their gestures, unaware of being observed. Yet, I couldn't help but smile inwardly at their subtle antics.

Around 6 o'clock in the evening, the resonant chime of the sacred bell summoned us back to the meditation hall. As the session commenced, Goenka Ji instructed us to focus on our breath once more. However, I found it challenging to maintain my concentration on the breath for more than a few fleeting moments. The practice felt monotonous to me, as I was accustomed to encountering captivating and profound experiences during meditation. Yet, in this setting, the simple act of observing the breath failed to evoke any significant response. Every five to ten minutes, Goenka Ji reminded us: Stay mindful and continue observing the breath. Bring your attention back to the breath gently. Don't let it slip away unnoticed.

Following that session, the coordinator played a video clip featuring Goenka Ji on the large white screen. Given the typical image of Buddhist monks with shaven heads and saffron or red robes, I anticipated Goenka Ji to resemble a traditional monk. However, as the clip began, I saw an elderly man dressed in ordinary attire. His appearance was unassuming; there was nothing about him that outwardly suggested he was a master or monk from the lineage of Buddha.

Following this, Goenka Ji commenced his sermon: The first day of this ten-day course has concluded, leaving us with nine days ahead. You all are embarking on a challenging journey; continue your practice with dedication. Drawing from my own experience and the experiences of millions of meditators, I can affirm that focusing on the breath is no easy feat. Yet, it is the path that leads you inward, allowing you to gradually experience the reality of your body and mind. Approximately 2600 years ago, Siddhartha Gautama, a remarkable individual, diligently practiced this approach on the land of Bharat and attained Nirvana. He transcended into the great Buddha, an enlightened being, and subsequently disseminated this exceptional approach globally for the betterment of all humanity. Vipassana is not confined to any specific religion; rather, it belongs to the entirety of humanity. The ultimate aim of Vipassana is to liberate you from the karmic residues accumulated over numerous lifetimes, to achieve liberation from the ceaseless turmoil that arises in the mind, and to transcend all forms of mental conditioning. However, it must be acknowledged that our mental disposition is often diametrically opposed to this goal. The mind has lost its capacity for tranquility and single-pointed focus, instead, it flits about erratically, much like a monkey leaping from one branch to another. Yet, patience is paramount. Simply acknowledging the reality of the present moment, where the mind has wandered from the breath, can swiftly bring it back to focus. Always bear in mind that forcing the mind can backfire, potentially causing it to rebel. Imposing on the mind breeds dissatisfaction. Thus, it's essential to approach the mind with tenderness. We must dissolve entrenched mental patterns with love and empathy. Therefore, persist in observing the natural cadence of your breath. Witness the truth of the present moment without trying to change it. Vipassana's essence lies in observing reality as it is, without manipulation.

Discourse continued for more than an hour, during which Goenka Ji shared profound insights about the nature of the mind. His words filled me with zeal once again, leaving me feeling uplifted. Following the discourse, we participated in another meditation session until 09:00 P.M., after which everyone returned to their rooms for the night.

With no dinner provided, hunger began to set in, but with only water available, I settled in for sleep. It had certainly been a long day for me. The next day followed the same routine, beginning with a meditation session lasting around two and a half hours, followed by breakfast.

Upon returning to my block after breakfast, I overheard a conversation taking place nearby. Despite the strict rules in place, I was curious as to who would dare to break them. It appeared that a resident from the room opposite mine was questioning others about an individual who had been washing clothes before 04:00 A.M. His sleep had been disturbed by the noise, leading to his frustration as he sought out the culprit. As I approached my room, he gestured towards me, asking if I was the one responsible for the disturbance. However, I chose not to engage and simply entered my room.

How could someone dare to flout the rules and disturb the entire ambience of the premises, all for their own benefit? Truly, such behavior was beyond belief. However, encountering various types of individuals is inevitable no matter where you find yourself.

Over the course of two days, I dedicated myself solely to the practice of focusing on my breath. Through this experience, I came to a newfound understanding of breathing, uncovering insights I had never realized before. I observed the intricate patterns of inhalation and exhalation, noting how at times, we breathe in through the right nostril and out through the left, and vice versa—there are moments when one nostril alone facilitates both inhalation and exhalation, while at other times, both nostrils synchronize in this rhythmic process. I also experienced the sensations accompanying each breath—the coolness as air enters the throat and the warmth as it exits, brushing against the upper lip.

While these observations may appear commonplace, in our yogic tradition, the dynamics of breath hold profound significance, intricately tied to our spiritual evolution and the awakening of our Kundalini. Yet, delving into this complex concept now would require a more in-depth discussion, perhaps better suited for some other occasion when we can explore it further.

Following the final meditation session of the day, the instructor present among us individually summoned each participant to discuss the duration it took to refocus on breathing once attention was diverted. Responses varied, with some indicating five minutes or more, while others mentioned two to four minutes. When it was my turn, I conveyed that it typically took me less than a minute to realign my focus on breathing. Through consistent practice over hours, my awareness had sharpened to the extent that I could discern within a minute when my attention had wavered. It seemed that very few, if any, had responded similarly, indicating a high level of attentiveness.

Unexpectedly, on the third day, a bizarre phenomenon began to unfold within me. While focusing on my breath, I found my mind slipping out of control, and a sensation emerged that the Vipassana Centre had transformed into a confining cage where I was confined for what felt like an eternity of ten days. The passage of time seemed to stretch indefinitely, making these ten days feel like an eternity. Restlessness gripped my mind, urging me to break free from the confines of the Centre, to engage in conversation, to use my phone, to listen to music, to read, and more. Despite being surrounded by others, a profound sense of loneliness crept in, exacerbated by the inability to communicate with anyone. The intensity of my longing for these simple pleasures baffled me thoroughly.

CHAPTER 13

ESSENCE OF THE PHYSICAL BODY

Centuries ago, nestled in the southern Himalayas, there existed a Buddhist monastery where an elderly master named Takeshi Yoji lived alongside his disciples. One day, a damsel from a nearby village approached the master and expressed, "My mind has been quite restless lately. All sorts of nasty and evil thoughts keep running through my head, often driving me entirely lunatic." She added ahead, "Despite several efforts to soothe my mind, I had no luck. Hence, I approached you, Master Yoji. Please teach me some easy-peasy technique so that I can conquer my mind and attain absolute serenity."

Master Yoji gazed at her smiling and suggested, "Well, in my opinion, you must listen to some music first." Master Yoji added ahead, "There is a seraphic waterfall flowing at the back of the monastery. The exceptional fact about this waterfall is that a nectareous tune of music is heard from its water when it falls to the ground. Go there and listen to that sense-appealing music."

Hearing this, a suspicion arose in the mind of the damsel because she had never heard about such a mystical waterfall in that region. Though she had no other choice so she headed towards the waterfall. After spending a while there, the damsel returned to the master and said slightly disenchanted, "I could not hear any musical sound there; instead, I could only hear the noise of falling water."

Master already knew that she would come and say this. He closed his eyes and responded tenderly, "There is music in the water, my child. Move back to the waterfall and listen to it."

Without asking anything ahead, the damsel returned and sat close to the waterfall. An hour later, she returned to the master and repeated her earlier statement. The master instructed her again to move back and listen to the music. This routine continued for a week, but the damsel didn't hear any tune of music. One evening, the damsel approached the master and expressed, "I guess I have figured out the nuisance; perhaps the relentless rush of the falling water is overshadowing the music. Is there a way to prevent this grueling noise of water from becoming a hindrance in my path?"

The master responded dearly, "There is no such trick, my child. You have to make your way through this. Now move back and listen to the music."

The damsel became pretty crestfallen and returned to the waterfall once again. For the next two days, she attempted various tactics to avoid the grueling sound of water, yet the harder she tried to evade it, the more the sound disturbed her mind. Even after making all the possible efforts, when she couldn't find any loophole, the poor damsel became pessimistic. Eventually, at night while lying down in her bed, she decided to leave the monastery and return home.

The next morning when the damsel was primed to depart, she saw that Master Yoji was giving a sermon to all his disciples. She thought that before leaving, she must listen to the last sermon of Master Yoji. Therefore, she went there and sat at the back of the disciples soberly. The master was talking about the challenges and hindrances on the path of self-discovery. While concluding the sermon, the master exclaimed, "Never get perturbed by any hindrance and nuisance that come your way, nor strive to run away or escape from it. Whatever is bothering you, first accept it with love. You can't achieve anything on the path of self-realization by force or coercion. It's not combat; you have to be in harmony with everything around you. Once you accept your barriers with love and cease to struggle against them, instantly you overcome them as smooth as butter. Acceptance is Nirvana."

Upon hearing the words of the master, the damsel realized her flaws. Expeditiously, she stood up and headed straight toward the waterfall. Reaching close to it, the damsel gazed at the falling water for a while and then sat down in a lotus posture by closing her eyes. Initially, she acknowledged that she could only hear the sound of water and not any music. After that, she ceased trying to hear music and struggled even with the sound of water. Soon, the noise of the falling water that had troubled her transformed into a sense-appealing melody. The damsel had immersed herself in the sound of water and transcended all limitations. The next morning, Master Yoji didn't see her in the monastery. For a while, he thought that perhaps she had run away. But when he walked to the waterfall to check, he found her sitting in an intense meditative state. Master Yoji approached her and placed his hand gently on her head. The damsel gently opened her eyes and said, "I was listening to the nectareous tune of music, master."

"You have conquered your mind," the master responded with a soothing smile.

Somehow, I managed to pass the third day of practice. Following the evening session, Goenka Ji began his discourse, announcing that the next day would mark our entry into the realm of Pragya (insight). The actual practice was slated to commence then, as he was going to initiate us into Vipassana. Over the preceding three days, we had diligently practiced Anapana to sharpen and refine the mind, preparing it to receive Vipassana.

Goenka Ji further elaborated, "As you progress through the process, your mind will gradually become more subtle. Alongside this, suppressed tendencies of the mind will also surface. I understand that many of you may feel like escaping, with your mind craving various distractions. I empathize with your situation; it's natural because the mind has been conditioned this way since childhood. It yearns for instant pleasure, and I acknowledge that there is no immediate pleasure in simply sitting and observing the breath. However, patience is key. We are undergoing this rigorous practice to break free from the conditioning of the mind. Stay steadfast on this path and avoid resisting your mind; instead, accept reality as it is. Harmonize with your mind and avoid creating inner conflict. Whenever your mind starts to wander, acknowledge its wandering. Then gently guide it back to the rhythm of your breathing. Be a witness to the present moment and accept it fully. You have all come this far; I wish you all success. May there be well-being for everyone, and may all beings attain liberation."

After listening to the sermon, I felt remarkably serene. Goenka Ji's comforting words dissolved the agitation in my mind. It was as if his words were a healing balm for my inner turmoil. I began to recognize the mistake I was making. Like the damsel in the story, I had been struggling to ward off unnecessary thoughts, unwittingly feeding my mind's restlessness. Afterward, we had a meditation session where Goenka Ji directed us to shift our attention from the breath to our nostrils, focusing on observing any sensations present. He explained that these sensations could range from subtle to intense—heavy, cool, warm, light, or various other feelings—and emphasized the importance of simply witnessing each sensation without reacting or responding.

As I began concentrating on my nostrils, unexpectedly, I felt a sensation as if something were swirling around the surface. Momentarily taken aback by this unfamiliar sensation, I paused for a while, unsure of what was happening. Just moments before, there had been no such sensation, and suddenly, I perceived a swirling motion around my nostrils, moving in an anticlockwise direction at a steady pace. Yet, remembering Goenka Ji's instructions, I acknowledged the sensation and continued to observe it with mindfulness, without dwelling on its nature.

At the end of the session, the instructor called each of us individually to discuss our experiences. Most meditators shared that they had felt only subtle sensations. However, when it was my turn, I described the specific sensations I had experienced. But the instructor didn't react much or offer an explanation for my unique experience. Shortly afterward, we all returned to our respective rooms.

The fourth day promised to be significant for all of us, as Goenka Ji was going to initiate us into Vipassana. I was eager to see what would unfold next, after three days of intensive practice leading up to this moment. By noon on the fourth day, we continued our regular practice as we had done for the past three days. After lunch, during our meditation session, Goenka Ji instructed us to chant a prayer, invoking our master's blessings to receive Vipassana. Following that, Goenka Ji recited some suttas and instructed us to sit completely still, like a rock, without making even the slightest movement.

Goenka Ji instructed further, saying, "Focus on a small point at the center of your head and observe closely whatever sensation arises at that specific point. Simply observe the sensation with a detached attitude, exactly as it presents itself. Our task is solely observation." He added, "Even if you experience intense pain in your body, remain seated quietly, regardless. Pain itself is a sensation—do not react to it. Just observe it and remind yourself that it is transient and fleeting; it will not endure. Through this practice, you will soon witness the sensation fading away. This is the undeniable reality and nature of sensations—they are impermanent. Stay mindful, observing whatever unfolds in the present moment, and you are bound to be successful."

As I followed Goenka Ji's instructions, I began observing a specific point in the center of my head. Within moments, I felt sensations akin to tiny creatures moving at that spot. After some time, Goenka Ji directed us to expand our focus to a broader area and notice if we could detect similar sensations elsewhere.

When I widened my observation to encompass more of my head, I detected the same sensation. Continuing with his guidance, Goenka Ji encouraged us to explore every part of our head, observing any sensations present. Gradually, as I extended my attention across my entire head; it felt as though numerous tiny creatures were moving throughout. Regardless of where I moved my attention, I perceived the same subtle sensation of these minuscule entities.

For a moment, it appeared that the sensation arose from my focus, but in reality, it had been present from the beginning. The difference was that I had not been aware of it before. After an hour, Goenka Ji instructed us to redirect our attention to the area around our face, and then gradually to our neck, shoulders, arms, chest, and the rest of the body. As I shifted my focus from my head to my face, I began to sense a subtle trembling sensation on my forehead, and then on my eyebrows. Moving my attention across different points on my face, I felt this subtle trembling sensation everywhere—on my eyes, nose, cheeks, lips, and chin. Similarly, I shifted my attention to my neck, then shoulders, arms, fingers, chest, abdomen, genitals, and legs.

In certain areas of my body, such as the fingers of my hands, I experienced trembling sensations intensely, while in a few areas, the sensations were subtle or absent altogether. Goenka Ji advised us that if we didn't perceive any sensation at a particular point, we ought to remain there for a minute before shifting our attention elsewhere. Often, within that minute, sensations would begin to arise, but if not, we were encouraged to proceed without lingering for more than a minute. Goenka Ji emphasized: You ought not to anticipate any specific sensation; rather, you ought to attentively observe whatever is occurring in the present moment, adopting the role of a watcher.

Methodically, I moved my attention from head to toe in a precise sequence, finding the process quite captivating and calming my mind. Occasionally, I encountered severe pain in my joints. However, as Goenka Ji had advised, I reassured myself that this pain was temporary; it would soon subside. True to his guidance, the pain invariably faded away shortly thereafter. And so, the day passed as I continued to experience sensations throughout my entire body.

Another issue that frequently bothered me there was dinner. Generally, humans experience stronger food cravings in winter as our body temperature drops, stimulating our appetites. Consequently, I often felt hungry at night before sleeping. One day, I found a way to alleviate this to some extent. During our tea break, fruits were served daily—sometimes orange, kinnow, apple, or banana. Instead of eating the fruit in the dining hall, I started bringing it to my room to consume before bedtime.

While a single fruit couldn't thoroughly satisfy my hunger, having something was better than nothing. Additionally, I found solace in the presence of a house gecko that lived on the front wall of my room. I silently spoke to it, imagining it could hear my silent words. Whenever I felt restless or lonely, I would glance at the house gecko and reassure myself that at least someone was there with me.

Over the following two days, we practiced systematically shifting our attention throughout our entire body, from head to toe. Afterward, Goenka Ji instructed us to alternate this sequence, moving our attention from toe to head and then head to toe. As I followed these instructions, after some time, I began to feel a nimble vibration throughout every inch of my body. I could even sense the vibration in the tips of my fingers.

It reminded me of what I had learned in biology textbooks—that cells are the fundamental units of life, and our physical body is composed of countless active cells. This knowledge, once theoretical, now became tangible as I felt the vibrancy of my cells. I witnessed firsthand how millions of cells perish and regenerate in a mere moment. In various readings and teachings, I have encountered the idea that the physical body is mortal, altering ceaselessly and it's not our true identity. Now, I became acutely aware of the impermanence of this physical form, witnessing the subtle change occurring rapidly.

A few hours later, I entered a state where I no longer felt any physical coarseness, only vibrations. All sensations of grossness had completely disappeared, leaving me feeling weightless, like a feather drifting in the air.

Upon conducting various experiments, modern science now acknowledges that nothing in this creation is truly solid or gross. At the quantum level, the concept of 'solidity' becomes blurred due to the dual nature of matter; wave and particle. Anything that appears gross or solid is merely a result of the ceaseless dance of subatomic particles—electrons, protons, and neutrons. Upon deep reflection, one can readily realize that the entire cosmos is nothing but an eternal dance—the dance of supreme energy. Indeed, I was experiencing this dance, and it would not be inaccurate to say that I had become one with the dance itself.

While observing my physical body, I could feel the subtle movements of particles. Then, for a fleeting moment, I transcended my sensations, attention, observations, and everything else, reaching a state where there were only undulating waves all around. There was no experience, no experiencer, yet I existed. There were no memories, no body, no mind, yet I existed. The sense of 'I-ness' thoroughly dissolved in that moment. Then, it felt as if springs of ecstasy had surged within me.

With that experience, I realized that I am not this body, nor my thoughts, nor even my mind. I perceived that my true identity was beyond all physical manifestations. When the session concluded and I opened my eyes, I noticed that my entire body was soaked with sweat. Despite such a chilly environment, sweat had formed on my body due to a rise in the body temperature.

Later that night, after Goenka Ji's discourse, the instructor gathered us to discuss our experiences. We approached him in groups of five, sharing our sensations. Some meditators spoke of warmth and lightness in their bodies, while others described subtle ordinary sensations they were experiencing. When I approached the instructor, he asked softly, "Did you feel the sensations in your body?"

I nodded with a tender smile and responded politely, "Indeed! I have read about these concepts in texts, but now I have lived through them. Until today, they were theories to me, but now they are in my experience. I have truly encountered the transient nature of this physical body, along with a glimpse of my true essence. It was immensely blissful."

My words captivated the attention of every meditator, filling the hall with astonishment. At that moment, all eyes were fixed on me, brimming with wonder and curiosity. The instructor, smiling warmly, acknowledged my experience with a nod before moving on to the next individual.

As I mentioned earlier, the sight of the snow-covered Himalayan peaks loses its thrill if you keep gazing at them for too long. Similarly, two days had passed, and we were still receiving the same instructions to move our attention throughout the body. Now I was eager to move forward and experience something more transcendent. Then, an unexpected incident occurred.

On the eighth day, my mind rebelled once again. Thoughts of leaving the Centre started to flood my mind. I wondered about what might be happening outside the premises. My mind began craving pleasure. Some suppressed tendencies and impressions of the mind were yet to surface. I thought that I had altered the old conditioning of my mind, but I was mistaken.

After the tea break, to soothe the inner turmoil, I went to the parking lot where my motorbike was parked. I stood there for a moment, gazing at it. The black color of my Royal Enfield had turned grey from the dust. 'Just two more days, and then we will go home,' I thought to myself as I looked at it.

That night, an unusual incident occurred at the Centre, known only to a few. The following morning, I observed the meditator who usually sat in front of me in the meditation hall standing at the instructor's door alongside the head coordinator. They seemed engaged in a serious discussion. I only learned the full story on the final day of the course when I approached the guy and asked why he had been standing there. Without hesitation, the guy disclosed that he had climbed through a wall and entered the women's domain. His revelation left me utterly astonished. Out of curiosity, I probed further, asking him, "What compelled you to take such a daring step?"

"I fell in love with a girl from overseas, a white girl, and I was desperate to see her. But when I jumped over the wall, the coordinator caught me," he replied, laughing unabashedly.

Initially, I dismissed it as a joke—how could such a thing be possible? However, when others corroborated his story, I was astounded. I have encountered many daring individuals in my life, but he was on another level altogether. His audacity was remarkable! Despite his actions, he showed no remorse. It was a disgraceful act. This serves as a reminder never to assume that only noble individuals inhabit sacred places. One must learn to coexist humbly among all types of people, remaining unaffected by their actions, much like the lotus flower that remains untainted by the ooze of a pond in which it blooms.

It was our final day at the Vipassana Centre. Throughout the day, we diligently practiced meditation. In the evening, we were shown a video about the 'Tihar Jail'. The video showed prisoners in Tihar practicing Vipassana meditation and sharing their profound life-changing experiences. They expressed gratitude for the opportunity to transform their lives and become virtuous individuals. Indeed! Witnessing this brought a sense of pleasantness to my heart.

Afterward, Goenka Ji imparted us with final instructions: The work is not yet complete. Ten days are insufficient for such profound work. You must continue practicing until you attain the ultimate goal—liberation from all limitations. Apply what you have learned here in your daily lives. The real test begins when you leave this Vipassana Centre and face the world. Only then will you truly understand if you have transcended your conditioning.

After a brief pause, Goenka Ji continued, "These courses at the Vipassana Centre are offered free of charge. We do not ask for any payment. However, this organization relies solely on donations. I am not asking you to donate, but reflect on the fact that you have lived here for ten days as a monk, provided with all necessary comforts, thanks to someone's generosity. Your contribution ensures that future meditators also receive the support they need during their practice. If you choose to donate, do it with the intention of benefiting others, not yourself. May all beings find welfare and liberation."

Later, I met Rishabh and other fellow meditators. We exchanged our experiences, insights, and observations from the past ten days. Shortly after, an individual approached me. His name was Kamaljeet, and he mentioned that he held a senior position in the Haryana Police Department. "I have been eager to meet you ever since the day you boldly shared with the instructor that you have experienced what you have read in books. It was incredible!" Mr. Kamaljeet continued while admiring, "I have never seen anyone state something like that so directly. It left quite an impression. You have no idea, but everyone here is talking about you. They all want to know your name."

I chuckled at his words, not sensing anything unusual in what I had said. After a brief pause, Mr. Kamaljeet expressed, "Listen, Madhusudan, what Goenka Ji preaches in his sermons is all well and good to a certain extent. We attend these meditation courses to calm our minds and to take a break from the daily grind. But in practical life, things don't always work that way. Love, compassion, mercy—all these sentiments can't solve every problem." He continued, "I am a police officer; I have a team of twenty to thirty people under me. Some of them are so unreliable that if I don't show strictness, they won't perform their duties properly. If I try to be gentle and polite, they will take advantage of me. I am certain I won't achieve the desired results that way. Unfortunately, I have to be tough with them because I also answer to my superiors. Hence my friend, here is my advice to you: It's good to be into these spiritual practices, but you have to be practical in life. You can't solve everything with sweet words. The world operates in a certain way, and you have to navigate that reality. Sometimes, you have to get your hands dirty to clean up the mess."

In response, I nodded gently in understanding and bid him farewell. By the way, what Mr. Kamaljeet said made sense to some extent. He wasn't entirely wrong in his perspective. If I were in his shoes, I might have similar views. However, the key factor here is intention. A Guru often employs tough love when their disciple makes a mistake, not out of opposition, but because they genuinely care for the disciple. The sincerity and intention behind our actions are crucial, as nature judges our karma based on these motives. Always hold compassion in your heart, even when circumstances require you to speak sternly.

Later on, a senior coordinator approached me and commended my commitment to the practice. He happily conveyed that even the instructor had taken notice and admired my dedication. He told me that the instructor remarked: This young man has the potential to become the next Buddha. If he remains steadfast and unwavering, he will attain Nirvana one day.

Following that, he encouraged me to continue on the path and maintain my practice. I respectfully bowed to him with folded hands and received his blessings.

The ten-day Vipassana meditation course came to an end, and it was time for me to return to the everyday world. I packed all my belongings into my backpack and tidied up the room. Goenka Ji's final words about charity deeply resonated with me, so I made a donation according to my caliber. Afterward, I gathered my belongings from the registration area and called my father to assure them of my well-being before setting off for home. I said my farewells to my fellow meditators and made my way to the parking lot where my Royal Enfield awaited, covered in dust. I cleaned it off and began my journey homeward.

Reflecting on those ten days, my time at the retreat taught me a great deal. I discovered insights into my own mind's nature and witnessed the evanescent nature of the physical world. Many long-held illusions were shattered, especially the idea that I could easily embrace a monk's path and renounce worldly attachments. It became evident how deeply my mind was entangled in material pursuits and habits.

Yet, ten days proved insufficient to thoroughly transform my mind's conditioning; ongoing effort would be necessary. While residing there, I came across a profound insight that we humans uniquely require engagement and stimulation to maintain mental equilibrium, unlike any other species on this planet.

Furthermore, I learned that Siddharth Gautam was not the sole Buddha; there have been many before him, and there continue to be several today. Becoming a Buddha is not a monopoly; anyone who achieves self-realization attains this state. Goenka Ji's teachings on Dhamma or Dharm were invaluable, emphasizing a moral way of life. His focus was on imparting an approach to experiencing reality in the present moment rather than getting entangled in philosophical debates. This aspect made their organization truly exceptional.

I didn't anticipate that these ten days would so profoundly shift my perspective and reflect the truth back to me. I realized that there was still much more to learn and experience; I had a long way to go. However, I resolved to continue chanting the name of Lord Ram because the peace and fulfillment I found in devotion to Lord Ram were unmatched by any other spiritual practice. The experiences during Vipassana meditation deepened my quest for ultimate reality, as I became aware of the impermanence of the physical realm. I began to wonder: Is there something eternal in existence? Is there anything that remains constant and unshakable?

Driven by these questions, I continued my journey in search of that eternal source—the Absolute Truth.

As time passed, I found myself irresistibly drawn to the profound and mystical practices of the Tantra tradition, captivated by its depth and transformative potential.

CHAPTER 14
A TANTRA PRACTITIONER

Among the diverse dimensions of spirituality, Tantra has often been misunderstood and misrepresented over the centuries, unfairly stigmatized in our society. It's significant to remark that Western interpretations and influence have played a significant role in this misrepresentation, sometimes intentionally distorting our cultural heritage and traditions. As a result, even in the contemporary era, ordinary people often react with apprehension upon hearing terms like Tantra, Tantric practices, Aghora, etc. However, upon closer examination, one discovers that Tantra is a deeply sacred, unassuming, systematic, and mystical practice with ancient roots that span cultures and ages.

The Tantra tradition is widely believed to predate both the Vedic period and Hinduism itself. This raises the question: Why does society harbor such apprehension towards Tantra, considering it an ancient, sacred, and systematic practice? Why has it been largely taboo and prohibited for so long, with people avoiding discussion and viewing it as inferior or malevolent? Why is it not widely practiced or recognized in our culture?

To understand these reasons, it's important first to grasp certain aspects of Tantra in its context. Before we proceed further, I want to clarify one important thing: I do not claim myself an accomplished practitioner of Tantra, at least not yet. My knowledge has been gleaned from Tantric scriptures, texts, and insights shared by several dedicated Tantra practitioners and scholars. However, my understanding in this domain is substantial enough that I cannot be misled or deceived in matters concerning Tantra.

The realm of Tantra is indeed vast, encompassing a lifelong journey of learning and practice. Yet, there are fundamental aspects that every seeker ought to understand about it. Let's begin with its meaning: the Sanskrit word 'Tantra' signifies a method, approach, or specific way of performing a particular task. Just as a methodical approach is used to achieve precise results in any endeavor, Tantra serves as a method or approach through which a seeker can attain heightened states of consciousness and transcend all physical and metaphysical limitations by merging with the Absolute. It is the path through which the finite can seamlessly merge into the infinite, realizing the true essence of the Self. By transcending body, mind, space, and time, Tantra aims to uncover the Supreme Energy within, marking its ultimate objective.

According to various Tantric scriptures, the Supreme Energy, the Divine Source, the Creator, the Absolute, or whatever term one prefers to use, is known as 'Adishakti' or 'Adya', meaning 'the first'. Adishakti represents the original source from which this entire existence emanates, often embodied as Mahadevi. As the origin of creation, Adishakti is revered as the Prime Mother.

From Adya emerged two distinct forms: Shiva and Shakti, representing masculine and feminine energies respectively. 'Shiva' symbolizes supreme consciousness inseparable from Shakti. These two energies function in tandem, each supporting the other. Hence, the diverse manifestations of Shiva and Shakti are revered as deities within the Tantric tradition.

The divine feminine is embodied as Kundalini Shakti, residing in a dormant state at the base of the spine in every individual. Tantra provides an approach to awaken this energy and ascend through the piercing of various Chakras present in our body, culminating in its union with Shiva, resulting in a state of oneness that leads the seeker to absolute unity. Tantra opens the gateway to boundless possibilities, enabling practitioners to attain virtually anything in the material realm: fame, wealth, luxurious living, prosperity, and whatnot.

Through Tantra, a seeker can achieve extraordinary feats beyond the imagination of ordinary people, such as longevity, perpetual youthfulness, voluntary transcendence, prophetic abilities, connection with otherworldly forces, various Siddhis, and many others. Yet, these are merely distractions that can lead practitioners away from the ultimate goal, engaging them in earthly pleasures rather than pursuing higher spiritual objectives.

Siddhis are the rewards bestowed upon a practitioner when they achieve milestones on their path, signaling progress in the right direction. This phase is critical in a practitioner's journey, requiring careful navigation forward. However, Siddhis tend to ensnare a practitioner in worldly pleasures, causing many to prematurely end their spiritual journey. These powers can either propel one to the pinnacle of spiritual growth or lead one to plummet by indulging in desires and cravings. Therefore, Siddhis are often likened to toxic substances that emerge from excessive practice, potentially obstructing a practitioner's path. Only a rare few, about one percent, ascend sincerely to the zenith, forsaking all temptations. This quality of a true practitioner is shown by their unwillingness to boast or show off their spiritual accomplishments before others.

Two indispensable components in Tantric practices are Yantra and Mantra. 'Yantra' simply refers to a tool, instrument, or specific object necessary for performing a task. In Tantric rituals, a Yantra can take various forms such as a picture, a deity's idol, a crystal, gemstones, beads, or other relevant objects. However, traditionally in Tantra, a Yantra is often depicted as a mystical geometric structure, meticulously crafted in two or three dimension on materials like metal, wood, paper, or even on the ground.

Each intricate shape and pattern within a Yantra holds precise symbolism related to the deity it represents. For instance, the Bindu or red dot at the center signifies the divine seed of creation, serving as the core or starting point of the Yantra. The downward-pointing triangle symbolizes feminine energy (Shakti), while the upward-pointing triangle represents masculine energy (Shiva). The hexagram or six-pointed star signifies the union of Shiva and Shakti, while lotus petals symbolize purity and absoluteness. The circle denotes continuity and the cycle of manifestation, while squares and rectangles represent the earth element and various directions. These shapes are commonly found in Yantras across different practices.

In Tantric rituals, Yantra is essential as it is revered as the 'abode of the deity' always associated with a specific Mantra. Additionally, a practitioner's physical body is considered the greatest Yantra, housing divine energy within.

'Mantra' is the vibrational energy essential for invoking a deity. Each deity possesses its unique Mantra known as the 'Bija Mantra' or seed syllable. These syllables, such as ॐ, लं, वं, ऐं, श्रीं, and others, carry potent sonic energy without specific translations or meanings. In Tantric tradition, a Bija Mantra represents the fundamental power of a deity, often considered the deity itself in the form of sound energy. There exists no deity without a corresponding Mantra, and vice versa; they are fundamentally identical, differing only in their mode of expression according to circumstances. Therefore, Bija Mantras are profoundly powerful and traditionally chanted only after initiation under the guidance of a Guru.

When a practitioner embraces a Bija Mantra, it is like sowing a seed in the soil of consciousness. Gradually, the divine energy within the seed begins to manifest in the practitioner's inner world, akin to a seed growing into a mighty tree. Thus, the practitioner attunes themselves to the deity, and what manifests within their Chidakasha can also manifest in the outer world, aligning the microcosm with the macrocosm.

To illustrate how the triad of Tantra, Mantra, and Yantra functions together: consider the physical body as the Yantra—a tool through which we navigate and interact with the world. The vital energy needed to sustain and function this body is likened to the Mantra. Similarly, the method or approach necessary for the body's functions represents Tantra. Put simply, a Mantra is essential for the consecration of a Yantra, and the entire spiritual process involved in this consecration is referred to as Tantra.

Within Tantra, there are generally two primary paths to follow: the Right-hand path known as Dakshinachara, and the Left-hand path known as Vamachara. These paths differ in their approaches and practices, yet both ultimately lead the practitioner to the same destination. Thus, neither path is inherently superior nor inferior; each holds its own significance. Let's delve briefly into these two paths:

- **The Right-hand path** – This is the path of orthodox, virtuous, and moral conduct that emphasizes on purity of body and mind including the external environment. The Vedic rituals and other forms of worship that we practice in our homes, shrines, and other sacred places are considered the Right-hand path practices. Other than that, various yogic practices such as Kundalini Yoga, Kriya Yoga, Siddha Yoga, Ashtanga Yoga, Samkhya Yoga, Bhakti Yoga, Raj Yoga, and others are also considered the Right-hand path. A practitioner is instructed to consume Sattvik and pure substances during practice such as fresh fruits, flowers, freshly cooked foodstuffs, fresh milk, honey, sweets, etc. This is the path for devotees, it is not mandatory to get initiation to follow this path. One can worship the Divine according to their convenience. This path involves practices that focus on gradual progression towards spiritual enlightenment by transcending the ego.
- **The left-hand path** – This is the non-orthodox, forbidden, and socially unwelcomed path in which there is no discrimination between pure and impure, positive and negative, ethical and non-ethical, auspicious and inauspicious. The practitioners believe that everything emanates from the Supreme Being so everything is divine in itself. Therefore, they don't loathe anything rather, accept everything as a source of energy. This path emphasizes thoroughly the inner purity of a being, it has not much concern with the purity of the physical body and the external environment. This path is not meant for everyone; one cannot willingly walk on this path. Only those who are initiated by an accomplished Guru, who itself

supposed to be a practitioner of the Left-hand path, can follow this path. The practitioner is supposed to offer and consume five forbidden substances during rituals known as the Punchamakra:

- *Mans* (meat)
- *Matsya* (fish)
- *Madira* (alcohol)
- *Mudra* (parched grain)
- *Maithun* (sexual intercourse)

One cannot avoid these five substances while following the Left-hand Tantra. Most rituals and Tantric practices on this path are performed in prohibited places such as cremation grounds, graveyards, dense woods, and other uninhabitable places usually after midnight. The practitioners are fond of such things that society considers forbidden and malicious. They move ahead on the path while embracing all the aspects of nature; they adopt what common folks avoid. The Left-hand path is highly disciplined and quite unpredictable as compared to the Right-hand path. It can ascend one to the ultimate reality and can also turn into ashes within a moment. There is no amendment for mistakes on this path, one inevitably has to confront the consequences. Well, as per the perspective of some Tantric practitioners, the Left-hand path is the actual Tantric path.

When learning about the two paths of Tantra, many seekers wonder why some prefer the Left-hand path over the Right-hand path when both lead to the same entity. Let's consider an analogy: suppose you want to extract water from the ground. You have two options, you can either dig a well with your hands or use machines to create a pit. Digging by hand may take months while using equipment can get you water in just a few hours. This illustrates the difference between the two paths. The Left-hand path is akin to using equipment to extract water quickly. In essence, the Left-hand Tantra is a direct and slightly rapid path to spiritual realization as compared to the Right-hand path.

Now, let's address the questions we posed initially. There are several reasons why Tantra is often considered taboo in our community. The primary reason is the practice of the Left-hand path. This path involves bizarre and mysterious rituals that appear sinister and extremely unsettling from a societal perspective. Such practices include animal sacrifices, worshipping in cremation grounds while smearing ashes on the body, consuming highly intoxicating substances, wearing rosaries made of human skulls, performing sexual intercourse during worship, offering raw flesh and blood to the deity and consuming it as Prasad, meditating while sitting on a corpse, and many others.

Ordinary people fear death, but Tantra practitioners sit among burning bodies and adorn themselves with their ashes. While an average individual shuns darkness, a Tantra practitioner is drawn to it, recognizing its equal importance to light. There can be no light without darkness. What society views as inferior, they embrace in a sacred form.

The truth is that our lack of appropriate knowledge about Tantra leads to misunderstandings of its mystical rituals and practices. We tend to see everything in dualities because of our mind: good and evil, positive and negative, black and white, day and night. In contrast, Tantric practitioners put their minds aside and perceive everything as unified, seeing the Divine in all things, beyond notions of good and evil, positive and negative. For them, every act is sacred because it is performed for the Divine. However, due to our ignorance, we mistakenly view these practices as gruesome and uncivilized ways of worshipping God.

Another reason is that for centuries, Tantra has been misused for nefarious and harmful purposes. Some practitioners in the past exploited their Tantric powers, inflicting terrifying acts on innocent people. This caused widespread fear, leading ordinary folks to view Tantra as evil. It is similar to how a sword can be used for protection or for harm, depending on the wielder's intentions. Fire can illuminate a path in darkness, but it can also burn everything to the ground. Ultimately, it depends on how one chooses to use it.

In the land of Bharat, there are several revered sites known as strongholds of Tantra practitioners, such as the Kamakhya Temple in Assam, Tarapith in West Bengal, Vishvanath Temple in Varanasi, Mahakaleshwar Temple in Ujjain, Chausath Yogini Temple in Madhya Pradesh, Dakshineshwar Kali Temple in Kolkata, and a few in the southern regions. These locations are believed to host divine energy in its potent, vibrant, raw, and natural form.

After the winter break, I returned to Haridwar. Alongside my academic studies, I delved deeper into certain profound aspects of spirituality such as Tantra. Through studying Tantric texts and listening to Om Swami's insights on Tantra, I gradually recognized that the methods taught by my Guru were themselves rooted in Tantric practices—I was creating events within my Chidakasha using the power of the Bija Mantra 'Ram' while employing my breath and body as a Yantra. Those events and experiences were as tangible and significant to me as the physical world around me.

During that period, I befriended someone named Sangam, a lively individual passionate about worldly pursuits. Originally acquainted through my cousin's circle of friends, Sangam often visited my aunt's place to see my cousin, eventually becoming my friend as well. He was actively involved with the RSS, a group dedicated to societal welfare, which led him into politics and social causes. Whenever we met, our discussions ranged from current events in science and religion to broader global issues. From his words, it was clear that he had great potential, but financial difficulties at the time restricted his opportunities and affected his life.

Typically, there are numerous ways for an individual to become wealthy. It's a different matter that some methods are ethical while many are not. Sangam initially pursued wealth ethically, but when things didn't work out, he chose an unconventional path. I call it an unconventional path because it's one that only a rare individual, one in a million would follow.

When I saw Sangam that day, there was a distinct charm on his face. He appeared quite organized. We were meeting after a long time, so I asked him what he was doing these days. Knowing I was a spiritual seeker, Sangam didn't hesitate to tell me that he was practicing Tantra.

It was slightly surprising for me because I never expected him to become a Tantric practitioner; he had once told me he was a sincere devotee of Lord Hanuman. However, I was glad to know that he was also on the path of self-realization, just like me.

This was the first time I was speaking with a Tantric practitioner in person, and I was eager to learn more about his practices and rituals. Sangam told me, he was initiated into Tantra by his uncle, who was also a practitioner. Making his uncle his Guru, Sangam was worshipping Goddess Matangi. His practice lasted forty-one days, during which he had to go to the bank of the river Ganga every night after midnight and recite the deity's Mantra a certain number of times while standing in the water. After that, he performed rituals requiring specific items, such as flowers, raw meat, and alcohol, as offerings to the deity. Hearing Sangam's words, I immediately realized that he was engaged in an extraordinary practice.

Scriptures such as the Rudrayamala Tantra, Tantrasara, Shakti-Samagam Tantra, and Devi Bhagavat Purana describe an enigmatic group of ten Goddesses known as the Das-Mahavidya. These ten goddesses are as follows: Kali, Tara, Lalita Tripura-Sundri, Bhuvaneshri, Bhairavi, Chinnamasta, Dhumavati, Baglamukhi, Matangi, and Kamala. According to these scriptures, all these goddesses are manifestations of Shakti, embodying Her various attributes.

Sangam was delving into something profound, as the deity he was worshipping is depicted as a vengeful, Tamasic form of energy in Tantric tradition.

Among the Ten-Mahavidya, Goddess Matangi is worshipped according to the Left-hand path. She is considered an outcast Goddess who favors polluted, abandoned, and impure things. Matangi is slightly more challenging to access compared to the other deities in the Mahavidya, and She is usually worshipped to attain supernatural powers.

Out of curiosity, I asked Sangam about his true objective behind worshipping the Goddess. He candidly told me that he sought to attain immense wealth and was performing this rigorous penance to please the Goddess. Hearing his purpose, I grew somewhat concerned for him.

Om Swami once said in his sermons that if a seeker practices Tantra to achieve Siddhi for fulfilling material desires, eventually the Siddhi itself can cause the seeker's downfall. Without renouncing ego and detaching from the material world, it is impossible to handle such powers responsibly.

However, I chose not to say anything to Sangam about this, as I didn't want to raise any doubts in his mind. Perhaps the Divine intended for me not to interfere with his destiny. Sangam also mentioned some peculiar herbs he used in his practices, such as Hatha Jodi, Kamal Gatta, and Rakta Kunja, along with other miraculous substances like Siyar Singhi and Indrajal, typically used to protect the practitioner from malevolent and supernatural forces. During our conversation, Sangam casually mentioned a twenty-claw turtle. He said that he was currently searching for such a turtle. As soon as he mentioned it, I remembered the turtle we had at home. I told him that I had a twenty-claw turtle. His eyes lit up, and he eagerly offered three lakh rupees for it.

Upon hearing the amount, I was taken aback. Initially, I thought he might be joking, but then he insisted that I call my father. I started considering the possibility of a significant deal, even though the turtle had been just an ordinary one for us. So, I promptly called my father to inquire about the turtle. But my father informed me that he had given the turtle to one of my uncles a few weeks earlier. When I called my uncle, he regretfully told me that he had unknowingly lost the turtle. My uncle explained that he used to let the turtle roam outside every few days, but one day it disappeared while he was occupied with other tasks after setting it free. In an instant, my excitement plummeted.

When I informed Sangam about the lost turtle, he started laughing. "It's not surprising that the turtle vanished. I know these turtles are not inclined to stay in one place for long. Finding such turtles is difficult, and even if you manage to find one, keeping them safe is an even greater challenge. He added, "You can have three lakh rupees in cash anytime for a twenty-claw turtle."

"Why is that specific turtle so important to you that you are willing to pay such a substantial amount?" I asked him, my expression reflecting curiosity. I was eager to unravel the mystery behind his interest in the turtle.

"This amount is trivial, my friend, but it's the most I can offer." Sangam explained further, "In reality, this turtle is invaluable because it is used in Tantric rituals associated with Goddess Lakshmi. It can serve as a Yantra in Her worship, drawing prosperity into one's life." He went on to advise, "If you ever find a turtle with twenty claws, never sell it or give it away. In fact, refrain from discussing it with anyone. The turtle embodies the Goddess Herself; as long as it remains within your home, your people will never experience financial crises."

After discussing more about his practice, Sangam bid farewell. Before he left, I offered him a friendly piece of advice to exercise extreme caution during his practice, emphasizing the unpredictability of his chosen path. I wished him good fortune as he departed.

For several months, we didn't keep in touch. During this time, I was deeply immersed in my spiritual studies. One day, I encountered Sangam again in Haridwar. He appeared gaunt and frail, lacking the vitality and radiance that once defined him. It seemed as though something had drained the sparkle and vigor from his body.

"What happened to you, my friend? How did you end up in this state?" I asked Sangam, expressing concern.

"A few days ago, I fell sick and had some serious health issues," he responded putting a synthetic smile on his face.

"Oh...! But weren't you involved in some Tantric practices? Did they bring you any fortune?" I asked, curious.

"It's all thanks to those practices," he chuckled.

I didn't catch the hint of sarcasm at first. Then, a moment later, he grew somber and uttered, "My Tantric practices ended up having the opposite effect."

"I'd like to hear the whole story. Please, tell me what happened," I said consoling him, placing my hand on his shoulder.

Sangam looked into my eyes and smiled before recounting the whole ordeal: Everything was progressing as expected. I was nearing the completion of my forty-one days of practice. According to my Guru, the Goddess was supposed to appear before me on the 41st day. It happened three days before the end of my practice. My Guru instructed me to perform a specific ritual in the evening. On my way back after completing the ritual, I had some offerings to deliver to someone from the outcast community. As I headed towards their settlement, I encountered an old, unkempt woman. She wore torn, dirty clothes, resembling a beggar. She blocked my path and asked for a bundle of Bidi (a type of cigarette). Although I had a bundle of Bidi with me along with the offerings, I didn't give it to her. Instead, I promised to buy her one from a nearby store. A small shop was just a few steps away, where I purchased a large bundle of Bidi.

However, when I turned to give it to her, she had vanished. I searched around thoroughly, but she was nowhere to be found. I brushed off the incident and returned home. Just before midnight, suddenly some of my limbs stopped moving. I couldn't sit properly or speak; it felt as though my tongue was tied. Gradually, half of my body became paralyzed. When my Guru learned about everything that had transpired, he informed me that the filthy lady was none other than Goddess Matangi Herself, who had appeared to receive the offerings. Due to my lack of insight, I failed to recognize Her. As a result, the Goddess became displeased with me, and in an instant, I lost the benefits of my worship. If my Guru hadn't intervened, it would have been difficult for me to survive. I am foolish and thick-headed; my Guru had previously mentioned during a casual conversation that the Goddess might test my devotion someday.

As Sangam recounted the event, his heart weighed heavily. I couldn't help but feel compassion for him. Trying to console him, I said, "Back when you first mentioned your Tantric practices, I intended to warn you. These deities are temperamental and unforgiving of mistakes. One ought not to approach them seeking material desires because even a minor slip-up can be disastrous for the practitioner."

"You are absolutely correct about that. I had no idea things could escalate to this extent," Sangam murmured. His condition was distressing; I had never seen such despair on his face.

"What are your plans moving forward?" I asked gently.

"I am looking for a job. I need it for survival," he chuckled softly while shifting his gaze away.

"May Lord Ram bless you," I prayed for him smiling while bidding farewell.

To some extent, I was aware of the consequences that Sangam was facing. I have personally witnessed the aftermath of Tantra practitioners who lost their sanity due to their practices. I remember a practitioner who would speak continuously for 24 hours as if conversing with an entity visible only to him. Another would wander the streets like a deranged person, verbally abusing anyone who crossed his path. I recall a practitioner in my mother's village who would howl every night, pleading with someone to leave him alone, despite living in solitude. Tragically, they all met brutal ends. Nearly all of them took their own lives; some embraced fire and burned themselves, while others jumped in front of moving trains and ended themselves.

At that moment, I couldn't comprehend how someone could lose their sanity due to worshipping God. Later, as I delved deeper into Tantra, I learned the true reasons behind their suffering. Sangam was fortunate; he survived through it all.

To delve deeper into the realm of Tantra, let me share with you an unsettling phenomenon that occurred to an ordinary individual who achieved a Siddhi through the grace of an Aghori.

CHAPTER 15

AN ECCENTRIC AGHORI

It happened in Kashi years back, there lived a man named Shreenath. He belonged to a Brahmin family, residing with his parents, wife, and son in an ordinary house. Shreenath was a mediocre fortune teller; he used to make his living by crafting horoscopes and performing some Vedic rituals. However, he was not the maestro in his field.

Usually, Shreenath used to anticipate a few things related to an individual's life just by observing their expressions, but he couldn't predict any extraordinary event that was about to happen in someone's life. For that reason, Shreenath wasn't counted among the versed fortune tellers in the city who could attract the crowd of householders. Therefore, Shreenath was in pursuit of some mystical power that could bring him fame throughout the entire city and abundant wealth.

One day, Shreenath was sitting near the bank of the river Ganga. He was engrossed in thoughts regarding his family and the future. In the meantime, he saw an Aghori who was passing through there. There was a certain magnetic force in the Aghori that Shreenath couldn't resist himself following him. The Aghori went to a nearby cemetery and sat next to a recently burnt pyre. Following him, Shreenath also entered the cemetery and sat a few steps away from him.

The Aghori took a stick and started to draw something in the ashes. Shreenath was gazing at him keenly. The Aghori was wearing numerous rosaries of Rudraksha beads around his neck along with a Mundamala (rosary made with skull beads). In his right hand, he was wearing a couple of silver bangles. Except for a black fabric tied around his waist covering his legs, the Aghori was wearing nothing. His long dreadlocks were tied like a turban on his head and his body was smeared in ashes. Apart from a messy sack, the Aghori only had a grubby metal bowl.

After a while, the Aghori stared at Shreenath but didn't utter a word neither did Shreenath strive to have a word with him. Both of them kept watching each other from a distance. Thenceforth, Shreenath began to visit the Aghori every single day. He always found him sitting among the pyres drawing something in the ashes.

Shreenath was familiar with the caliber of Aghoris; he knew well that if the Aghori took pity on him, he could eat the jam with a golden spoon. Therefore, he began to make efforts to please the Aghori by bringing him edible offerings. However, the Aghori paid him no attention. Every day, Shreenath would visit the Aghori, place the food at his feet, sit beside him for a while, and then return home. Before eating the food Shreenath brought, the Aghori would look at him and laugh fiercely. Only then would he pick up the offering, place it in his bowl, and start eating.

A month passed like this, but the Aghori didn't utter a word to Shreenath. One day, abruptly Shreenath's son fell sick; the toddler had a severe fever. Shreenath's wife asked him to stay home because she was quite anxious about their son's health. Shreenath agreed to her request and stayed at home. He couldn't visit the Aghori that day, Shreenath was so worried that he didn't even think of the Aghori. His entire family was concerned about the toddler. Haplessly that day, their only physician was also out of the city.

In the evening, while keeping cold water strips on the forehead of his son, unexpectedly Shreenath fell asleep. While sleeping, he had a weird dream in which he saw that the Aghori was calling him; he was calling his name aloud sitting in the cemetery. Shreenath woke up from sleep in a flash and looked around. He found himself in the room with his son. In the next instant, he recalled the Aghori and made up his mind to visit him instantly. Without any further delay, Shreenath told his wife that he had to leave right away for some urgent work and he would return soon. Having said this, Shreenath ran toward the cemetery to see the Aghori. When Shreenath reached there, the Aghori welcomed him, saying, "Jai Mahakaal! Oh, you have come. Come on, sit next to me."

It was the first time when the Aghori was talking to him. Shreenath was sitting next to him but in his head, he was still thinking about his son. "Hahaha...You can relax, your son will be fine. Now you have come to me, everything will be great," the Aghori uttered roaring with demonic laughter.

Hearing about his son, Shreenath was stunned for a moment. But then he thought that for an Aghori, mind reading was merely a child's play. A few moments later, an exceptionally elegant lady approached them with two bottles of wine along with some cooked meat. She approached and sat cozily in the lap of the Aghori while placing the stuff on the ground.

Following that, the lady poured the meat into the bowl of Aghori and started feeding him with her hands. Shreenath was staring at her as if he had not seen such a charming woman in his life. She had dark long curly hair and a fair complexion. Her eyes seemed to be a replica of the eyes of a reindeer. Her nose was adorned with a round golden nose pin and her lips seemed as if loaded with red wine. She was adorned with delicate, gleaming jewels on her neck and arms, which perfectly complemented her red robes.

The well-grown body of the lady was magnetizing Shreenath; he had entirely forgotten about his wife and his son who was in a critical situation. Her beauty seemed to leave him in a state of numbness. Just in the blink of an eye, the Aghori engulfed both bottles of wine and then he picked the lady up in his arms and started dancing. Shreenath was perplexed seeing all this, that scenario was beyond his intellect. A while later, the lady took leave from them. As she left Shreenath couldn't resist himself to ask the Aghori, "Baba, if you don't get offended, may I ask something?"

"Certainly, my son!"

"She didn't seem your daughter. Who was she and why did she bring you all that stuff?" Shreenath asked with some hesitation.

"Oh, you nut! How could she be my daughter? Just because I am looking old and she is pretty young?" the Aghori uttered in a mild scolding manner. He added ahead, "Don't mistake her for a human; she is a mighty Yakshini (demi-goddess). Through rigorous penance, I have attained her, and now she serves me akin to a consort. She fulfills all my desires, both physical and, to some extent, transcendent."

Shreenath was listening to him attentively. It was fascinating for him to witness some ethereal entity in person. Now it was quite dark so Shreenath took leave from the Aghori and headed towards home. But the captivating appearance of the Yakshini lingered in his eyes; he was thinking about her all the way. When Shreenath reached home, he saw that his son was playing leisurely just like any healthy lad. He was delighted to see his son healthy. Later on, his wife told him that an unfamiliar physician came home a few minutes later when he left home. Nobody among them saw him ever before neither did he talk to anyone. He just put a medicine in the toddler's mouth and left.

Shreenath wasn't certain about it but he knew somewhere that the anonymous physician was none other than the Aghori. The next day, Shreenath visited the Aghori with some delicious sweets. Seeing him coming, the Aghori started roaring with laughter. "How's your son now?" the Aghori asked comically.

"He regained his health, Baba," Shreenath responded bowing his head at the feet of the Aghori.

"It's all the play of Mahakaal, Jai Mahakaal!" the Aghori started roaring again with laughter.

Then the Aghori put the sweets in his bowl and started consuming them. He was quite pleased with Shreenath and well aware of his desire.

At night, Shreenath was lying on his bed, thoroughly absorbed in the thoughts about the Yakshini. It seemed as if she had done some spell on him. Now Shreenath aspired to attain the Yakshini but he didn't dare to mention it to the Aghori. In the meanwhile, he fell asleep and had a bizarre dream—Shreenath saw that he was sitting with the Aghori in the cremation ground; numerous pyres were burning around them.

"I am impressed with your service, my son. Therefore, I feel compelled to grant you, my Siddhi," the Aghori expressed followed by his laughter. "Are you ready to attain that Yaksini?"

Shreenath nodded instantly and said yes. The Aghori started chanting and then after a moment, the Yakshini appeared there and sat among them. She looked immensely beautiful and delighted, adorned with all sorts of jewels just like a new bride. The Aghori gave her a look and then started laughing like the thunder of clouds. Thereafter, he poured some alcohol from a bottle into his bowl and took a deep sip. Then he leaned towards the Yakshini and released all the alcohol filled in his mouth on her.

The Yakshini started burning instantaneously and within no time, she turned into dark smoke. The Aghori placed the bowl in Shreenath's hand and asked him to swallow the rest of the alcohol in one sip. Shreenath followed his instructions and vacated the bowl in one sip. Instantly the dark smoke started revolving around Shreenath and then penetrated his body.

'Jai Mahakaal!' The Aghori started howling. Then he put his hand over the head of Shreenath and said, "Just like the Yakshini serve me till today, now on she will serve you. I have given you my Siddhi, don't approach me now." Stating that the Aghori disappeared and all the burning pyres became tranquil.

The next morning when Shreenath woke, he remembered the dream thoroughly but he considered it nothing more than a dream. Then he went to the cremation ground to see the Aghori but he didn't find him there. Shreenath returned home after a few hours while assuming that the Aghori must be wandering somewhere. But it was quite queer for him because the Aghori never left the cemetery. Shreenath was entirely unaware of the impending phenomenon. He had brushed off the events of the previous night as a mere dream, but he started to feel an eerie presence around him as if he was never truly alone.

In the dead of night, Shreenath heard a whisper in his ears. 'Shreenath... Shreenath...' a voice was buzzing in his ears. Abruptly, he woke up and gazed around. He surged the flame of the lamp and strived to clear his sight. But no one was there, everybody was sleeping deeply. There was utter tranquility all around. Shreenath thought that it might be his delusion but then he heard his name again. It was a female's voice. Now a phobia had started creeping in his mind. "Who is this?" Shreenath asked in a shivering tone.

"It's me, Shreenath," someone mumbled in his ear.

"Who...? Please show yourself." Shreenath was sweating in fear his voice was shaking.

"Oh! How could you forget me? We just met yesterday."

"Yakshini...?" he inquired apprehensively.

"Yes, Shreenath. I am your Yakshini."

"It means... it wasn't just a dream..." Shreenath thought to himself. He became overwhelmed thinking about her.

"I am in your service now," the Yakshini uttered giggling.

"You have to leave for now. If someone heard your voice, it would be chaos," he murmured anxiously.

Hearing the concern of Shreenath, Yakshini's laughter echoed through the room, and then she said confidently, "Don't fret about it, no one could hear my voice except you."

"But why can't I see you?" Shreenath asked gazing up-down and hither-thither.

The Yakshini erupted into laughter again and then responded in a seductive tone, "You have to feed me first."

"At this time!" Shreenath uttered a little dazed. "It's midnight..."

"Yes! And this is my mealtime," she chuckled.

"Okay! Wait for a while, let me see in the kitchen what I can find there for you."

"Hahaha...How innocent you are, Shreenath! You think that just like mortals, I feed upon such mundane fares as cooked veggies and rotis?" she asked him bursting into laughter.

Shreenath was utterly unaware of all these things. He didn't have any idea of what the Yakshini was talking about.

"You have to feed me some freshly cooked meat along with some alcohol," the Yakshini articulated in her captivating tone.

"You feed on such things!" Shreenath's voice quivered with shock. He was taken aback by what he had just heard.

"Yes, I am fond of these things," she said gratifiedly.

Shreenath's ear refused to accept what they heard. He couldn't even fantasize that such a bewitching entity would consume all these nasty things. As a matter of fact, Shreenath was thoroughly unfamiliar with the nature of the Yakshini.

"But where will I get these things at midnight?" Shreenath asked her after a brief moment.

"I know a place from where the Aghori used to bring meat and liquor at night. I could take you there," the Yakshini replied gently followed by giggling.

Shreenath had no other choice, unwillingly he had to venture out at midnight. The Yakshini guided him along the way. Eventually, Shreenath reached a place where he found a store of liquor and cooked meat. Swiftly he took the stuff and returned home. After reaching home, Shreenath arranged the stuff on a plate and sat in the hall.

"Come on, please accept it," Shreenath urged the Yakshini to enjoy the meal. But as soon as he asked her to consume the meal, she couldn't help but laugh.

"You are truly gullible, Shreenath." The Yakshini added ahead, "You have to consume it first only then I would consume it through your body."

"But how can I consume all these things? I have never touched such kinds of substances ever before. You have to consume it on your own," Shreenath refused her straightaway; after all, he was a Brahmin.

However, the Yakshini didn't become wrathful by his gesture; rather she was impressed by his sobriety. Following that, she started to explain to him articulately how things would work for both of them simultaneously: From the moment that Aghori bound me to you, we became one. Now, only death can separate us. We depend on each other for our needs and actions. Whatever you consume, I will consume as well. This is the only way you can nourish me. We must care for each other. You continue to feed me, and I will fulfill all your material desires. This mutual arrangement is how things will work. Therefore, you must first boost my energy, only then can I serve you in any way you desire.

After hearing Yakshini's words, Shreenath pondered for a while. It was out of the ordinary thing for him. But he was compelled to do it with no other choice. So he lifted the bottle in his hand and gazed at it for a moment; thereafter he closed his eyes, put the bottle in his mouth, and kept it upside down until all the alcohol went down his throat. He gulped down the whole bottle in one go and then cleaned the plate of meat in the blink of an eye.

From that day onwards, the course of Shreenath's life altered miraculously. Within a couple of months, he became the most versed fortune teller in the city. Whatever he used to utter from his mouth became truth. Folks from far and wide started coming to see him after hearing about his astrology skills.

Gradually Shreenath started being counted among the dignified and well-heeled individuals of the city. Shreenath was living his dream life but as time passed, he became addicted to alcohol. He began remaining intoxicated day and night and as a consequence, his health started deteriorating. With time, he realized that now his body was not as potent as it used to be. On the other hand, by degrees, the Yakshini started to reveal her true color. As Shreenath's body was losing vigor, the Yakshini was gaining control over his mind. She had started dominating him because now he was incompetent to control her. Shreenath's family was quite concerned about his health; the physician refused him firmly to consume a drop of alcohol. He also wanted to cease all this, but his mind wasn't in his command anymore.

Eventually, Shreenath realized that he made a blunder but now it was too late to regret it. That Yakshini had become the bone in his throat. She yearned to remain vibrant and active all the time without any interruption, and for that, she demanded more and more alcohol along with flesh.

Gradually, the Yakshini started threatening Shreenath because she had perceived that Shreenath was willing to cease feeding her. Therefore, Shreenath sent his entire family away from the city so that they could not get harmed by her. Now neither did Shreenath uphold the power of Yakshini, nor he could escape from her. Helplessly, he kept cursing the Aghori all the time; blaming him for everything. Shreenath had grasped why the Aghori granted him the Siddhi without asking. The Aghori also aspired to be free from the Yakshini because he had also become feeble and incapable of restraining her.

One day Shreenath became so agitated with the Yakshini that he decided to be free from her either way. He started racking his brain thinking that there must be some way by which he could get rid of her. Abruptly he remembered the words of the Yakshini: Only death can isolate us.

Thinking about it, Shreenath burst into tears and started roaring in anguish. A few minutes later, his sight fell on the wine bottle placed beside him. He picked it up and broke it against the wall. The bottle shattered into pieces from the bottom end. Shreenath was holding the broken bottle in his hand; his eyes were blood-red from which tears were flooding. Then he put the sharp side of the bottle on his neck and strived to cut his throat. All of a sudden, his hand froze. The Yakshini didn't want him to commit suicide under any circumstances. Shreenath pushed himself with all his strength but couldn't move the bottle even an inch. Struggling with his hand, he became unbalanced and fell on the floor. Within no time, blood started gushing from his neck. When he fell on the floor, the broken glass went straight into his throat and he breathed one's last. Thus eventually, Shreenath got free from that knavish Yakshini.

If truth be told, I have no intent to terrify you with such incidents. I just want you to know the facts so that you can choose consciously which path to follow for spiritual attainments. Every Siddhi or spiritual power is obtained at a certain price. A seeker ought to be aware of the consequences of their steps. It is significant to know what is supposed to be done, but it is even more significant to know what is not supposed to be done. There are some paths from where there is no return; once you move toward that direction, you will not be able to turn back even if you want to.

A few months later, I accomplished my graduation degree. Now I was looking ahead to go for post-graduation. It was the month of August 2019 and I secured admission for post-graduation studies in Microbiology at Gurukul Kangri Vishwavidyalaya.

After getting admission, I relocated from my aunt's place to Khanna Nagar colony on street no. 2 along with my friend Mayank Bharadwaj. Well, we have been friends since our graduation days because my roll number came before him in the classroom, so we used to sit together. And now, both of us got admitted to the same branch of the Life Science Department at Gurukul Kangri.

In Khanna Nagar colony, we rented a flat with two rooms and a small hall. In one room, we used to do everything; eating, sleeping and many more. In the other room, I used to study scriptures along with my spiritual practices. One night, as usual after performing my daily practices, I went to sleep. While sleeping, I had a phenomenal dream.

There are various concepts and notions among humans regarding dreams. Periodically, people all over the world have put forward their perceptions about dreams. Some rational minds believe that dreams are nothing but the projection of our memory which is packed in our subconscious mind; either we dream of such things that we yearn for or that we are scared.

Some folks believe that whatever we think about intensely while we are awake, similar events keep appearing in our mind while we sleep because our brain remain active all the time. Some neglect dreams considering them the cocktail of our past information. A few believe that our dreams can be the portal to a parallel universe or an alternate reality; we could touch different dimensions during dreaming. Many cultures believe that dreams can be prophetic, providing insight into the future about forthcoming events.

To a large extent, all these theories seem rational because the experiences of dreams are always individual. Hence, nobody can deny them thoroughly. However, in Western culture, the majority of people consider dreams merely a play of mind which makes no sense. But it's not the sheer truth about dreams.

In the realm of spirituality, dreams are considered exceptional and significant events. In our Upanishads, the dream is described precisely as a state of being. There are five states of being mentioned in the scriptures:

- *Jagrati* (Awakening)
- *Swapna* (Dreaming)
- *Sushupti* (Deep Sleep)
- *Turiya* (Absolute Awareness)
- *Turiyateet* (Transcendental)

These five states of being are commonly recognized as the five states of our human consciousness: Conscious, Subconscious, Unconscious, Super-conscious, and Supreme-conscious.

When we are in the state of awakening, what we perceive through our senses, we consider as reality. However, as we transition from the state of awakening to the dream state, our perception of reality undergoes a profound alteration. At that moment, what we perceive through our mind in our inner world becomes reality for us.

Similarly, when we come out of the dream and open our eyes, that reality vanishes in a flash. The dream that we were living considering reality ends as soon as we open our eyes. But while dreaming, we remain entirely unaware of the physical reality; it doesn't exist for us in the dream state. Now the question arises: What will you consider as reality?

The answer to this question is not supposed to be this or that. It's not about opinion; we must contemplate it only then we can reach close to the truth. The world we perceive around us is just because of our senses and memory. What if our senses cease to work for a while; suppose we stop being able to see, hear, speak, smell, taste, and touch, will we be able to perceive this world in the same way as we do usually? If our memory is wiped out for some time, will we still be able to see the world as we normally do?

Well, you certainly know the answer. The Upanishads, along with our great philosophers, have articulated that this world is merely an illusion as it appears to us something but it is something else in actuality. The sky appears blue but it's not blue; stars appear only at night but they remain there all the time.

Truth is unchangeable, yet the truth of the physical world is constantly shifting. What if this vast existence is merely a dream of the Supreme Being? And when it awakens, the entire drama could end in an instant...

Ultimately, there is no fundamental difference between the dream state and the waking state; both are dynamic and subject to time and space. The Tantra practitioners believe that dreams play a pivotal role during our spiritual journey, acting as the medium through which the ethereal and divine entities establish communication with us. Usually, a practitioner gets guidance and indications from the deity or their master in the state of the dream. It's a state readily accessible to such entities because it's the only state in which an individual dwells in the middle ground; neither thoroughly awakened nor in deep sleep. When an entity or deity doesn't make it physically to their devotee, at that time they make contact with them in the dream state.

As per some Tantric texts, there is a particular deity associated with dreams known as Swapneshwari Devi. She is believed to dwell in the realm of dreams and is invoked by the practitioners to seek answers and guidance from their dreams relevant to their spiritual practices. The Goddess appears in the dream and gives some instructions or indication regarding their concern. With the assistance of the Goddess, one can exercise control over their dreams. Some Tantra practitioners worship Swapneshwari Devi with the specific intention of preventing dreams, thereby shielding themselves from unwelcome entities.

Based on my personal experience, I can affirm that some dreams are not merely dreams; they hold profound significance surpassing ordinary reality. Such dreams leave indelible imprints on our psyche, lasting for a lifetime. A mortal often strives to understand and explain things through logic and rational thinking; however, some things transcend logic. Sometimes, it isn't practical to make sense of everything using our intellect. As a matter of fact, if we lack the ability to comprehend something, it doesn't mean it is without meaning.

Something similar happened to me in that dream; something, that surpassed my comprehension. In my dream, I witnessed an anomalous Aghori. Before we proceed, allow me to give a brief overview of the Aghoris and their lifestyle.

A practitioner who engaged in an enigmatic Tantric practice known as 'Aghora Sadhana' is referred to as an Aghori. It is the mystical cult of extreme Tantra practitioners. The word 'Aghori' is derived from the Sanskrit word 'Aghora' which implies that which is not intense, which is not sophisticated, absolutely fearless, and that which is the way to the Divine Light.

Among the countless forms of Lord Shiva, one is portrayed as an Aghori and is renowned by various names such as Adinath, Shankarnath, Suyambhunath, Bhoolenath, and Aghoreshwar (Lord of the Aghoris). In this way, Lord Shiva Himself is revered as the first Aghori. However, some traditions believe that Lord Dattatreya is the originator and primordial Guru of Aghoris.

The Aghora tradition is believed to have originated as

a distinct branch of the Nath Sampradaya, with Adinath considered the first Aghori. Some Aghori lineages trace their heritage back to Guru Matsyendranath and Guru Gorakshanath.

The Aghoris worship different aspects of Lord Shiva and Shakti such as Bhairav Baba, Mahakaal, Goddess Kali, Tara, Kamakhaya, Bhairavi, and some other relevant forms. All these manifestations are the destructive forms of Lord Shiva and Shakti. These deities are competent in the destruction of one's fear, lust, greed, ignorance, karmic bond, ego, false identity, and many others. Hence, Aghoris worship these fierce forms of God to transcend all these limitations.

Aghora is entirely a Vamachara or the Left-hand path practice. The Aghoris embrace all the forbidden things so that they can transcend all the aspects of nature and attain union with the Divine. An individual who transcends the state of duality or discrimination becomes an Aghori; the absolute. When an individual transcends their ego, relinquishes the notion of 'I', and merges into the entirety, they embody the essence of an Aghori.

Aghori is the natural state of a being. When a being is born, there is no discrimination in its head; it doesn't identify itself with something. Later on, the world starts to put labels on it such as gender, name, caste, religion, profession, and on and on. Therefore, Aghoris are fond of rawness; they perceive everything around them as energy. They always remain aligned with nature.

An Aghori is a true alchemist who is a maestro in transmuting the nature of the substance such as turning the Tamsic nature of alcohol into Soma (divine elixir), pure Sattvik. Aghoris dedicate their lives solely to their practice. Every action they take revolves around their spiritual pursuits. They are just unbelievable; thoroughly beyond the comprehension of ordinary minds. Aghora is a direct path to spiritual realization but walking on it is extremely courageous. After all, one requires courage to renounce ego and look beyond it.

I retain a clear mental picture of that dream in my head—the surrounding was engulfed in darkness and I was sitting with an eccentric Aghori who was smeared thoroughly in white ashes. We engaged in a fire ritual while sitting face-to-face beside a riverbank. In the light of the blazing flames, I could see things around me to some extent.

The Aghori had fashioned his black and grey dreadlocks into a makeshift turban atop his head. He sported a peculiar Tilak adorning his forehead and his eyes appeared large, round, and tinged with red. Around his neck, he was wearing some Rudraksha beads along with a Yantra and a Mundamala. There were big round metal earrings in his ears and both of his arms were loaded with silver bangles. He appeared quite skinny; there was barely flesh on his bones.

Around the fire pit, there were several bowls made with banyan leaves in which some particular stuff was placed to offer in the sacred fire. The Aghori was offering Ghee in the sacred fire while chanting certain Mantras intensely and I was offering the other stuff with him. He was so engrossed in the ritual that he didn't even glance at me.

After a while, when the ritual was accomplished; the Aghori took a bowl in his hand and put some offerings in it along with a burning coal from the firepit. Then he stood from his seat and headed toward the river. I was sitting in my seat and observing him just like a watcher.

The Aghori floated that bowl into the river and then he turned toward me. For a brief moment, we gazed at each other and then he vanished in the blink of an eye. When I woke up in the morning, I felt like I was physically there with the Aghori just a while ago. The dream felt incredibly lifelike to me; I spent a week contemplating this phenomenon, yet nothing seemed to click for me.

A week later, another extraordinary event occurred during the night. On that day, I was completely alone in the apartment. Mayank had gone to his village for a few days.

After completing my chanting, I went to bed as usual. We often kept the hallway light on to prevent complete darkness in the apartment.

In the dead of night, I suddenly awoke from a deep sleep, feeling as though something had jolted me awake. The room had an eerie chill, causing uncontrollable shivers to run through my body. The sound of my heartbeat reverberated loudly in my ears, my pulse racing, and I felt an unsettling presence in the room.

After a brief moment, I became conscious and gazed around, there was an exotic mist all around inside the room. The door of the room was partly open, and the ceiling fan was also running at its full pace. Despite that, the mist was present there and I was experiencing a rather frosty sensation.

Though I wasn't seized by fear, I felt a ghoulish intuition. Amidst the mysterious mist, my vision obscured, yet I keenly sensed an ethereal presence surrounding me. A seeker often perceives things more intensely through their senses beyond hearing and vision. Immediately, I sat in the lotus posture, closed my eyes, and began chanting the name of Lord Ram.

Thereafter, I started to feel a sensation of relief; my pulsation had returned to its natural rhythm. Following that, I opened my eyes and observed my surroundings. There was no mist in the room; everything was back to natural.

Based on my intuition and signs, I had gained an inkling that it was a sinister entity that approached me but it proved incompetent of causing any harm. Indeed, this was the divine grace. Such events represent the potential of spiritual practices, shielding the seeker from any malevolent force, regardless of its strength. In due course, I learned from a Tantric practitioner that when a seeker reaches a certain milestone during their practices, they start to magnetize some ethereal entities; the practitioner begins to draw the attention of unearthly forces toward themselves. It depends on the tendency of the entity whether it will aid in spiritual growth or strive to make a foray against the practitioner. I didn't express concern about this phenomenon because I was aware that no matter how diligently these entities attempted, they wouldn't be able to tame my hair. I had faith in Lord Ram; I was in the refuge of the Almighty.

A few days passed and then one night, I had another dream. It was none other than Om Swami himself who appeared in the dream. He was sitting in the lotus posture wearing saffron robes and I was sitting next to him at his feet. As usual, he wore a serene smile on his face.

Although Om Swami may not be my official mentor, he has served as one in many ways because I have gained valuable insights from him. Anyone who imparts knowledge to you, regardless of the method, becomes your mentor. Indeed, all of nature itself serves as our mentor. On that particular day, Swami appeared in my dream to offer valuable advice. "What is it that you desire, my dear?" Swami asked me dearly.

"I aspire to achieve something extraordinary," I expressed while bowing at his feet.

Hearing that Swami gazed into my eyes smiling and after a brief pause, he suggested, "To achieve something extraordinary, you have to do something extraordinary."

After uttering these words, Swami disappeared. Our dialogues were encoded in a way that only I or Swami could grasp. Immediately, I woke from sleep and scanned the darkened room. I felt Swami's presence as vividly as my own life force. Yet, what truly resonated with me were his words.

Deciphering our dialogue, I expressed to Swami that my aspirations lay not in earthly possessions but in attaining the Supreme Being, the essence of all existence. In response, Swami advised me to exert strenuous efforts, as this yearning was no ordinary desire. He pointed out distractions in my life that were hindering my progress. Subsequently, I made a significant decision regarding my spiritual practices, which left my father thunderstruck.

CHAPTER 16
ONE-DAY MONK

I was thriving in life. Things were going exceptionally well during that period. While pursuing my post-graduation, I became acquainted with some other students with whom I used to hang out frequently from place to place in the mountains; just consider that I was on cloud nine. But after having a word with Om Swami, things changed.

I grew indifferent to the ordinary aspects of life. Over time, worldly pleasures no longer stirred my enthusiasm. It was the month of December, and the date for our 1st-semester examination had been announced. Subsequently, Mayank and I started preparations for exams accordingly. I was good at academics but during those days, I didn't feel like studying at all. It seemed as if I was involuntarily pushing myself to engage in deeds that I wasn't supposed to do. Only the words of Swami continuously echoed in my head: To achieve something extraordinary, you have to do something extraordinary.

A notion was consecutively popping up in my mind: I'm merely misspending my precious time in academics and relevant endeavors. This is not the life I envisioned, nor the deeds I was meant to accomplish.

The speck merely aspired to merge into the dune. The only thing that I was yearning for was that peerless source which is the epicenter of this vast cosmos and for that, I needed to concentrate thoroughly on my practices without any hindrance. A certain devotional ambience and a company of dedicated seekers were all I required.

Three days before my first exam, I arrived at a decision; a decision, I was aware would not be appreciated by my loved ones. Despite that, I didn't consider anyone and with a lot of courage, I decided to relinquish everything and become a monk.

The fact is, I didn't have such an intent to join any cult or lineage, nor did I aspire to follow someone. Instead, I merely wanted to relocate to such a place where I could do my penance composedly. Since I was following the path of devotion in a pure Sattvik approach, therefore I believed that a place imbued with a devotional ambience would be a great call for me.

After giving it considerable thought, I figured out such a place. Well in the name of devotional ambience, there was a name that frequently kept on flashing in my head, the ISKCON Temple. There were two major factors behind it; first, I was quite familiar with the culture of ISKCON, and second, they were the worshipers of Lord Ram along with Lord Vasudev Krishna. I don't mean precisely that form of 'Ram' I worshipped, but rather Shri Ramchandra.

See, Ram is Ram; it doesn't matter how one adores Him. It is thoroughly a matter of individual conscience. Anyway, for me only Ram was prominent. Fortunately, one of the ISKCON Temple was there in Haridwar also which made it more convenient for me as I didn't have to travel elsewhere. Thus, I had created a scenario in my mind; now I had to work further accordingly.

When the contemplation of all these things was going on in my mind, I was seated studying some topics, while Mayank sat beside me, observing his academic notes. "I have reached my limits, my friend. I can't continue doing this any longer," I uttered at once, turning towards Mayank. "It's just the deterioration of time, none of these actions seems rational to me. This is not my rightful place. If I keep on wasting my precious time like this, how would I accomplish the ultimate objective of my life? Enough of these entanglements; now it's time... I have made up my mind to renounce everything and embrace the path of monkhood, solely dedicated to my objective."

Mayank was momentarily taken aback to hear such words abruptly from me. For him, this was as if lightning thundered in the sky without any chance. Instantly, he closed his notes and gave me a bewildered look. "Is everything okay with you; why are you talking like this out of the blue?" Mayank inquired, showing a hint of concern. He added ahead, "I comprehend you have been immersed in spirituality for quite some time, but your sudden decision to become a monk caught me off guard. It is an unusual step, my friend; so before moving ahead, I urge you to reflect on it mindfully."

"I have given it through consideration and now I'm genuinely committed to this decision. Out of ignorance, I have spoiled several years of my brief life. I don't have plenty of time; therefore, I have made up my mind," I stated assuredly.

Mayank presumed that I had made this decision hastily without mindful consideration. Hence, like a reliable comrade, he was striving to soothe me. A moment later, Mayank asked peering into my eyes, "Are you certain about this?"

I responded to his question with a gentle smile and a nod. Following that, Mayank adopted a somewhat serious demeanor. "Then, when are you thinking of departing?" he murmured.

"Today, within a few hours."

Hearing that, Mayank started looking away; it seemed as if he was pretending to act natural. However, he appeared rather displeased and thoroughly disagreed with my decision. "See, I am no one to tell you what you are supposed or not supposed to do; nevertheless, as a friend, I want you to take some more time and think about it profoundly," Mayank suggested submissively. "Just stay tonight and move ahead with your decision the following morning."

"If you say so, I will stay tonight and think about it," I uttered honoring his words. However, deep inside I knew that nothing would alter; I was not going to change my mind, no matter what.

The moment I shared my decision with Mayank, I began to experience the sensation akin to that of a bird breaking free from its cage and soaring into the boundless blue sky; perhaps because I was about to transcend all the mundane boundaries and lose myself from all the bonds that were holding me up in any way.

This is the essence of the monk's ecstasy: they have liberated themselves from mundane attachments, leaving behind all ties that bound them to the world.

I passed that night by assuming things that were about to alter in my life from the following morning. There was much to forgo both internally and externally and similarly, there were certain things that I needed to adopt. However, internal renunciation was inevitable.

If truth be told, renunciation is always internal because we cannot thoroughly abandon things externally. We possess a physical body, and to sustain it, we rely on nature. Thus, a genuine monk remains dispassionate about the external world while performing their duties without being attached to it; it's great if there is bread and jam to eat on the plate and it's also great if there is merely a dry bread on the plate.

The aim is to quench the appetite, not to please the tongue.

The next morning, I informed Mayank that I had decided to adhere to my decision. He didn't utter a word in response, though I could read his face; he wasn't pleased at all. And how could he? After all his best friend was about to leave him forever. None of us ever anticipated that one day we would have to bid farewell so suddenly. I told Mayank about ISKCON Temple and urged him to drop me there. Well, he agreed to take me there; maybe because it was the last help, I was seeking from him.

Thereafter, I packed my bag with some daily use stuff such as the Bhagavad Gita, a couple of ordinary robes, toothpaste and brush, my Aadhar Card, mobile phone charger, slippers, some cash, and a diary. This much was sufficient, I wasn't going for a voyage. Then I took off my wristwatch, my silver bangle, and other accessories; I felt there was no purpose in wearing all these accessories anymore.

Only a handful of people were there in my life who had been close to my heart. Among them, one was standing next to me and the others were my father and Bhojraj Bhaiya. Now only these two remained, whom I wished to inform of my departure and bid farewell.

Upon packing my stuff, I took my phone and called Bhojraj Bhaiya. After greetings, I told him that I had decided to embrace the path of monkhood, so I was going to be a monk. Bhaiya was also amazed at hearing my words. He strived to know whether I had made this decision in haste. However, he knew from the inception that one day I would embrace this path. Bhaiya was well cognizant of the necessity of this decision. The agony of an injured individual can only be truly understood by another injured individual.

"May you succeed on your path. Godspeed, my friend," Bhaiya blessed me and hung up the call.

Following that, I left for the ISKCON Temple with Mayank which was around half an hour away. Everything was falling apart yet, I was glad. I wasn't much concerned about my family because, by the grace of Lord Ram, I had a brother who could look after them. There was nothing to be concerned about, all of them were doing great in their lives. Hence, I could cozily proceed on my spiritual journey.

At roughly 09:00 A.M., with the aid of Google Maps, we reached the ISKCON hermitage which was some distance away from their shrine. This hermitage wasn't as spacious as those that I had visited in the past years; it was a modest three to four-story building with approximately ten to twelve rooms. On the ground floor of the building, there was a small office where a monk, aged around fifty, was seated.

"Hare Krishna, Prabhu Ji!" we bowed to the monk, smiling with folded hands.

"Hare Krishna!" the monk greeted us smiling in response.

This is how devotees greet each other in the ISKCON. Then I expressed straightaway the purpose of coming there. Hearing that, the monk became glad and asked us to sit. "I am glad to hear that you want to walk on the path of devotion at such a young age. May I know about your profession?" the monk inquired mellowly.

"I'm pursuing post-graduation in Microbiology from Gurukul," I responded delightfully.

"That's pretty cool! Well, you can keep on with your education along with your devotional service. We don't have an issue with that rather we require well-educated youngsters like you to join us so we can expand the divine message of the Bhagavad Gita in the entire world," the monk uttered affectionately.

"I appreciate that but I don't want to entangle myself in mundane anymore. I want to avoid all the distractions and focus thoroughly on my spiritual journey," I said articulately.

"Well, that's your individual choice," the monk murmured.

After a brief pause, thinking for a moment about my family, I uttered, "I have a query, Prabhu Ji."

"Go ahead without any hesitation."

"Can I see my family whenever I want after becoming a monk?" I inquired slightly hesitating.

"Certainly! You can see them, even it would be great if your family also joins our community after you." The monk continued, "You can become an inspiration for them. There is no such restriction in our community. All sorts of devotees come to us every year. Some stay here because they find serenity in the devotion of Lord Krishna, some stay here because they become mesmerized by the ambience of our ISKCON, and some others because of our appetizing Prasad (meal)."

The monk chuckled and added, "Some devotees stay here forever, and some return to the mundane after spending some time. Also, there are some devotees whose minds are not stagnant; they keep coming and going here. However, we don't have an issue with any of them neither we bound them for anything. But before you become a monk, the consent of your parents is necessary for us. It is not supposed to happen that tomorrow your parents approach and start accusing us that we have brainwashed their naive child and turned him into a monk. These sorts of things often happen here so we want to avoid such unpleasing plights. That's the only concern from our side."

"Don't worry about that, Prabhu Ji. In my situation, that's not likely to happen. There are no problems within my family," I reassured with confidence.

"Very well! I need to submit your Aadhar ID as per the protocol."

"Certainly!" Instantly, I took out my Aadhar Card and handed it to the monk.

"Thanks! Now you can move to the room and have some Prasad if you are hungry. Govind Das will show you around and make you familiar with our schedule," the monk instructed while pointing toward a guy who was reading the Bhagavad Gita sitting beside him.

Thereafter, I turned to Mayank; he was avoiding my eyes. It seemed as if he was pretending to be a maestro in controlling emotions. However, his eyes had turned red from restraining his tears. Now it was the time to bid last farewell to my dear friend. I showed my gratitude to him verbally for everything by holding his hand and then he embraced me firmly for a while. "If you need anything ever, I am just a phone call away. I never assumed this moment would ever come… peace out, my friend," Mayank said in a dolorous tone.

There was a hint of nostalgia in Mayank's voice. I knew he was quite miserable; he wanted to hold me back for the sake of our friendship but even if he wished to, he couldn't. Unwillingly, Mayank welcomed my decision and stood by my side. This embodies the essence of a genuine friend. On the other hand, I was also trying to suppress my emotions; it wasn't as though I had become utterly stone-hearted. After all, we enjoyed a long period of bliss together.

Farewells are never effortless. People frequently endeavor to conceal their feelings and emotions during such moments as they are reluctant to appear vulnerable, especially men. Mayank left from there keeping his sentiment suppressed within his heart and I walked upstairs following Govind Das.

Govind Das was a nearly twenty-five years of age nigrescent, tall, and bony guy who had joined the ISKCON a few days back. He told me that he had escaped from his home and arrived here because his family forbade him from worshipping Lord Krishna. Govind Das attended school only up to sixth grade and then began working at a tailor shop. I noticed that the senior monks in the hermitage did not treat him with the same regard as they treated me.

In this era, if you are not well educated and don't possess a high educational certificate then perhaps you may not receive soft treatment even in these sorts of places.

Govind Das showed me the cooking area where I had some Prasad; they addressed the meal as the Prasad of God.

"We do everything on our own here, therefore after having the Prasad, you have to clean your dishes and place them in their respective place," Govind Das instructed me.

I nodded, signifying my comprehension. In the meantime, Govind Das asked me if I knew how to prepare the meal. I mentioned to him that I could prepare vegetables, but I wasn't skilled at rolling rotis.

"Great! Henceforth we will prepare the Prasad together," he said inhaling deeply.

I suppose Govind Das had been single-handedly preparing meals for everyone until now. Following that, he showed me a room on the top floor where there were four single sets of beds, along with a wardrobe, a table and chair, and an attached restroom.

As I told you earlier, the hermitage had limited space so just a handful of monks resided there. Govind Das pointed towards a bed and asked me to take it. I placed my backpack on the bed and sat there for a while. A few minutes later, I thought that now I ought to inform my father. I took my phone and dialed his number.

Initially, I presumed that my father wouldn't react much upon hearing about my decision to embrace asceticism because he was aware that I had been on the devotional path for a few years and usually I kept on visiting ashrams, monasteries, and shrines to see monks and yogis. However, I was mistaken about my father.

After a few rings, my father received the call. Followed by greetings I expressed to him politely, "Father, I arrived at an ashram this morning."

"Appreciable! Explore and learn something new out there," he encouraged endearingly.

My father was unaware of what I meant by that. Therefore, I got straight to the point and said, "Henceforward, I will stay here with the monks." I added ahead, "A senior monk has told me that I can visit home to see you every three to four months. I guess I would not face any inconvenience here."

"What do you mean by that? I didn't grasp any of it," my father stated in a bewildered tone.

"Yes Father, I have decided to embrace monkhood. Therefore, from now on, I will reside among the monks in this ashram, dedicated entirely to my spiritual practices," I stated, mindfully enunciating my words.

"Let's skip this silly pranks. Take all the time you need there, and when you are done, come back to your flat before evening," he uttered emphatically.

"I have made up my mind, father. I can't return to my flat," I flatly refused and added, "I just wanted to inform you so that you would not worry about me."

"See, I am sitting with someone at this moment, I will talk to you soon about this," my father said in a slightly anxious tone and then hung up the call.

My father's tone hinted at a slight agitation, indicating that my words had stirred some unrest in him. Before he or anyone else could strive to contact me, I turned off my mobile phone.

There were some lingering questions in my head that were necessary to address in order to walk ahead firmly, subsiding all the sentiments. Thus, I took out my diary from the backpack and wrote three questions: Why am I here? What is the purpose behind all of this? What will be my reward for doing this?

Thereafter I wrote the answers to these three questions precisely one by one:

- I am here because I require a certain ambience where I can heed entirely on my spiritual evolution, away from worldly distractions and hindrances.
- The purpose behind doing all of this is to reach the ultimate truth; the Absolute.
- Someday, I will uncover my true identity and unite with the source transcending all the limitations; the individual speck will merge into the whole dune. I will become complete.

Before making a crucial decision in life, keep one thing in your head: You must have a precise answer to your 'Why' and 'What'. Once you have the answer, make your move. This is the ultimate Mantra of decision-making.

I had my answers; now I was geared up to step ahead. The monk told me that after a few days, they would shift me and Govind Das to another ashram in Gujarat for our initiation and further training. For the next three years, we had to reside there while serving and learning about monkhood. Thereafter, we could choose to serve at any of the ISKCON ashrams across Bharat as per our choice. Till then we had to live and serve here in the Haridwar.

The core teaching of ISKCON is service, rooted in the belief that the primary purpose of humanity is to serve. Serving God, specifically Lord Vasudev Krishna, and all that belongs to Him, which encompasses the entire world, is regarded as the supreme duty, Dharm. This path leads to pleasing the Lord and attaining His grace.

Govind Das familiarized me with some other monks in the ashram. One of them provided me with a long Japa Mala (rosary) made with Tulsi wood and taught me how to chant the 'Hare Krishna Maha-mantra' on it. He explained: The point where the threads meet in the rosary is marked by a distinct bead known as Sumeru, a representation of the divine Mount Meru, the abode of God. A devotee is not supposed to cross or count the Sumeru bead while chanting and upon reaching the 108th bead or the one before Sumeru, one ought to reverse the direction of the rosary.

In the Hare Krishna Maha-mantra, the word 'Hare' implies 'take away', so while chanting the Mantra we pray to the Lord Vasudev Krishna to take away all our flaws and bestow us your devotion. I noticed that the monks there always carried their Japa Mala in a small sack and kept on chanting the Hare Krishna Maha-mantra while strolling, sitting, or performing any other activity. All of them were extremely passionate about their devotion.

In the evening, the monk instructed us to visit the shrine which was around one kilometer away from their ashram. Govind Das was familiar with the location so I walked with him to the shrine. On the way, he told me some more things that the monk explained to him regarding devotion.

When we reached the shrine, I saw that it wasn't crowded at all. Usually, the ISKCON shrines attract a large gathering of devotees. Despite its small size, the shrine was pretty posh. Outside the sanctum sanctorum, there was a magnificent idol of Srila Prabhupada. Firstly, we paid obeisance before Srila Prabhupada, as he was the founder-acharya of the ISKCON society. The devotees associated with the ISKCON earnestly adhere to his teachings and ideals.

The evening adoration had yet to begin. A young monk was offering food and fruits to the Lord from behind the curtain. Another monk was arranging things for the adoration. The chants of Lord Krishna were softly resonating in the background. I was sitting on the floor with Govind Das, we were waiting for the curtain to be removed so we could have the Darshan of the Lord.

Meanwhile, some other devotees approached and sat with us. After a few minutes, the curtain was drawn back with the echo of a conch shell revealing a majestic scene: Lord Vasudev Krishna seated alongside His brother Shri Balram and His sister Devi Subhadra. These exquisite idols were the replicas of the wooden idols, established in the Jagannath Temple in Odisha.

All the devotees bow their heads on the feet of the Lord together. Then one of the monks initiated the ringing of a sacred bell while waving a holy lamp before the Lord, while another monk began serving the Lord by wielding a white sacred whisk, known as a Chaur. The remaining devotees were joyfully singing hymns in perfect harmony.

The idols of the Lord were being treated with utmost care as if they were living entities themselves. Including their edible stuff and water, all sorts of decorous arrangements were made for them. An air conditioner and two wall fans were installed in the sanctum sanctorum so that the Lord would not feel inconvenient in summer. At specific times in the morning, the family of the Lord were roused from slumber, bathed, adorned, and presented with food and water. Likewise, at designated times in the evening, they were gently laid to rest. However, all this was not happening merely because of the devotee's faith or the devotee's perception of the reflection of God in these idols, but rather there was a particular comprehension behind doing all these practices.

In Hinduism, there is a remarkable perception regarding idol worship. Usually, if you ask a Hindu, why you people worship these inanimate statues? Certainly, you would receive various explanations based on their faith, beliefs, and sentiments. But this is not the precise justification. I'm not implying that people who worship idols out of faith and sentiment are ignorant. However, most of them are unaware of the profound wisdom and rational motive behind 'idol worship'.

I want you to understand that for Hindus, our devotion is not to lifeless idols but to the omnipresent divine energy that pervades all existence. When a stone idol of a deity is installed in the shrine, the chief priest performs a ritual which is known as 'Prana Pratishtha' before starting to worship it. Unless the sacred ritual of Prana Pratishtha is formally performed, an idol is merely an ordinary stone.

'Prana' implies the 'life force' and 'Pratishtha' implies 'consecration'. It is a pious ritual in which the idol of the deity is consecrated through the purification of elements which is known as Bhuta Suddhi. 'Bhuta' implies 'the element' and 'Shuddhi' implies 'purification'. This ritual of Bhuta Siddhi is performed to stabilize the five elements: Air, Water, Fire, Earth, and Ether or Space. Following that, the energy of the deity is invoked by chanting certain Mantras, while urging the deity to permeate into the idol. It's a whole methodical Tantric approach. Before initiating the ritual, the eyes of the idol are covered with fabric, and when the entire ritual is accomplished, the priest places a mirror in front of the idol before removing the fabric. As soon as the priest removes the fabric from the eyes of the deity, the reflection of the deity falls on the mirror and it shatters into pieces because of the intense energy of the deity. Humans don't have the caliber to endure the first sight of the deity, therefore, they place a mirror.

After Prana Pratishtha, life is breathed into the idol and then it becomes the living form of the deity. The idol turned into an active Yantra in which the core energy of the deity dwells. Hence, the devotees across Bharat serve the idols of the deities appropriately because after Prana Pratishtha, they are no longer an inanimate stone.

After the adoration, a monk started distributing Prasad. It was an ambrosial sweet dish which is known as Kheer in the northern region and Payasam in the south. It is prepared by boiling rice in milk with sugar or jaggery.

After having it, I realized why the monk said that some devotees stay here for the Prasad. Indeed, it was savory. Even I wanted to have a whole bowl of it but it was a Prasad which means one can only have that in a limited amount.

A while later, we returned to the ashram. In winter, the sunset occurs a bit earlier. At around 07:00 P.M., darkness had already fallen, and everyone had finished dinner by that time. I was strolling outside the room and then casually I switched on my phone to check something.

As soon as I switched it on, instantly uncountable missed call notifications popped up on the screen. Among them, there were mostly from my father, brother, and Bhojraj Bhaiya. My decision to become a monk was a piece of breaking news for all my acquaintances.

Before I could turn off the phone again, it started buzzing. It was Bhojraj Bhaiya on the call. I answered the call and he asked me to talk to my father immediately. His accent of words made me slightly apprehensive. In the depths of my heart, I beseeched Lord Ram for everything to be well at home. Then I called my father without thinking for a moment. He received the call and started sobbing vehemently. Words were barely emerging from his mouth; within no time my father burst into tears.

"Please! Return home, my son. Don't do this to me. I have never prevented you from anything nor will I prevent you in the future. Do whatever you want, but please stay with us. If you say, I will build a shrine for you in the village. You can stay there cozily and perform your worship over there; no one will disturb you. If you are not ambitious towards your academics, that's also admissible. You aren't required to do anything, just come back to me. Don't abandon us just like your mother," my father expressed dolorously.

The words of my father were filled with such immense anguish that they stirred my heart to its core. I could have endured anything except the tears in my father's eyes. Rarely have I seen my father's eyes brimming with tears. The first time I saw him in such profound agony was when my grandsire departed his life, the second when my mother took her last breath, and now at this moment, due to my actions.

Indeed, there is no suspicion that an individual is responsible for their own pleasure and suffering. Nevertheless, if your family has nurtured and instilled virtues within you, then regardless of circumstances, witnessing them in agony would be unimaginable; your heart will never approve of it. When you endure the caliber to move the mountains for your loved ones then how could you bear their sufferings? How could a child attain serenity when his parents are in deep anguish? Your spiritual teachings won't allow you to ignore it and move ahead.

I was caught in a profound dilemma. However, I wasn't someone who prioritized my own needs over the tears of my father. I became miserable and started sobbing with him and then I told him that I would come to see him.

There was no sense of spiritual development when I realized that my father was in grief because of me. In sooth, it was beyond my anticipation that my father would become such miserable upon hearing about my renunciation. All night long, I pondered whether I could face my Lord if I turned a blind eye to my father. Would my Ram be pleased and embrace me if I disobeyed my father? I could hear my inner voice legibly; it was answering all my queries.

The next morning, I went to the monk in the office and told him about my father. The monk didn't ask anything ahead and he just allowed me to return home. "The portals of our ISKCON are always open for you, son. You can visit us whenever you want in the future," the monk said dearly while handing me my Aadhar ID.

Afterward, I took my backpack from there and headed towards my apartment. I kept my arrival a secret from Mayank because I wanted to astonish him and witness his joy upon seeing me. When I arrived at my apartment, I found that my whole friend circle was gathered there.

The instant they spotted me, their joy became boundless. Each of them leaped over to me and enveloped me tightly in their arms. One of them was my friend Shubham Pandey, who became so overwhelmed that tears started rolling out of his eyes when he embraced me. All my friends were slightly mad at me for how I abruptly left everyone and went away. None of them ever anticipated that I would leave in this manner to pursue a life as a monk because I never let the individuals around me realize that I was different from them in any way; I always had the knack for effortlessly connecting with people of all kinds.

Honestly speaking, I never sought attention for being different from others because of my spiritual attainments; I used to be like anyone. Except for those who were close to my heart, no one knew about my spiritual life. Whenever the spiritual ego started to surge within me, something or the other happened that made me realize that I was nothing more than a speck. Indeed, it was grace!

After that, my fellows asked me to assure them that I would never depart in such a manner again. Their conduct was beyond anything I could fantasize about; I had no inkling that these individuals cared for me to such an extent. Thereafter, as usual, we all had a great time and enjoyed ourselves immensely.

In the meantime, my friend Mayank pointed out to me that we were not adequately prepared for the exam scheduled for tomorrow. He started to blame me comically for all this. A while later, someone from my family informed me over the phone that my father had not swallowed even a morsel of food since the moment he heard about my departure. Then I called my father and briefed him about my return and assured him not to worry as I would come to see him tomorrow after the exam. Upon hearing that, my father breathed a sigh of relief.

Following lunch, Mayank and I approached one of our friends to ask for assistance with preparation for tomorrow's exam. Somehow, we managed to review some significant topics and appeared in the exam the next morning.

In the examination hall, the teacher handed me the question paper and then I started running my eyes at the questions. Reading all the questions thoroughly, I turned to Mayank who was sitting a certain distance away behind me. As I turned, I saw that he was already looking at me. We started giggling looking at each other.

Well, I'm certain that you must be familiar with that gesture. Yes! There were a lot of questions that were out of our range. But as soon as I started writing the exam, out of the blue, visuals of the topics that I had studied during lectures started emerging in my mind. Thus, I managed to attempt all the questions and then headed toward my village as my father was looking forward to seeing me.

By the time I reached home, it was almost night. I found my father standing at the door and as I approached him, he pulled me in a warm embrace. That day I realized how much my father loved me; it was apparent in his eyes. To justify my intention, I aspired to present an explanation before him but he was not in the mood to listen to anything. My father was simply pleased to have me by his side.

The next morning, when I was looking for a book in my wardrobe, I saw that all the books were missing from their spot. Even the books and scriptures that I brought with me were also missing from my backpack. Undoubtedly, my father was behind it. He had kept all the books away from my sight because according to his perception, I had decided to embrace the path of monkhood after being influenced by those spiritual texts. My father was quite a naive individual. But now the time had come to sit with him and talk openly in this regard.

While my father was having his afternoon meal, I approached him and asked gently, "What do you think about me, Father? What kind of person am I in your sight?"

"You are a virtuous soul," Father replied smiling graciously.

"Good to hear that from you but do you know how did I become this way? What encourages me to be a noble being?" I asked him benignantly. Following that, Father started listening to me attentively.

"Tell me one thing, what do we do with the soil before sowing seeds in the land?" I asked him gently. "Don't we work on the soil to make it fertile?"

My father nodded in response. Then I continued, "We add a variety of manure, fertilizers, and other nutrients to the soil so that our seeds can flourish well." Father nodded to my point. Then I added further, "Often some unwanted weeds also emerge with the crop; we remove them because they could influence the yield of our crop. Similarly, our mind is also like soil. We have to work on it to make it immaculate and unclouded constantly. These books work as manure and nutrients for my mind. With the help of these scriptures and spiritual texts, I gain wisdom and always strive to apply that wisdom in my life so that I can become a noble individual while eliminating all the flaws. Books are just like my mentors. Therefore, I urge you Father, don't entertain the idea that all these books are negatively impacting my mind."

Hearing my words, my father started pondering. Eventually, he agreed with my words but, he was my father; one step ahead of me. Before returning my books, my dear father put a condition before me. He asked me to make a commitment that I would not renounce home ever in this manner and along with that I would live my life as a householder. However, I was not less than him; after all, I was his son. So I gave him my word in a tricky manner, saying, "I assure you, Father, I won't leave home until you are with us. I will remain by your side."

Following that, my father returned all my books pleasantly. When some of our acquaintance folks came to know about the whole incident, they were amazed. Everyone started to give me deep knowledge, as per their intellect. Some said that the path of monkhood is merely for forlorn individuals who don't have anyone to look after. Some said that only those who are not wealthy become monks.

These unblessed people were making the mistake of considering the monks as beggars. A few said that one who runs away from their duties chooses to become a monk. I heard these sorts of talks from every second person I met after that incident. However, I didn't feel like I needed to explain to everyone. They would never comprehend it; such an insight is attained by divine grace.

The reality is that accidents or coincidence simply don't exist; Lord Ram had alternative plans for me. Regardless of what occurred, I accepted it as the Will of the Divine and proceeded forward. I had firm faith in my heart that the cosmos would help me in one way or the other to evolve on the spiritual path.

After meeting my father, I returned to Haridwar and appeared sincerely in every exam. In addition to worldly achievements, I remained committed to my spiritual path. One noon, while scrolling the screen of my mobile phone I encountered a clip in which a fortune teller was briefing certain exceptional insight about the 'water element' that I never heard of or read before.

CHAPTER 17

MYSTICAL POWER OF WATER ELEMENT

In the physical realm of this vast cosmos, whatever exists is composed of five vital elements that are elucidated as 'Punch Mahabhuta' in our Vedic scriptures. These five elements are Ether (Akasha), Air (Vayu), Fire (Agni), Water (Jal), and Earth (Bhumi). These five elements embody the fundamental energy that shapes the core structure of all entities, including humans, animals, birds, insects, plants, microbes, and any inanimate form. Therefore, all kinds of living and non-living objects are subject to these elements which operate ceaselessly in nature in some way or the other.

As an illustration, mankind consumes the energy of the 'Earth' element, in the form of vegetables, cereals, pulses, fruits, etc. that provide density and firmness in our physical body. Apart from that, the presence of gravitational force is attributed to the Earth. Similarly, we consume Air in the form of oxygen which is required for our respiration. Plants and trees consume it in the form of carbon dioxide for the process of photosynthesis. We consume the energy of the Fire in the form of sunlight which is required for the production of vitamin D and the soundness of our bones. The digestive fire, known as Jathar Agni, is present in our body and is responsible for metabolic and reproductive functions; it also regulates the temperature in our body. Apart from that, this entire world is visible only because of the 'Fire' element.

Water is said to be the liquid vital force of nature. Almost 70-72% of our body is Water. All the fluids such as blood, lymph, milk, saliva, sweat, and more, present in our body are primarily composed of Water. Ether, which is loosely implies the space in which everything exists. It is the only element that imbibes all the elements therefore, it is the primordial element in the creation. In this way, all these elements operate collectively in nature.

This provides a brief glimpse into the functioning of these elements within our physical body. Now let's move on to the subtle body (sensory body from where feelings and thoughts arise) and have a brief insight into how these five elements are associated with our subtle body in their subtle form.

In the yogic culture, grossly we found the description of seven chakras or seven energy centers in our body. At the perineum or base of the spinal cord, the Muladhara Chakra is located where the cosmic energy i.e. Kundalini Shakti is coiled in a dormant state. This Chakra is also known as the fundamental Chakra which is associated with the 'Earth' element. It provides structure to our subtle and gross body.

In the same alignment at the pubic area, the Svadhisthana Chakra is located. This Chakra is associated with the 'Water' element and it is responsible for the craving of creation or reproduction in the body. Above that, at the naval, the Manipur Chakra is located. This chakra is associated with the 'Fire' element and because of that it is the center of transformative energy. Above that, in the center of our chest and close to the heart, the Anahata or the Heart Chakra is located. This Chakra is associated with the 'Air' element which connects one to the cosmic vibrations, Nada.

Above the Heart chakra, in the center of the throat, the Vishuddha Chakra is located. This chakra is associated with the 'Ether' element which transforms everything in the pure form. Hence, it is referred to as the purification center. Some yogis depict the Ether as the closest form of the Supreme Being, as everything emerges from it and merges into it eventually. Ether is the only unalterable and eternal element therefore; it remains in its pure state. Every yogi undergoes the Bhuta Shuddhi ritual to purify these five elements within their bodies.

Of the five elements, Water, Fire, and Air exist in highly dynamic forms in nature, making them easily accessible to humanity. Mastering the energy of these three elements enables one to control nature. This mastery grants an individual transcendental power, capable of both beneficial and destructive outcomes beyond imagination. In essence, one can transform a mere droplet of water into a precious pearl and possess the ability to extract every last drop from any living being.

One afternoon, while browsing online I came across a captivating video clip that immediately caught my eye. It was a video clip from an Astrology and Numerology seminar in which a fortune teller was talking about the arcane power of the 'Water' element. He mentioned: The water we consume has tremendous power. It possesses a tendency to resonate with the intensity of our thoughts and sentiments; as a result, it acts in a certain way within our body. When we consume water while creating an intense thought in our mind regarding healing, it remarkably starts to heal and cure our ailments. Hence, whenever you engage in spiritual rituals such as prayers, worship, or chanting, always keep water with you in a metal container. Copper is ideal, but any other metal will suffice if copper is unavailable. By doing this, the water will absorb the vibrancy and energy of your sacred practices, transforming into mystical nectar that can deepen the intensity of your practice and devotion. Upon accomplishing your rituals, it is recommended to consume this water cozily.

It was an enthralling disclosure about the potential of water that sparked my desire to grasp the entire picture of the subject. Thereafter, I began to explore this topic and discovered articles describing experiments suggesting that 'Water' is a living element with memory. While wandering on the Internet, I encountered a Japanese researcher, Dr. Masaru Emoto who conducted a series of experiments observing the substantial effect of the atmosphere, words, chanting, music, and prayers on the crystalline structure of water molecules.

In the course of these experiments, Dr. Emoto achieved remarkable outcomes. His team witnessed the transformation of the crystalline structure of water droplets in response to alterations in their surroundings. The droplets formed certain aesthetic and harmonious patterns when surrounded by soothing sounds and prayers. In contrast, when awful and unpleasant sounds played in the surroundings, the droplets formed certain grotesque and unsettled patterns.

Based on these experiments, Dr. Emoto concluded that human consciousness can influence the vitality of water molecules. Likewise, these water molecules can also influence human consciousness. This indicates the potential to harness the mystical power of water for both healing and harm.

After perceiving the entire concept, the dots started connecting in my head. I recalled how some sages, yogis, exorcists, priests, and occult practitioners would harness and manipulate the power of water. In ancient times, our powerful sages and yogis possessed the remarkable ability to curse malevolent beings with nothing more than a splash of water, while they could purify a soul with the same simple gesture. Since the beginning, they possessed the knowledge of exercising the arcane power of water through the potential of their penance.

When Yajna or Homa (fire ritual) is performed in houses, the priest asks to put some water specifically Ganga Jal (river Ganga water) in a copper or brass pot close to the fire pit. After the rituals, the priest sprinkles water from the pot upon the folks present there and then instructs the host to sprinkle the rest of the water in the entire house for purification. The essence lies in the fact that water imbibes the energy of the Yajna, and its influence extends to every individual or place it touches.

I have witnessed exorcists and priests performing specific rituals involving water to heal those afflicted by possession and chronic ailments. Usually, they used to chant some spell or Mantra and then blow in the water; sometimes they used to write it on a small chit and then dissolve the chit in the water. After that, they provided the water to the victim for consumption and it worked as it was supposed to.

In my childhood, I used to think that such people possessed mystical or talismanic water that they used to heal those who sought their help. Now, I understand the secret behind their miraculous water. This sparked a thought in my mind: If they have these abilities, what's preventing me from doing the same?

Upon acquiring profound insight, I started practicing to exercise the energy of water. While chanting, I initiated the practice of keeping a copper pot filled with water before me and consuming it upon concluding the chanting. Before swallowing the water, I created a thought in my mind: This pious water would shield me from demonic entities and enhance the potential of my spiritual practice.

After each chanting session, I would perform this action. But after some time, a suspicion arose in my mind—I didn't observe any remarkable surge in my practices. There were no indications that could assure me of the effectiveness of this approach. To confirm its efficacy, something ground-breaking needed to be attempted.

A few days later, I visited my village to spend a weekend with my family. During that time, there was a lady in our family who used to look after our house. But for almost a week, she was running sick. On a daily basis, our family doctor came to see her but it seemed that things were out of his grip. All the relevant medical test reports were normal hence the doctor was uncertain in her case. Her health condition started getting worse day by day. Even the medicines were not providing much relief. That lady's body had become such pale that she lay on her bed just like a spiritless being. Every individual in my house was concerned about her health.

Even today, in the rural areas of Bharat, folks are so superstitious that if things are not working as they are supposed then they start to associate it with dark magic, occult, paranormal, and supernatural kinds of stuff. My family members were in a similar state; people nearby started to suggest that we must take her to some exorcist or tantric; she could be possessed by some demonic entity.

When every second individual in the village started talking like this then eventually my father approached me seeking my thoughts on this matter. I didn't want my family to get entangled in the supernatural matter; I didn't want them to believe in all this. At that moment, a thought sparked in my head: This is the ideal moment to confirm whether I can wield the power of water. Let's experiment to see if water truly possesses any mystical power or any healing properties.

After pondering for a moment, I expressed, "Please give me 24 hours, let me see what I can do for her. I have faith that there will be no need to take her anywhere. However, if I fail to do so, you are free to take her wherever you wish."

My father relied on my words, knowing that if I said something, it held substance. In the evening, I sat firmly in my room by applying the lotus posture. I kept some water in a small copper pot which my father used to carry to Lord

Shiva's shrine each Monday. Before initiating my chanting, I beseeched Lord Ram to allow me to perform it for the lady and then I started chanting intensely.

Around thirty-five to forty minutes later, I opened my eyes and held the pot in my hand. For a moment, I gazed at the pot, and then by bringing it close to my lips I whispered: She will be safe and sound after drinking this pious water. Whosoever entity is behind her miserable condition will free her immediately and she will be vigorous again. Precisely, this water is going to heal her. May Lord Ram take pity on her.

After uttering those words with immutable faith, I blew into the water in the name of Lord Ram and then approached the lady without delay. She was lying on her bed in a pathetic state. With the support of my hand, I made her sit and asked her to swallow the water. "What's in it?" she murmured.

"Just swallow it and by tomorrow morning you will feel better," I said sympathetically.

But she hesitated for a while. "Believe me, it will cure your agony," saying that I handed over the pot in her hands.

She started engulfing it sip by sip and then after a while, she fell asleep. The next morning as soon as I woke up, she was the first thing on my mind. Although I had unwavering faith in its efficacy, I sought confirmation. My father was sitting in the courtyard, basking in the sunlight. I approached him and asked curiously, "How's she doing now?"

My father was looking quite pleased, and he responded with a cheerful demeanor, "She is feeling significantly better since last night. But what spell did you hit on her? She told me that you gave her something to drink last night," he asked further in wonder.

It appeared from the look on my father's face that he was filled with a mixture of wonder and curiosity, indicating a keen interest in knowing more. "All this happened because of Lord Ram's generosity. I didn't do anything, I'm just a medium," with a feeling of gratitude, I uttered.

This is how these sorts of approaches work appropriately; one ought not to reveal what and how they make things function to others. Indeed, I was over the moon hearing that. Yet, I was eager to see the lady by myself and hear that from her mouth. So I went straight to her room. Gazing at her, my heart filled with ecstasy; she was sitting in her bed like any normal individual, enjoying her breakfast. "Hello there! How are you feeling now?" I asked her tenderly while passing a smile.

"I have been feeling quite easeful since last night. For a week, I have been having nightmares but last night, I had a quality sleep," she replied beamingly. "But I want to know, what was in that water which you gave me last night?"

Pouring out gratitude to Lord Ram I responded, "Nothing... It is the clemency of Lord Ram. You must be grateful to Him."

She smiled feeling relieved. Everyone in my family was amazed and eager to know what spell I blew on her. A lady who had been in bed in a miserable state for a week, how could she become healthful overnight? However, I didn't want to enlighten anyone in this regard but rather urged them not to reveal this phenomenon to others. But in villages, these sorts of things spread just like ink in water.

Faith is the most ergastic emotion that exists in the cosmos. If you have unabashed faith in something, it will work for you certainly; it is bound to work, I'm stating it from my experience. We worship God and visit shrines; we have never seen God with our bare eyes. All we have witnessed is various representations of God in the form of idols and pictures. Nevertheless, we have faith that God is present among us, watching over everything. While standing in shrines, we share all our joys, euphoria, agony, pain, grief, sorrow, and other sentiments, trusting that God hears and responds to our expressions. To be honest, I wasn't relying on the power of water; instead, I was placing my trust in Lord Ram.

Now, there was no room for doubt regarding the potential of water. Thereafter, I started to employ the power of water to cure all sorts of ailments. From boyhood, I had hypersensitivity to soap and other foam-producing substances. Whenever I used to apply such material on my face, if erroneously the foams came in contact with my nose area, instantly I started to sneeze abysmally for the whole day. Thus, I used to apply face wash on my face avoiding my nose area. Nevertheless, the allergic reaction started often. Because of that, I used to feel out of countenance among my fellows and in public gatherings.

What happened once, the Professor was delivering a lecture on a particular topic, and I was sneezing ceaselessly. The issue wasn't that I was sneezing, the issue was my sneeze was pretty loud which disturbed the flow of Professor. As a consequence, the Professor sent me out of the classroom.

More often than not, I sought advice from those who were knowledgeable about it; I came to know that it would take years to treat it with drugs. I always make an effort to steer clear of medications and drugs whenever feasible. Perhaps upon hearing this, you may not find my hypersensitivity a major concern, but trust me, I have suffered with this for several years. Only the injured can feel the pain.

One morning while having a shower, I was standing with my palms pressed against the wall. Water was sprinkling all over my body from head to toe. Out of the blue, a thought arose in my head: Can't I cure my hypersensitivity with water?

Immediately closing my eyes, I started to create an intense thought in my head: I'm harnessing the healing power of water to eliminate the cause of hypersensitivity from my body. The cause of my sneezing is about to be cured. From now on, I will not sneeze because of this allergic reaction. This pious water is healing every cell of my body.

I'm healing... I'm healing... I'm healing.

For a couple of days, I fervently recited these words while standing under running water in my washroom. You won't believe it, within no time my hypersensitivity vanished away as if it had never existed. My sneezing came to a halt absolutely. Since that day, I started to heal my health issues such as fever, cold, pain, and any other injury with the power of water. Sometimes I used this approach to heal some of my acquaintances.

Over time, I came to grasp that harnessing the healing power of water demanded immense focus and intensity. I realized that it wasn't supposed to be used frivolously for minor discomforts; instead, it was supposed to be incorporated into my spiritual practices. Sometimes later, I decided not to harness the power of water for healing anymore. However, nature didn't approve of that.

It happened to me one day, I fell sick. A high fever gripped my body and because of that an unbearable pain started in my limbs. In the beginning, I paid no heed to it by thinking that it would be cured on its own. Issues such as cold and fever weren't like a day moon to me; I had tolerated much extreme discomfort. But when a couple of nights passed alike then one of my friends showed concern.

She bought me some drugs and encouraged me to consume them. However, the drugs were not availing much; as long as their effect remained in my body, I felt sound but later, the temperature surged again. My condition became worse and I was feeling utterly feeble. While standing, I was sensing dizziness. Even the food didn't feel pleasurable to me.

Then my friend made up her mind to admit me to the hospital, yet I refused because I wasn't financially sound at that time so that I could pay for the hospital bills. Neither did I inform my family; they would have worried in vain. She kept on encouraging me to go to the hospital. Then I said to her dearly, "Give me a night, I will be well and sound till the following morning."

However, she didn't agree, so I urged her that if I did not feel safe and sound till morning, she could take me to the hospital. Upon hearing that, she didn't utter a word and left annoyed.

Unwillingly that night, I had to heal myself. I took a glass of water and uttered some intense words: The profound vitality of this water is restoring my well-being; I will be in good health until morning arrives. As I rise the following morning, I anticipate a surge of vitality coursing through my body once again.

Saying that I blew into the water and engulfed it in one sip. The following morning, when I woke up, I was experiencing a noticeable improvement in my health compared to before. Within two days, I thoroughly recovered from that fever without any medication.

Water, Fire, Air, and Earth are all vital elements in nature just like any other entity, sustaining life in this creation. Across the world, there are places where the energies of elements such as Earth in the form of soil, Air, and Fire are utilized for healing purposes.

For months, I kept on practicing harnessing and shaping the energy of water to elevate my spiritual evolution, and then after some time, I progressed further and gained insight into the mysterious capabilities of the mind.

CHAPTER 18

IMMENSE CALIBER OF THE HUMAN MIND

Nature has originated the entire cosmos legitimately. If we consider solely our planet then we will find that from vegetation to animals, from mountains to oceans, from rivers to dunes, from rains to snow, from summer to winter, from day to night, and land to sky everything possessed an unparalleled uniqueness. There are millions of wondrous species prospering on earth. Among them, human beings are the most sophisticated species ever to exist. Rather it would be pretty rational to mention that humans are the most prominent creation of nature on this planet earth.

However, have you ever wondered about the idiosyncrasy that isolates us from all the other species? Has this thought ever struck your head, what makes us humans the dominant or leading species on this entire planet? What is it that only humans are capable of doing at a fundamental level? Perhaps some of you may argue that we humans have evolved ourselves over time. We have infinite intelligence through which we have discovered and developed all kinds of resources to facilitate our lives; in this era, we humans have better and more convenient ways of survival than any other species.

Well, there is no doubt that at this time, humans are living the most convenient life as compared to yesteryears. What haven't we humans discovered, developed, and innovated; we ceased hunting and discovered better ways to prepare our food. We built fabrics to shield ourselves from the harsh climate. In contemporary times, humans are less preoccupied with defending themselves against other animals and natural catastrophes since we reside in robust concrete structures. With time we have developed all means of transportation and highly evolved systems of communication.

To somewhat, we have control over the domains of land, water, and air. In order to function in this world methodically, we constructed society, norms, and laws. However, it remains a fact that all the innovations and developments humans have achieved so far are merely aimed at fulfilling their needs in a more refined manner. Despite modifying our methods of operation, akin to any other species our objective remains unchanged: to thrive under challenging circumstances.

Intelligence isn't an exclusive gift to humans from nature; instead, nature has endowed every living creature with this capacity. A lion knows how to quietly wait and ambush its prey, while a deer is quick to sense when it needs to be alert and uses its instincts to escape danger by running away. Plants and trees are experts at capturing sunlight to make their food. Every species naturally knows how to reproduce, showing that the intelligence of nature works perfectly throughout the entire universe.

Fundamentally, there is not a highly notable divergence in the requirements of humans compared to other beings. Every other species requires food, water, air, mating, and shielding themselves against threats for their survival. The entire mankind employs its own strategies for accomplishing life goals, just as other species have their distinct approaches. Even though, I would say that there are several animals who live a far better life than the majority of humans because they are more connected to their roots i.e. nature. They possess a profound understanding of the laws of nature, which humans have, to some extent, neglected.

Inherently, animals can perform almost all the activities that humans do nevertheless, human beings have a privilege or it would be more apt to say, a blessing from nature that no other species on this planet ever had: the capacity for recalling information and visualizing possibilities.

Everything humans have constructed this far is a result of their potential to visualize and memorize. We can visualize anything that exists in the creation and store any information in our memory for a long period. Humans can recall their bygone time and visualize their future or forthcoming events while biding in the present moment. We have the capacity to maintain a conscious state for any duration we wish, regardless of external influences. In contrast, animals and other species lack such abilities; instead, they are primarily driven by instinct.

There is a popular saying: 'Eat, drink, and relax'. You all must have heard this saying some time or the other. What's fascinating is that while this proverb was coined by humans, it doesn't necessarily reflect human behavior. An animal can lie peacefully with a full stomach because its concerns revolve solely around essential needs like food, reproduction, shelter, and sleep. As long as an animal is gratified with these essential needs, it can remain in a state of meditation; doing absolutely nothing. But this is not the case in humans; we can't remain serene just by eating, drinking, mating, and sleeping. We tend to think about all sorts of things when we are pleased with our necessities. Human beings require something to keep themselves engaged; it could be a physical object or just an internal thought. Now, the question is: What prevents us from maintaining contentment by merely meeting our essential requirements?

The answer to this question is straightforward, though it may not be readily apparent. Mankind possesses something that stands as the most exceptional and potent tool in this world. This sophisticated tool is none other than our 'evolved mind' which renders humans the matchless creation of nature. It's solely due to our evolved minds that mankind leads the race for survival and dominates as the ruling species on this planet earth.

Besides its ability to visualize and recall information, the human mind harbors immense capabilities such as perception, discrimination, sensing, manifestation, cognition, action, reaction, and control. However, nobody yet has comprehended the functioning of the human mind thoroughly because it is not a physical object. It is akin to the air, all-pervading within the body.

Some philosophers and intellectuals argue that the mind is merely a manifestation of thoughts. You may have heard such quotes: No thought, no mind; if you can control your thoughts, you can control your mind, and many others. Some scientific studies claim that the mind is nothing but the functioning of the human brain. Though, it's not the sheer truth about the mind.

In the Bhagavad Gita, Lord Vasudeva Krishna depicts the mind as the master of our five sensory organs and the true 'Self' or soul as the master of the mind. Therefore, in order to reach the Self or to attain self-realization, one must transcend the senses and surpass the mind. The overall concept of spirituality is focused on transcending the mind. Thus, the ancient sages devised various practices of yoga and meditation to aid in the understanding of the mind, as mastery over anything can only be achieved through absolute comprehension. Therefore, instead of seeking control over something, one ought to strive for a deep understanding of it. Once you understand something, you become free from it.

As per our Vedic scriptures, the mind is depicted as the fusion of four components:

- **Buddhi**
- **Ahamkara**
- **Manas**
- **Chitta**

Buddhi – It is also known as our intellect. It is the property to discriminate or dissect the physical world into dualism for instance right and wrong, day and night, positive and negative, rational and irrational, darkness and light, and so on. Intellect is engaged in our decision-making, judgments, and choices, drawing upon the knowledge and information stored in our memory.

Ahamkara – It is loosely translated as the 'Ego' though; it is not always considered in the negative sense such as arrogance; rather it is essential for a being to operate in this world. In essence, Ahamkara embodies the essence of an individual's identity, the fundamental sense of I-ness required for one's existence as a being.

Manas – It is responsible for our feelings and sentiments which may be stimulated by the external environment. It is the cause of sensations in our physical body such as pleasure, agony, anger, envy, enthusiasm, and so on.

Chitta – It is the subconscious mind which is the warehouse of numerous impressions. It is the cosmic intelligence that governs everything inside our physical body and functions all day and all night. Chitta is the attribute that makes us aware of both internal and external objects, it is also responsible for the manifestation of our thoughts. Chitta is beyond Buddhi, Manas, and Ahamkara. It is the pure consciousness through which the whole existence is linked together.

Usually, when we strive to comprehend the functionality of the human mind, we distinguish it into two sections: the conscious mind and the subconscious mind or the rational and the irrational mind. You may have heard various technical and logistic elucidations about the conscious and subconscious mind. Nevertheless, allow me to decode it as easily as ABC.

The conscious mind is the part of mental processing that we are aware of at any given moment. Hence, whenever we act intentionally or with mindfulness, our conscious mind is active during that period. For instance, we can intentionally raise our hands and legs in the air, take a deep breath, blink rapidly, or purposefully smile at someone.

On the other side, the subconscious mind operates below the level of awareness; when we perform all these above activities without conscious awareness or as a matter of habit, like frequently moving our hands while speaking with someone, breathing naturally, blinking naturally, or smiling unexpectedly, it is our subconscious mind that is in operation. In essence, our subconscious mind governs our natural actions, whereas our conscious mind directs our intentional or thought-out actions.

The majority of significant functions in our physical body are regulated by our subconscious mind such as our heartbeat, pulsation, blood circulation, respiration, digestion, excretion, etc. It operates in a magnificent way akin to a miracle. The knowledge and information we perceive from our surroundings through our sensory organs are also stored in our subconscious. Apart from that, everything we come across is imprinted on the screen of our subconscious mind whether we are aware of it or not. To give you an idea, as soon as we catch the aroma of cooking in our nose, we instantly recognize that food is being prepared nearby because that aroma of cooking food is already there in our subconscious.

Everything is linked up in this cosmos; hence the imprints of this vast existence are already present in our subconscious mind. Our mind is the treasury of all the answers and wisdom that we seek in the outer world. Therefore, there is no question that the mind has tremendous power.

Intentionally, some mystical aspects of the mind have remained hidden from humanity since ancient times. Certain knowledge is meant to be kept secret because if such extraordinary information falls into the wrong hands, the consequences could be dire for all of existence.

However, in this era, things function in a different manner. Therefore, the Siddhas, sages, and other mystics have decided to take pity upon humans and share some of their mysterious wisdom and insights with the world, allowing even ordinary people to transform their lives. One such insight was the mind's remarkable ability to manifest thoughts and words into physical reality.

If we look at the evolution of innovations, all that mankind has created this far has originated as ideas or thoughts within the mind; primarily we have created all that in our minds later it comes into existence. So there is no question that the world around us is simply a manifestation of our own minds.

In the Tantric tradition, it is widely believed that if you can contemplate something, you also possess the potential to bring it into physical existence. Therefore, if one masters the art of manifestation, one gains the ability to bring forth anything within the boundless expanse of the cosmos. Aghoris, yogis, some saints, and sincere tantric practitioners have been well-versed in the art of manifestation for centuries. They possess the requisite knowledge to manifest a thought, belief, idea, or word within the mind before bringing it into physical existence. This knowledge permeated the world, thanks to the Guru-disciple tradition.

The mastery of manifestation is reserved for those with a singularly focused mind, as it demands a focused and unwavering mental concentration. Upon learning about such phenomenal powers, an individual can effectively heal severe illnesses such as cancer in a relatively short period. Such an individual can bless anyone with immense wealth, health, longevity, vision, and offspring regardless of medical opinions.

I have encountered stories of extraordinary Nath yogis who wielded the power to manifest their words into reality almost instantly. They would wander the earth akin to a walking marvel, manifesting miracles throughout their journey and imparting blessings upon households they encountered. Consider this: Everything we perceive in the world is merely a reflection of our minds. Thus, one holds the ability to reshape reality through the power of the mind.

The workings of the cosmos are governed by its own unique mechanisms. After acquiring knowledge of the water element, I was eager to advance along my journey. Several days later, while reading a text relevant to the subconscious mind, I learned about the power of manifestation. I found this concept particularly captivating. Although I was harnessing the power of the mind since the beginning but wasn't thoroughly aware of its operations.

Therefore, I began my pursuit to acquire knowledge on the subject. Following that, I acquainted myself with the conscious and subconscious mind, and within a short span, I initiated practice to wield the power of the mind purposely. I would sit in a meditative state, as tranquil as still water, and then consciously direct my thoughts toward my aspirations. With firm command over my subconscious mind, akin to a strict master, I began visualizing my thoughts manifesting. Soon after, they transformed into reality with surprising swiftness.

Using the power of manifestation, I have successfully cured several diseases on numerous occasions. Apart from that, whenever I aspired to possess something particular, I consciously thought about that and my mind perceived it as a command; within a few hours somehow or the other, that thing would appear before me. When I sought insight on a certain topic, a command would trigger the appearance of that knowledge in my memory out of the blue; well, it was always there in my mind.

Over time, I became adept at influencing the psyche of other individuals—all my desires seemed to materialize effortlessly; it was as if the Divine was attentively fulfilling each of my longings.

Time was passing at its own rhythm. After my mother's departure, the family needed someone who could take over all the responsibilities she used to handle. Therefore, my entire family and relatives unanimously decided to arrange the marriage of my younger brother, Vishwa. He was two years my junior, and there were two primary motivations behind arranging his marriage; first, Vishwa was determined to engage in farming alongside my father in the village, so his spouse would also live with him in the village. On the other side, I aspired to pursue a career in a bustling city, and if I were to marry, everybody knew that eventually, I would have to relocate with my partner. Another reason was: I'm the second child of my parents; I have an elder sister, Srishti.

In our tradition, marriage typically begins with either the eldest or the youngest child. I was satisfied with the decision made by my elders as it settled the family and household matters. Now, I could leisurely pursue my objectives.

It is believed that time flies by swiftly when all is flowing smoothly. On the one hand, I had accomplished my post-graduation and at the same time, preparations for my brother's marriage were on. In the meantime, I was offered a position as a Microbiologist at a molecular laboratory in Haridwar and I willingly accepted the offer.

A couple of months later, my brother tied the knot. My father was over the moon during that period, and the entire family was filled with sheer delight. Vishwa's consort, Siya gradually took over all household duties and after a year, God blessed the couple with a baby boy. Gladly, I bestowed upon the baby boy the name Advait, signifying the Absolute. In the village, my father arranged a splendid welcome ceremony on the arrival of the newborn. Our family and friends from the village and beyond came to offer their blessings for the newborn's long and healthy life.

Generally, in villages, when a newborn and the mother arrive home after being discharged from the hospital, they are provided an isolated room for the next six days. Access to that room directly from outside the house is restricted for everyone; only with certain precautions can one observe them from afar. Six days later, following certain rituals, the mother and the newborn are shifted into their respective room.

The underlying cause is that during those six-day period, the newborn and the mother are particularly vulnerable to unworldly entities. In the course of pregnancy, the mother magnetizes certain ethereal entities toward her womb because there is a new life thriving in her womb. This presents an opportunity for such entities to cross into our realm, enabling them to acquire a physical form and fulfil desires achievable only in corporeal existence. Hence, they tend to possess the mother and the newborn smoothly. To shield the mother and her child from evil entities, certain talismans are tied to their bodies, usually in the neck. I also used to wear such a talisman around my neck when I was a toddler. In urban areas, merely a handful of people follow these rituals but, in the villages, people are quite aware of all these things.

That day, because of the ceremony, the mother and the newborn came in direct contact with numerous individuals and nobody took any precautions. In the depths of night, while sleeping, the mother of the newborn was haunted by a nightmare that unsettled both, the mother and the infant. Both of them remained awake throughout the entire night, unable to find any rest. The newborn was quite restless, frequently crying throughout the night. The following morning, Siya shared her nightmare with my brother along with some other ladies in the house. Upon hearing this, concern spread throughout the family regarding her dream, and discussions arose about seeking help from an exorcist or obtaining a talisman from a reputable practitioner for both the mother and her baby.

In the meantime, my brother sought my advice on the matter. He told me that her consort had some nightmare last night that left her terrified. He elaborated that the women in the house suspected a paranormal origin and were insisting on consulting an exorcist. It became evident to me that the situation was deeply unsettling. "You don't have to worry about anything as long as I'm here," I reassured my brother by laying my palm on his shoulder.

Subsequently, I entered the room where the mother and newborn were resting. Siya sat on the bed while the newborn slept peacefully. I grabbed a chair next to her and initiated the dialogue by asking about her health to make her comfortable to talk about this. I then encouraged her to recount the dream in its entirety, ensuring she didn't leave out any details.

Siya took a long gasp and then started narrating the dream. "Last night while sleeping, I witnessed a tall and skinny lady wearing black robes standing at the entrance of this room," she said pointing towards the entrance. She added ahead, "I asked her, who are you, and why are you standing there? Her response was a haunting laughter, sending shivers down my spine. I felt an overwhelming urge to scream in panic, but my voice seemed to be trapped in my throat. Gradually, the woman approached close to my baby, and then she placed some Batasha (white sugar candies) alongside some contaminated items on the infant's chest. Instantly, the baby began to cry. I awakened from slumber and found the room empty. Somehow, I managed to make the baby asleep and then I drifted off to sleep. However, as soon as I fell asleep, that eerie figure reappeared, horrifying me once more with her sinister laugh. Throughout the entire night, I struggled to scream, yet felt utterly helpless. The entire incident felt incredibly vivid and tangible to me."

As I mentioned previously the ethereal being strives to connect with us in the state of dreams. Something similar happened with her. Upon hearing her, I perceived that certain evil ethereal being strived to possess her last night and certainly, it would strive to bother both of them again. Such unworldly forces tend to harm us whenever they find suitable circumstances. To shield the mother and the baby, I needed to perform a ritual called Kilan; it's a mystical approach to shield an area so that evil ethereal energies couldn't enter. However, I had never been in such a situation before, so I had not experienced it previously. Nevertheless, I had faith that I could do that.

For a while, I closed my eyes and directed my mind to impart the knowledge needed to create a protective shield around the newborn and the mother. Suddenly, as if out of nowhere, the thought struck me that I would need turmeric. I asked my brother to bring me quickly some turmeric powder.

As per Hinduism and Buddhism, turmeric is considered one of the highly auspicious ingredients that signifies purity and wellness. It contains immeasurable healing properties.

Vishwa swiftly went into the cooking area and brought some turmeric powder in a bowl. Then I asked him to add a few drops of water to it. Subsequently, with the bowl held in my left hand, I closed my eyes and beseeched Lord Ram for the ability to carry out the task. With a one-pointed mind, I started chanting while blending turmeric with water in an anti-clockwise rotation with the help of my ring finger. I was receiving all these instructions from my inner consciousness, the Chitta.

After chanting intensely for a while, I manifested a thought in my mind: I'm crafting a formidable energy shield around the mother and the newborn, empowered by the resonance of my chant. This shield will safeguard them from any malevolent entities, both in the present and the days to come.

Afterward, I opened my eyes and inscribed 'Ram' on both of their foreheads using turmeric paste.

There are various other sophisticated approaches for conducting Kilan as per traditions; the one I mentioned here is just one of them.

"You don't have to worry now. From now on, no such horrible dreams will come to you. Just chant the name of Lord Ram and have faith in Him; He will guard you and your child," I assured Siya with brimful conviction.

She showed her gratitude with a gentle smile. While leaving the room, I inscribed 'Ram' on both sides of the door with the remaining turmeric to shield the entrance and the room. My brother came out along with me and I explained to him, "There is no need to approach any priest and exorcist. I have secured them with a divine shield; no power can even bend their hair. If you visit anyone in this regard, mark my words, they will certainly link this phenomenon with dark magic and occult. Then they will direct you to conduct certain rituals which you have to do unwillingly. So stay away from such people."

Vishwa attentively absorbed my words. From that day forward, both the mother and the baby have been thriving. After that phenomenon, I aided some other of my acquaintances while harnessing the power of mind.

After some time, I came to realize that whenever I utilized my abilities to manifest something, I was generating new karma for myself. By healing or shielding others, I was also taking on their karma. Due to that, I was forming a Runanubandha (karmic debt) with each one of them. Therefore, I had to move ahead letting go of it all; I had a long journey ahead of me. The speck was still a considerable distance from the dune.

Around six to seven months later, I switched my job and relocated to Gurgaon, (NCR) where I joined a pharmaceutical company as a Microbiologist. One day, my friend Mayank contacted me and shared his intention to visit the Kedarnath

Temple in October with some of his companions.

I had been eager to visit the Kedarnath Temple since my graduation days. Almost every Hindu in Bharat dreams of visiting the Kedarnath Temple at least once in their lifetime. Without a second thought, I asked him to count me in.

Kedarnath Valley is such a place where one can witness the heaven on earth. The Himalayas abound with mystics, where the profound and enigmatic experiences are so highly captivating that one cannot help but believe in the existence of a higher power after witnessing them firsthand.

In the heart of the Himalayas, I came across something similar. It was an event that left some devotees in awe, others questioning its authenticity, and a few of us, myself included, bowing in reverence and devotion.

CHAPTER 19

KEDARNATH AND THE DANCING DEITY

Kedarnath Temple is one of the pious pilgrimage sites dedicated to Lord Shiva. It is situated in the Kedarnath town in district Rudra Prayag of Uttarakhand. Kedarnath is considered part of the 'Char Dham' signifying the four sacred shrines of north, which also encompass Gangotri, Yamunotri, and Badrinath. It is believed that the breezes that grace the area of Kedarnath originate from heaven. And rightfully so, it is situated in the lap of the majestic white Himalayas at an altitude of approximately 12000 feet above sea level. As per the scriptures, a mythological lore is behind the construction of the Kedarnath Temple.

Legend has it that after the combat of Mahabharata, the Pandavas set out in quest of Lord Shiva for the atonement of their sins. They traveled to Kashi, the city of Lord Shiva which is familiar as Banaras or Varanasi these days. But they couldn't find the Lord there, as He was offended by them because of the massive destruction of humanity in the combat. Lord Shiva didn't want to see them; therefore, He took the morph of a giant bullock and hid somewhere in the Himalayas. Somehow the Pandavas learned about it and then they headed toward the Himalayas. When they reached there, Bheem who was second among the Pandavas saw a bullock wandering in the ranges. He instantly recognized it as Lord Shiva. As soon as Bheem addressed it, the bullock started merging into the ground. Without delay, he hurried towards the bullock and grasped its tail firmly with all his strength.

Consequently, the bullock emerged in five distinct locations of the Himalayan ranges within the segments; the arms emerged in Tungnath, the face in Rudranath, the abdomen in Madhyamaheshwar, the hairs in Kalpeshwar, and the hump in Kedarnath. Thereafter, the Pandavas constructed these five shrines which are renowned as Panch Kedar. Following this, Lord Shiva was pleased and graciously bestowed His blessings upon them.

Due to heavy snowfall, from November to April, the portals of the shrine remain closed and when the snow starts melting in April, the portals are reopened for the devotees. Among all of us, two of our companions, Abhishek and Prashant had previously visited Kedarnath. They were well-acquainted with all aspects of Kedarnath; hence they took on the role of guiding us.

One week earlier, one of them created a chat group on social media and shared all the essential details regarding travel budget, number of travelers, departure spot, date and time, and also the necessary stuff to carry in backpacks. Abhishek provided us clear instructions to avoid carrying unnecessary items in our backpacks, as we were all preparing for strenuous trekking; the lighter our backpacks, the easier the trekking would become.

However, the dilemma was finding garments capable of keeping me warm and dry, as the temperature over there remains quite low due to high altitude and frequent rainfall.

Despite keeping it to a minimum, my backpack had become somewhat sizeable.

Initially, I returned home from Gurgaon and collected my Royal Enfield. With the wind as my companion, I embarked towards Paonta Sahib, Himachal Pradesh, as it was the initiation point of our journey, and most of our companions, including Mayank, resided there.

After a delightful ride of nearly two and a half hours, I reached there. The day before departure, until the evening, we all gathered in Paonta Sahib. It was a group of eight people; except for three, we all were familiar with each other since our post-graduation days. In those days, all these five stars of Gurukul were shining in the pharmaceutical companies.

We enjoyed a cup of tea along with some Aaloo Paratha while sharing anecdotes from our corporate lives. It seemed upon hearing them that we were all on the same page because we all had similar issues in our working life. The cause of all the issues was that we all were doing something that we didn't love to do. We were just dragging our bodies from morning to evening so we could pay our bills. It wasn't the life that we had envisioned after the accomplishment of our academics.

This journey was also essential for all of us as we sought a temporary escape from our daily routines. However, I had an additional objective to visit Kedarnath. There exist certain locations around the globe where the divine energy is notably vibrant; visiting such places catalyzes a profound spiritual evolution, forever changing your being.

I have heard numerous narratives of individuals who visited places such as Mount Kailash, Mahakaleshwar Jyotirlinga, Maa Kamakhya, Jagannath Puri, Kashi, and many more; they encountered the divine energy, which forever changed the course of their lives. Kedarnath was one such spot.

The distance between Paonta Sahib to Kedarnath is about 310 km. In flat terrain, this distance may seem ordinary, but in mountainous regions, it's significant, nearly double compared to flat terrain. The following morning, we departed from Paonta Sahib at 04:00 A.M. We had three motorbikes and a brand-new scooter.

I was riding my Royal Enfield and Kakraan was sitting behind me, Abhishek and his cousin were together on another Royal Enfield, Prashant and his friend were on a scooter, and Mayank and Yash were on a new Honda motorbike. Advancing at the speed of the wind, we navigated the serpentine roads carved amidst lush green mountains until we arrived in Srinagar; a beautiful town in the Pauri Garhwal district of Uttarakhand.

Around 10:00 A.M., we reached there and had breakfast in a small restaurant. It was a picturesque day; the clear blue sky served as a backdrop to the brilliant sun. For an hour, we stayed in Srinagar and then started our journey again. Now our upcoming destination was Devprayag.

Devprayag is renowned for the confluence where the Alaknanda River and the Bhagirathi River merge, continuing their journey as the revered River Ganga. When we reached Devprayag, we encountered a gathering by the roadside. The people were engaged with their mobile phones and cameras clicking photographs and videos. We also parked our motorbikes at the roadside and approached the other side of the road to see what captured the attention of folks there.

On one side of the road stood a towering mountain, while on the other side lay a deep chasm. The crowd was gathered around, peering into the depths of the chasm. I walked to the opposite side and gazed into the chasm below. Observing the profound chasm, my heart swelled with joy. It was a breathtaking scene, where two rivers of distinct colour blended together, continuing their journey as one. The water of one of those two rivers was clear and greenish, while the other flowed with murky, muddy water. There was a small shrine at the merging point where devotees were performing rituals.

We savored the view for some time before making our way towards Sonprayag; as we were committed to reaching Sonprayag before sunset because doing so would allow us the opportunity to proceed to Gaurikund in the evening and secure suitable accommodation for the night. According to this itinerary, we could have initiated our trek from Gaurikund in the early morning. Both Abhishek and Prashant had commendable itineraries, and we were determined to ensure their success. However, plans don't always unfold as expected, no matter how well-crafted they may be. When life is uncertain, you must not assume that things will be certain.

We rode our motorbikes as fast as we could on the serpentine mountain roads. During our journey, we also encountered landslides at multiple locations along the way. However, with the grace of God, we continued to progress safely. The path and the scenery surrounding it were as captivating as they were perilous. I guess 'Wynorrific' would be an appropriate term to depict it; a single misstep could lead you into a deep ditch. On one side, cascading waterfalls enhanced the beauty of the mountains, while on the other side, sections of the road were incomplete, requiring us to navigate through mud, sand, and stones. Even where the road existed, only one vehicle could pass at a time.

Roughly an hour before Sonprayag, we found ourselves trapped in a dense traffic jam. A giant waterfall was falling right in between the road which created a deep pothole in the road and unfortunately, a four-wheeler fell in that. As a consequence, hundreds of vehicles were stuck there, standing in a queue one after the other on both sides of the road. After an hour, eventually, somehow we managed to escape from there though we had wasted more than an hour due to the dense traffic jam.

It was almost 6 o'clock in the evening when we were about to arrive at Sonprayag. Despite the delay, we still had enough time to reach Gaurikund, so we adhered to our plan. Some distance away from the town; the police officers forbade us to move ahead with our motorbikes. They directed us to park our vehicles in the newly constructed parking lot, which was still in progress, and proceed on foot from there.

Abhishek briefed us that when he visited here last year, there were no such restrictions at that time. The devotees could have entered Sonprayag along with their vehicles, but now they weren't permitting us. After a while of discussion, we had to swallow the pill. We parked our vehicles in the parking lot, which was nearly one kilometer away from the town, and continued our journey on foot from there.

Sonprayag was jam-packed with devotees, almost every age individual was present there at that time. There was a vantage of four-wheelers to take the devotees from Sonprayag to Gaurikund. Therefore, we rushed to approach the four-wheeler stand so we could hire one for Gaurikund. But once again we had to face the hindrance. The police officers forbade us to move ahead because of the deficiency of accommodations in Gaurikund, hence they were not permitting anyone to go ahead.

Upon hearing that, a momentary chill dampened the euphoria within us. Despite our diligent efforts, we failed to reach our destination. Everyone became slightly morose but deep down I knew that if the Almighty didn't want us to reach there then it must be for a reason certainly. We gazed at each other's long faces and took a U-turn from there. Now the hunger and exhaustion that we were ignoring for a long while were glaring in our faces.

"Forget about everything, let's find a room and have some food first," Abhishek uttered softly.

We consented to this suggestion and followed him to a spot where a caretaker showed us the room. However, the room was overpriced but we didn't have plenty of alternatives at that moment; all the hotels and guest houses were nearly loaded even in Sonprayag also. Therefore, we didn't ponder much while taking that room on rent. Following that, we settled our belongings in the room, cleaned up by washing our hands and face, and then headed to find something to eat.

There were only a handful of eateries in the entire town, and all were quite crowded. Fortunately, we found some space in an eatery. Without thinking much, we entered there. When we were having the meal, two men arrived at the eatery. Both of them were wearing a rain cover, despite that they were thoroughly wet and shivering from the cold. When they were asked where they were coming from in this condition, they replied that they were coming straight from the Kedarnath Temple. One of them added further, "Due to the heavy rainfall, the temperature in Kedarnath fell to -4o degrees. Somehow, we managed to reach Gaurikund but we couldn't find a place to stay there. Therefore, we have to come here under compulsion."

Upon hearing that, we felt grateful. If we had reached Gaurikund, we would have encountered the same situation; Lord Ram saved us. Every event unfolds for our ultimate good. Now the plan was that we would wake up at 3 o'clock in the early morning and then proceed hastily towards the Gaurikund.

After dinner, we had a cup of tea and then off to the room to sleep. The following morning, we awaken to the sound of our phone alarms. We hastily got ourselves ready; had some tea with biscuits, and then checked out from the room around 04:00 A.M. We rushed through our preparations to avoid waiting for the four-wheelers. However, when we set out of the room, we witnessed a lengthy queue of devotees waiting to reach the four-wheeler stand.

Looking at the lengthy queue, Prashant asked us if we would like to proceed on foot to Gaurikund. The distance between Sonprayag and Gaurikund is hardly 5 km. Driven by enthusiasm, we exclaimed, 'Yes! Why not, it's just 5 km away.' We proceeded alongside the queue, but the police officers once again obstructed us at the same spot where they had halted us the previous evening. Meanwhile, we strived to have a word with them. Prashant told them that we didn't want to hire the four-wheeler rather we aspired to move on foot, so let us go. But the officers didn't allow us and asked us to wait by standing in the queue like everyone.

When we returned to the location from where we intended to proceed on foot, we found that the queue had become even longer. We couldn't enter the middle of the queue hence, we had to walk till the end of the queue. It was much longer than we assumed. Eventually, we reached the end of the queue which was near the parking lot. I could bet that the entire queue wasn't less than 3 km long.

The rising sun's beams were distinctly visible as they pierced through the mountains. It appeared as though nature was bestowing its blessings upon the region of Kedarnath Valley, extending its hand in grace. Enthralled by this wondrous spectacle, we advanced at an ant's pace. It took us three long hours to reach the spot from where the four-wheelers were transporting the devotees. Without any further delay, we hired a four-wheeler at fifty rupees per person, and passing under the mountains and waterfalls ultimately, reached Gaurikund.

Gaurikund serves as the initial point for embarking on the arduous 16 km trek to the Kedarnath shrine. From here you can take a palanquin or mule/ponies to reach the shrine. Even the government has also provided the convenience of a Helicopter service from Phata to Kedarnath base camp, though for that you must be wealthy. But the thrill you will experience while trekking is unparalleled by any other experience.

We initiated our ascent along the path, echoing 'Har-Har Mahadev!' with countless other devotees. As we ascended along the trail, the view grew ever more enchanting. The waterfalls descending from the mountains resembled streams of milk. For the first time in my life, I witnessed numerous waterfalls in succession. I didn't feel the need to drink packaged drinking water because there were several springs at every short distance. Whenever I felt thirsty, I would quench my thirst by consuming the pure, crystal-clear chilled water flowing directly from the natural spring.

As we continued our ascent, our climbing stamina began to diminish. Gradually as per the pace, our entire group had become isolated; some of our fellows had gone ahead of us. Yash was with me and both of us were climbing leisurely.

The milestones along the way were quite confusing. I came across one milestone that read 'Kedarnath 9 km', and after climbing for half an hour, I encountered another milestone with the same distance of 9 km. With backbreaking efforts, we continued our journey; pausing periodically to rest, eat, and hydrate along the way. Although the trek was incredible, I encountered something along the way that utterly dismayed me—I encountered three dead bodies of mules on the roadside.

In Kedarnath, the owners of the mules are extremely brutal with them. They don't provide adequate nourishment to the mules, instead, they compel them to carry people and heavy loads on their backs throughout the day without adequate rest. Consequently, some mules succumb to fatigue and weakness along the journey. Therefore, it's a humble urge, if you ever visit the Kedarnath Temple or any other such pilgrimages then don't hire animals to carry you or your belongings. Undertake the penance of climbing mountains on foot, and you will surely receive the fruits of the pilgrimage. Lord Shiva itself is known as the 'Pashupatinath', Lord of animals. How could Lord Shiva bless us if we don't possess compassion for animals in our hearts? In this way, our devotion to the Lord is just in vain.

After putting in a tremendous effort, eventually, we reached the base camp of the Kedarnath Temple, thoroughly exhausted. My body felt completely drained, and I was also experiencing pain in my feet. On arriving at the base camp, we realized one thing articulately; the trek wasn't merely 16 km long, instead it was approximately 22-24 km long. It took us nearly ten hours to get there.

At the base camp, I witnessed something that will stay with me for the rest of my life. Reaching there, I had an unobstructed panoramic view of the majestic Himalayas—I mean, how can something be so breathtakingly beautiful!

The immense Himalayas, cloaked in a blanket of snow, loomed majestically with their peaks reaching skyward. A few years back, during my visit to Dhanaulti, I briefly caught sight of the Himalayas from the car window, but it lasted only a couple of seconds. At that moment, I became utterly numb. Everything came to a halt for me; all the thoughts just vanished for a few minutes from my head and it felt as if I was falling into the void.

With all my heart, I longed to witness that scene one more time, and in the valley of Kedarnath, God granted me that desire. I sat by the roadside, entranced by the view of the Himalayas; I yearned to engrave that spell-bounding vista into my soul, my eyes fixated upon it unwaveringly. Indeed, there was an irresistible allure beckoning me closer. I felt an undeniable sense of connection to this place as if it were where I truly belonged.

A while later, my concentration was interrupted by the sound of some musical instruments. As I glanced back, I noticed some local residents playing music and proceeding towards the shrine with enthusiasm. Two individuals were bearing a splendidly decorated palanquin upon their shoulders.

The mountains of Uttarakhand are the abode of various deities. There are certain divine entities present there in their natural, vibrant, and dynamic manifestations; local folks have been worshipping them since time immemorial. They believe that these deities guard their forest, fields, cattle, and their families from disasters and other natural destructions.

Certain mysterious rituals are conducted from time to time in mountains where these deities are transported in palanquins to other locations for worship, such as the riverbank or another shrine. That palanquin was carrying such a deity, and the local folks were transporting it to pay homage to Lord Kedarnath. Following the palanquin, we too proceeded toward the shrine.

As we approached the shrine premises, we observed a throng of devotees engaged in capturing the marvelous scenery. Every inch of the shrine was adorned with meticulous decoration; the exterior was enveloped in a vibrant array of marigold flowers. The sound of drums and bells was echoing in the surroundings.

Somehow, avoiding the dense crowd, I reached the steps of the shrine and then I blessed my eyes with something that some of you might find hard to swallow once you hear about it. It was the same group of local folks that I noticed a few minutes back; with joyous fervor, they played drums and rang bells, while the palanquin they carried on their shoulders bounced briskly in the air.

Initially, I assumed that those bearing the palanquin were intentionally trying to make it bounce in the air. However, when I observed it keenly, I realized that the palanquin was bouncing on its own and those men were merely striving to hold it with their whole potency. In a matter of moments, the palanquin started running in a circle and following that, swinging from side to side almost as if it was dancing to the beat.

The palanquin swung vigorously from side to side, causing the men holding it to sway along with its motion. That phenomenon left almost everyone utterly amazed. There were no mechanisms within the palanquin to induce its movement, nor were the carriers intentionally swinging it. It was the divine power emanating from the deity that caused the palanquin to dance with such exuberance.

However, the sight of the dancing palanquin didn't startle me, as I had been told about similar occurrences by a friend before. During my first job in Haridwar, I had a friend named Jayasurya who belonged to Gopeshwar, a township in the Garhwal hills. He once shared a video clip with me, showcasing his hometown, where a palanquin carrying their local deity was seen dancing.

Afterward, he recounted an extraordinary event that occurred in their town several years ago: Once some local folks were carrying the palanquin of Naina Devi, from one shrine to another, accompanied by music and dance. All of a sudden, the palanquin started dancing vigorously in the air, causing the men carrying it to lose their grip. Subsequently, the palanquin levitated and started moving forward on its own. Everyone hurriedly chased after it, regaining the grip. After an arduous effort, they eventually managed to regain their grip. Hence, the carriers held onto the palanquin firmly to prevent it from levitating during the dance.

The first time I caught a glimpse of it on his phone, I couldn't have slept the whole night; I was astounded because I couldn't grasp how a palanquin could dance and levitate seemingly without any logical explanation. But now I was witnessing it with reverence and bowing before it; not every individual is fortunate enough to experience such uncanny events in their lives.

In the mountainous regions of Uttarakhand and Himachal, there are numerous shrines dedicated to local deities worshipped by the residents. Some notable deities include Mahasu Devta, Golu Devta, Naina Devi, Nanda Devi, Surkanda Devi, Kunjapuri Devi, Narsingh, Bhandari Golla, and Anayari. When summoned by the residents, these deities demonstrate their presence through specific responses and bestow blessings on their devotees.

Eventually, after a while, the palanquin departed from the shrine ground. Following that, I reunited with the rest of my companions, who had arrived there ahead of me. The sun had disappeared behind the Himalayas; it was time for the evening prayers. The shrine grounds were bustling with devotees, all eagerly awaiting the evening rituals. We joined other devotees in sitting on the ground on the outskirts of the shrine, while some stood queued up, waiting to enter the sanctum sanctorum.

The atmosphere around us was shifting; the temperature was steadily dropping, causing my body to start shivering. Shortly after, the prayers of Lord Kedarnath resonated through the speakers. Along with that, two aged monks appeared and began playing giant Damru raising their hands. Perhaps both of the monks belonged to the Naga cult; they had adorned themselves with bulky Rudraksha rosaries and covered their entire bodies in ashes. One of them had tied the thick hair knot on his head while the other monk had untied his hair. Their wrist was loaded with thick silver bangles. What was truly striking was seeing them withstand the cold with little clothing, while I, wearing a branded bomber jacket, found myself shivering. The temperature was dropping beyond my tolerance; I was freezing while sitting there on the ground; my teeth were clashing together. When I couldn't find a way to protect myself from the cold, I decided to warm my body from the inside.

Nature has endowed our minds with the capacity to regulate the temperature of our inner body, ensuring the accurate functioning of our organs under optimum temperature. Hence, I employed the power of my mind to accomplish this. With closed eyes, I began reciting the name of Lord Ram, aiming to concentrate my mind. Following that, I manifested an intense thought in my mind: The warmth is spreading throughout my body, banishing the cold entirely from my senses. I am feeling warm... I am feeling warm... I am feeling warm.

In no time, a feeling of warmth washed over me, and soon after, my body ceased its shivering. It was as if the cold had never existed. Following the worship ceremony, rather than proceeding to enter the shrine for the Darshan, we opted to rest.

Entering the shrine required waiting in a long queue for over an hour, and none of us had the energy reserves left in our bodies to endure it. Therefore, we decided to have the Darshan of the Lord early in the morning. Afterward, we made our way to the rented room, and upon arrival, everyone collapsed onto the bed without delay. Yet, our day was far from over; it seemed the Supreme had yet more in store for us.

Around half an hour later, we set out for dinner; it was around 9 o'clock. We entered a restaurant and feasted until our stomachs were touching our throats. As we stepped out of the restaurant post-dinner, Prashant quickly spotted that the line to enter the shrine had unexpectedly shortened. He gazed at his watch; it was 10:00 P.M.

The closing hours for the Darshan were set between 10:00 and 10:30 P.M. Without doing further calculation, Prashant uttered, "There is still a chance for us to enter the shrine. The portal is about to close and there are only a few devotees left in the queue. If we're lucky, we might be able to enter the shrine quickly and easily.

In an instant, we formulated a fresh strategy: Two of us would swiftly head to a nearby store to purchase offerings for everyone, while the rest would proceed directly to the queue.

The police officers were directing the devotees to enter the shrine one by one. However, they were not polite to the devotees queued up. While standing in the queue, I was anxious about the two guys who had gone to buy offerings; what if we entered inside and they hadn't arrived yet? Hence, I repeatedly glanced back, checking if they were on their way.

As we reached closer to the portal of the shrine, the police officers began pushing the devotees back, intending to close the entrance by placing barricades. As a consequence, the devotees started pushing themselves ahead forcefully thus, we approached the steps of the shrine. As soon as they began to inhibit the devotees from moving ahead, I became more worried as I didn't know whether my companions were inside the barricades or not.

The surroundings were pretty crowded, merely heads were visible all around. Meanwhile, a hand surged toward me holding a small bag of offerings. I raised myself on tiptoes and glimpsed that it was Kakraan. Upon spotting him, a wave of calm washed over me; I offered heartfelt gratitude to Lord Ram.

After entering the shrine, I started to observe every subtle thing keenly; I had never visited such an old shrine before. The interior architecture boasted a captivating uniqueness. The walls and pillars of the shrine were constructed from a diverse array of stones, each possessing a rugged texture and a slightly dark hue. Apart from that, idols of some deities were carved into the pillars; everything seemed quite antique. I was touching the walls and the pillars with my palm to experience the energy imbibed in the shrine. However, I didn't perceive any gross sensation there.

The priest and the policeman were not permitting anyone to linger inside or to have the Darshan peacefully; instead, they swiftly escorted the devotees out. I felt quite uneasy witnessing that, but I was powerless to intervene. Afterward, eventually, I experienced what I had traveled so far to witness: the divine presence of Lord Kedarnath, enshrined in the form of a Shivalinga at the sanctum sanctorum of the shrine.

Upon setting my eyes on the Shivalinga, I immediately felt a profound vibration emanating from the depths of my heart, swiftly coursing through every inch of my being; I could sense the vibrancy of the Shivalinga in my body articulately. Feeling overwhelmed, I bowed down to the Lord with all my heart.

Just before the priest escorted me out, I positioned myself next to him in a corner. With an earnest heart, I yearned for an uninterrupted view of the Lord. So I fixed my gaze upon the Shivalinga, immersing myself in its divine presence without a single blink.

This Shivalinga was unlike any Shivalinga I had encountered before; it was out of the ordinary. While a Shivalinga is typically cylindrical in texture, akin to an upside down 'U'; this one appeared somewhat triangular, reminiscent of a bull's hump. Through my gaze, I conveyed the depth of gratitude I felt for being present there.

At that moment, nobody interrupted me, as though I had suddenly become invisible to everyone around. The priest and the policeman were escorting everyone out individually, yet none of them seemed to acknowledge my presence, despite the fact that I stood right beside the priest. Indeed, all this was the grace of Lord Kedarnath.

For more than a couple of minutes, I kept on standing there, fixing my sight on the phenomenal form of the Divine. Following the serene Darshan, I bowed once more to the Lord before departing from the sacred shrine.

Upon stepping out from there, I sensed a revitalizing energy infusing through my entire being; all my exhaustion had vanished as if it had never been there. I expressed profound gratitude to Lord Ram for the magnificent Darshan, continually thanking Him within the depths of my heart.

All my fellows were waiting for me near the outskirts of the shrine. Thereafter, we headed towards our rented room. Through the night until morning, Kedarnath was drenched in heavy rain. We all felt grateful for the Lord's grace because if we hadn't received the Darshan at night, we would have had to awaken at 03:00 A.M. the following morning and endure the rain while standing in the queue. The morning after, we all awoke at a leisurely pace. Refreshed by a restful night's sleep, we found ourselves brimming with energy. However, our legs were still pretty stiff. But we were good to go.

Following that, we made our way to the Bhairavnath shrine, nestled at the summit of a mountain. From that vantage point, we marveled at the expansive, panoramic view of the entire Kedarnath valley. Then we witnessed the remarkable statue of Guru Adi Shankaracharya which was situated right behind the Kedarnath Temple.

The purpose of my journey to Kedarnath was fulfilled. As the moment to leave approached, my eyes remained captivated by the grandeur of the Himalayas. I couldn't help but wonder if there were yogis engaged in meditation within the secluded caves of those ancient mountains. While heading towards home, I harbored a sentiment deep within me that someday, the Himalayas would call out to me once more, beckoning me to spend additional time amidst their serene embrace, engaging in meditation upon the Eternal.

After a period of time, a profound scholar of Vedanta introduced me to the highest wisdom available in the physical realm about the Supreme Being—the Upanishads. It served as a pivotal moment, forever reshaping my spiritual voyage toward new horizons, where the ultimate mystery of this cosmos unfolded before me like an open book.

CHAPTER 20

A MILLION GODS AND GODDESSES

Since prehistoric times, the land of Bharat has always been a stronghold of diversity. Over the ages, this land has witnessed the flourishing of diverse religions, traditions, lineages, and cults. Certain religions migrated to this land from distant places, while others originated here, growing over time to become established ideologies or sects.

However, the tender-hearted and generous natives of Bharat have consistently honored and acknowledged every religion and ideology whether it was migrated or originated on this land, as discrimination in the name of religion, sects, or ideologies was entirely alien to us. Instead, we embraced the worship of various gods and goddesses harmoniously under one roof. However, it was equally acceptable for someone to be a non-believer. The concept of discrimination was never inherent in the core of the natives of Bharat; it was introduced to us by external influences.

Even in present times, when you visit a Hindu household, you will observe that if there are six family members, each peacefully worships a different deity. Upon entering their place of worship within the home, you will encounter idols of various gods and goddesses adorning the space; there will be Lord Shiva sitting along with Goddess Parvati, Lord Ganesha along with Goddess Lakshmi, Lord Hanuman along with Lord Sita-Ram, Lord Krishna along with Shri Radha Rani, and various others. Despite that, you won't observe any conflict among the family members in the name of God.

In my family, I have witnessed that my mother used to worship Goddess Durga, while my father is a dedicated devotee of Lord Shiva. Apart from that, we have our family deity, commonly referred to as Kuldevi or Kuldevta; my family also worships them with dedication.

During the Vedic era, all individuals were categorized, into four Varna (classes) based on their attributes and deeds: Brahmin, Kshatriya, Vaishya, and Shudra. The society adhered to specific morals and codes of conduct, known as Dharm, which defined the roles and responsibilities that were to be followed by these four classes.

The Dharm of the Brahmins were to recite and teach Vedic scriptures, conduct rituals, and guide society in matters of spirituality. The Kshatriyas were tasked to provide protection and maintain order. Their Dharm involved defending the kingdom, administering justice, and leading in times of battles. The Vaishyas were primarily engaged in agricultural, commercial, and economic activities. That's why, their Dharm included trade, commerce, agriculture, and animal husbandry. The Shudras were involved in service-oriented roles. Their Dharm revolved around serving the other three classes, providing essential services, and supporting the functioning of society.

These moral duties or the Dharm were considered essential for the smooth functioning of society and were expected to be followed sincerely by each class. In this way, each class held significance within its designated Dharm, without any notion of superiority or inferiority.

Likewise, nature operates according to its inherent order, just as the cosmos operates in accordance with its own cosmic principles. In a nutshell, everything in this massive cosmos functions as per its codes of conduct or Dharm; there are specific laws governing all occurrences in this existence. The day rises at a particular time and sets at a particular time; the earth revolves around the sun at a certain pace and the moon revolves around the earth at a certain pace, the fire offers warmth, and water provides coolness, demonstrating that everything operates according to its Dharm. Therefore, this eternal order was known as Sanatana Dharm; the universal code of conduct.

Regrettably, over time, mankind has distorted the true essence of Dharm. In contemporary times, it is commonly interpreted as a religious denomination or sect. We have become ensnared in the web of ignorance, losing sight of our true essence. In reality, the natives of Bharat had never classified themselves into distinct sects until interactions with cultures beyond their borders occurred. The notion of sectarian identification was spread primarily from the external world. When the folks of other lands established a connection with the people of Bharat, they introduced their ideology of 'One God, One Religion' to them.

Soon after they recognized that the ideologies and beliefs of the natives of Bharat were distinct from their own. However, it was impracticable to them; how could folks who believe in different gods or more than one god flourish together in harmony? Hence, they started questioning our beliefs. They began to inquire: What is your religion, how do you identify yourself? Why do you worship such a variety of gods? Isn't one God enough for you?

That was the moment when uncertainty started to take root in the minds of the even-minded people of Bharat regarding their beliefs. The term 'Hindu' was also introduced by traders and travelers from other lands. Some historical texts documented that the Persian and Arabic traders during the medieval period introduced the term 'Hindu' to refer to the civilization thriving beyond the river Sindhu which is also familiar as the river Indus.

In the context of today, many Hindus are unaware of the concept of a multitude of gods and goddesses. Consequently, they lack an understanding of why Hinduism embraces countless deities and the significance behind worshipping such a diverse pantheon. Allow me to articulately decode the enigma behind the existence of a million gods in Hinduism; this is a concept of significant importance to comprehend; particularly for the seekers.

Merely a handful of mortals have grasped it and delved into detailed discussions about it. In the past, some so-called intellectuals have misinterpreted the scriptures and entangled themselves and others in words. As a consequence, they were deprived of the quintessence. Those individuals began to consider themselves scholars merely by reciting the scriptures, yet they remained distant from the true meaning. However, there is an earth and heaven of difference between knowing something and perceiving it truly.

Before we take a deep dive into the enigmatic concept of a million gods and goddesses, let me craft a base for you so you would perceive everything as simple as ABC. Allow me to unfurl a captivating story woven with profound insights and compelling wisdom.

It happened a long time ago, there lived a Brahmin family in Thiruvananthapuram in Kerala. The whole family held a deep devotion to Lord Narayana. One day by the complaisance of God, a radiant girl graced the family with her presence. The parents celebrated her birth as a festival, and around a week later, they brought her to the Sree Padmanabhaswamy Temple to seek the blessing of Lord Narayana along with the naming ceremony. As the priest of the shrine cast his gaze upon the newborn, his eyes lit up with joyous fervor. "The mistress of the three worlds itself has arrived in your family; what name would be more appropriate for this girl than Kamakshi," the priest uttered in an ecstatic tone.

Upon hearing the name of the baby girl, a wave of joy swept through the family members, and everyone began praising the name. Following that, the grandmother of the baby girl urged the priest to make some predictions about her forthcoming life. The priest smiled and nodded approvingly, remarking, "She will evolve into a great sage. Once she comes of age, you are supposed to send her to an ashram to attain spiritual wisdom."

Upon hearing that, the girl's father smiled and responded with folded hands, "Certainly! As you wish, Swami Maharaj."

Time passed rapidly and as soon as the moon phase increased on the bright side, in the same way, Kamakshi grew up while playing in her house. She was pretty curious about things around her and possessed the caliber to learn anything swiftly. Kamakshi's father remembered the priest's words, though he was hesitant to send her to any ashram. One day he visited Sree Padmanabhaswamy Temple, where he encountered a mystic, Sumaya Amma.

Sumaya Amma was an ascetic and cognizant of all four Vedas. She was well-renowned in the southern land. Kamakshi's father approached her and bowed down at her feet to seek her blessings. Amma blessed him by placing her hand on his head. "It's time my dear, do you remember the words of the priest?" Amma asked smiling.

Kamakshi's father was stunned for a moment; he looked at Amma with wide-opened eyes and then folded his hands in devotion. "I am here for Kamakshi, now take me to her," Amma expressed while tapping on his head.

Following that, Kamakshi's father took Amma to his home. Upon arriving he introduced Kamakshi to Sumaya

Amma and asked her to seek Amma's blessings. Kamakshi bowed to the feet of Amma with folded hands. With affection, Amma gently caressed her soft cheek and then asked her to gather her necessary belongings. Kamakshi asked her father softly, "Where are we going?"

Her father smiled and responded, "Amma is taking you along with her. She will educate you well so that you may become a great scholar and seeker."

Thereafter, Kamakshi walked pleasantly with Sumaya Amma. She brought Kamakshi to the Agasthyamalai hill where she lived in a small cottage. A few days later, Amma started educating her in scriptures along with yoga practices. Sumaya Amma was an extraordinary Guru; whenever she needed to impart profound teachings, she would generously illustrate using examples from nature. One day Amma visited the town to buy some usual stuff. She took Kamakshi along with her. Upon reaching the town, they approached a sculptor who used to make several objects out of clay. In his store, there were various idols, toys, and pots of different textures and sizes. "What are these, my dear?" Amma asked Kamakshi pointing to the clay pots.

Kamakshi gazed in the pointed direction and then responded, "These are the pots, Amma."

Amma nodded and then she pointed to the idols and asked, "What about that?"

"These are magnificent idols," Kamakshi responded gently.

Following that, Amma pointed towards the toys and Kamakshi replied accordingly. "Absolutely, but what if I say that all these beautiful objects that you are watching here are merely clay?" Amma posed her question in a manner that seemed contradictory.

"Clay!" Kamakshi exclaimed, sounding perplexed.

"Yes, my child. There is no difference between these pots, idols, and toys. Now look carefully," saying that

Amma picked up a pot and broke it to pieces by slamming it on the ground. Following that, she kicked an elephant idol, causing it to break. In the same manner, Amma repeated the action with a toy. Kamakshi and the sculptor were merely witnessing that event, however, both of them couldn't perceive anything.

"See! In reality, there are no pots, no toys, not even any beautiful idols. It's merely clay around us. The sculptor has simply transformed the clay into various forms. Although they may seem distinct in appearance, they all originate from the same clay." Amma added further, "Similarly, what we perceive in the external world isn't precisely as it appears. At the fundamental level, there is no differentiation; you, me, and the sculptor we all are one at the core. Just like the clay, there exists only one Supreme Entity manifesting in different forms."

Kamakshi and the sculptor humbly bowed to Sumaya Amma, expressing their gratitude for such a profound insight.

In the sacred texts of the Atharva Veda, Yajur Veda, and Brihadranyaka Upanishad, the Supreme Being is vividly described as Trayastrimsati Koti. In simpler terms, according to these scriptures, the Supreme Being possesses 'thirty-three Koti' of forms. However, the meaning of the Sanskrit word 'Koti' has not been clarified in these texts. Some Hindu scholars and priests believe that the meaning of Koti is referred to as 'type or category' whereas some other believes that the meaning is referred to as figure 'crore'.

Due to this uncertainty, there is always a contradiction among Hindus; some believe that there are thirty-three categories of gods and goddesses, while others emphasize that there are three hundred and thirty million gods and goddesses. Though both sides believers are misled by ignorance.

Whenever our sages have addressed a subject in the scriptures, they have presented it in a profound coded manner, demanding thorough contemplation for absolute comprehension. This discrepancy arises from the fact that scholars of the past often focused on the literal words rather than delving deeply into the intended meaning.

The Sanskrit word 'Koti' holds dual meanings, signifying both type or category and the numerical value crore. Hence, those who maintain that there are thirty-three distinct categories of gods and goddesses are completely justified in their perspective, and similarly, those who assert that there are three hundred and thirty million gods are also unquestionably valid in their belief. Let us endeavor to perceive it profoundly. According to the Vedas, there are thirty-three individual classes of deities including:

- **Twelve Adityas,**
- **Eleven Rudras,**
- **Eight Vasus,**
- **Prajapati**
- **Indra.**

* The Adityas are personified solar deities, corresponding to the twelve months.

* The Vasus are the elemental deities that represent the different aspects of nature as water, fire, air, etc.

* The Rudras are vital energies in the body along with Jeeva (being).

* In some texts, the mention of two Ashwini Kumar (physicians of deities) is found instead of Prajapati (progenitors of mankind) and Indra (supreme monarch).

In this manner, there are thirty-three individual deities altogether. You can find the names of all these individual deities in the table given below:

Thirty-three Categories of Gods in the Vedas

Adityas	Rudras	Vasus	
1.Vishnu	1.Aja	1.Anala	**Prajapati Indra**
2.Aryaman	2.Ekapada	2.Ap	
3.Indra	3.Shambhu	3.Soma	
4.Tvashta	4.Twastri	4.Hamsa	
5.Varuna	5.Shasta	5.Dhara	
6.Dhata	6.Bhima	6.Dhruva	
7.Bhaga	7.Virupaksha	7.Pratyoosha	
8.Parjanya	8.Ahirbudhnya	8.Prabhasa	
9.Vivasvan	9.Kapali		
10.Anshuman	10.Pingla		
11.Mitra	11.Vilohita		
12.Pushyan			

Now that we have covered thirty-three classes; let's unravel the mystery of the million gods and goddesses.

In our Vedas, Upanishads, Bhagavad Gita, Purana, and various other holy scriptures; we come across an extensive description of innumerable characteristics and attributes of the Supreme such as 'That' serves as the creator, protector, and demolisher of everything present in the cosmos, 'That' possesses subtlety akin to a mustard seed while encompassing enormity on the scale of thousands of mountains, 'That' reaches the heights of the sky and delves as deep as the ocean; 'That' is the ultimate seed, the source of all beings, and 'That' is the ultimate womb from which everything comes into existence, the glory of Supreme is so immense that millions of suns appear as mere twinkling stars in its presence and so forth.

Taking into account these myriad qualities and attributes, the Supreme has been portrayed in countless names and forms. If I strive to explain it through an illustration: When the Supreme is portrayed as the creator of the cosmos, we recognize this manifestation as Lord Brahma. When the Supreme is described as the sustainer and protector of the cosmos, we recognize this manifestation as Lord Vishnu. Likewise, when the Supreme is depicted as the demolisher of the cosmos, we recognize this manifestation as Lord Rudra or Lord Shiva.

Following the same order, when 'That' is referred to as the omnipotent, we recognize it as the Mahadev, supreme among all Devas. When 'That' is characterized as immensely powerful and profoundly devoted, it is identified as Lord Hanuman. When 'That' is portrayed as the supreme ruler of heavenly beings, it is recognized as Indra Dev. When 'That' is depicted as the peerless dancer, it is recognized as Nataraja. When 'That' is described as the most dignified monarch on the earth, we adore it as King Rama. When 'That' is depicted as benevolent and indulgent, we worship it as Lord Narayana. When 'That' is depicted as the self-existent one, it is identified as Shambhu. When 'That' is mentioned as the first yogi, it is acknowledged as Adiyogi and when 'That' is portrayed as possessing an enchanting persona, engaging in Raasleela, and upholding righteousness, it is recognized as Lord Vasudev Krishna.

In the same fashion, when 'That' is represented as extremely ferocious, it is identified as Goddess Kali. When 'That' is described as the bestower of wealth and prosperity, we worship it as Goddess Mahalakshmi. When 'That' is described as the mistress of knowledge and wisdom, we recognize it as Goddess Sarasvati.

Likewise, when 'That' is described as the slayer of the demons then we recognize it as Goddess Durga. When 'That' is described as the embodiment of auspiciousness and the remover of obstacles, we all worship it in the form of Lord Ganapati. When 'That' is portrayed as an amalgamation of both masculine and feminine energy in one form, it is identified as Lord Ardhanareshwar. When 'That' is described as the deity of death, we recognize it as Yamaraj, and when 'That' is depicted as the semi-divine god residing in the celestial realms then we recognize this manifestation as Yaksha, Naga, Gandharva, Apsara, Dikpala, and many others.

Lord Shiva, Lord Vishnu, and Goddess Kali are portrayed in millions of diverse manifestations based on their unique characteristics. As a result, Hinduism recognizes millions of gods and goddesses, each embodying different facets of the Supreme Energy.

Let me recount my own experience; in my younger years, I also embraced the notion that there are countless gods and we all venerated various gods according to our specific needs or circumstances. As if we need strength and potency, we can approach Lord Hanuman. If we desire to be sapient then we are supposed to worship Goddess Sarasvati. If we require riches and grandeur then we are supposed to please Goddess Lakshmi and Kuber. If we want to avoid the hindrances then we ought to seek out the help of Lord Ganesh. If you desire a cherished life partner, it's suggested to honor Lord Shiva by fasting on sixteen Mondays, and so on.

Frequently, I struggled with determining the supreme deity between Lord Vishnu and Lord Shiva; I used to be pretty perplexed: Did Lord Vishnu create Lord Shiva, or did Lord Shiva create Lord Vishnu?

Being a devout follower of Lord Shiva, I firmly held the belief in His supremacy. Whenever someone asserted that Lord Vishnu held greater significance than Lord Shiva, it would evoke strong feelings of resentment within me. Ah! That's just how children tend to be. These teachings have been passed down to us from our parents and ancestors; they used to portray God like that. However, as I delved deeper into spirituality, I gradually came to realize that my previous perceptions relevant to God were entirely misguided.

While embarking on my quest to comprehend God, I discovered that the concept of millions of gods or diverse deities is not rooted in reality. Upon deeply contemplating the knowledge of the Upanishads, all my beliefs got scattered. Following that, I came to the realization that the notions I held in high regard were merely surface-level; they lacked profound roots.

Ultimately, my journey led me to a profound realization: Within this expansive cosmos, there exists but one entity—the captivating essence that reigns supreme. The array of deities before whom we bow our heads humbly are simply distinct manifestations of the same Supreme Lord. The word 'Ram' implies, that who resides in every particle of this existence.

Just as one form of soil possesses the competence to nurture various trees and plants; correspondingly, another form of that soil, with its remarkable versatility manifests into pottery, sculpture, bricks, tiles, and other building materials. Both forms emerged from the same source i.e. ground. In the same way, the Supreme possesses the competence to manifest itself in infinite forms and variations; it doesn't matter what name you give to it or in what form you love to worship it.

Whether you recognize it as the Creator, God, Ishwar, Paramatma, Brahm, Supreme Energy, Supreme Knowledge, Ultimate Reality, Ultimate Truth, Supreme Source, or any other title; it is one and only entity, and there is no uncertainty about it. Even in contemporary science, the acknowledgment resonates: There exists a singular energy; dynamically expressing itself through myriad forms and functions.

Wherever life thrives on Earth—be it on land or water, it springs from a common origin. Altogether, all the facts indicate that there is only one core source of this entire creation. This prompts inquiry: How, when, and why did the notion of more than one God or multiple gods disseminate throughout the world?

Across the ages, Earth has witnessed the birth of several enlightened beings. Among them, there are a few names that are well familiar and renowned in the world such as Gautam Buddha, Adi Shankaracharya, Mahavir, Jesus Christ, Guru Nanak Dev, Kabir, Lao Tzu, Bodhidharma, Rumi, Mohammad, Kinaram, Saint Gyaneshwar, Swami Ramakrishna, Paramhansa Yogananda, Maa Anandamayi, Ramana Maharishi, Shri Aurobindo, Osho, and many more.

Upon achieving enlightenment and perceiving the Supreme Truth, they embarked on a journey to share the profound nectar of their experience and wisdom with those around them. In this way, the folks began to embrace their dialogues and guidance. With their wisdom, these enlightened beings profoundly impacted the lives of countless individuals, guiding them toward self-realization.

Though change is perpetual in nature; as a consequence, with the passage of time, circumstances began to shift. Certain followers shifted their focus from the teachings and path illuminated by their mentors to idolizing the mentors themselves. Instead of glorifying their wisdom and practices, the disciples started glorifying the individual; following that, they formed isolated religions and sects in the name of their masters. The followers failed to grasp the intended direction of their master's gesture, instead fixating merely on the gesture and misunderstanding its significance.

I don't believe that the Buddha ever stated he was a Buddhist, or that Mohammad proclaimed himself as Muslim, Guru Nanak Dev identified as Sikh, Jesus emphasized his Christianity, or Mahavir claimed affiliation with Jainism. None of these great beings ever professed that God could be attained solely by following them. They never stressed that a certain path is the exclusive path to self-realization. Prior to the passing of these enlightened beings, no sects existed in their name; all these sects and cults emerged only after their departure. The Buddha, Guru Nanak, Mahavir, and others never instructed their followers to erect idols and shrines in their honor or to worship them globally after their demise—the Buddha opposed idol-worship, yet today around the world, no other figure has as many idols as Buddha does. His teachings centered on the pursuit of truth, empowering individuals to lead meaningful lives amidst mundane activities.

These transcendent entities present varied methodologies to attain the singular supreme reality. However, over time, individuals have manipulated their teachings and become ensnared in their own self-created concepts and beliefs, tailored to their convenience.

Today, if you inquire someone, 'Who are you?' I'm certain that numerous individuals would define themselves by their religious affiliations; now merely beliefs are their identity. Undeniably, the conflict in the entire world is just because of beliefs; some believe that there is God, while others believe that there is no God. Certain argue that their beliefs are superior to others while others are struggling to prove their superiority. Precisely, both are lost.

See, it's just a belief, regardless of how deep-rooted it is. One has to feed their beliefs to keep them sustained and alive. While the reality is utterly aloof from it. Therefore, only those who have the potency to question their beliefs, walk on the path of self-discovery, which is beyond any religion and sects.

We all admit that God is almighty. Okay! you can call it whatever you find favorable. Let's refer to it as 'Energy', sounds scientific and legitimate! At the core, every religion, sect, cult, and organization acknowledges the existence of a supreme, infinite energy from which everything is believed to have manifested or been created. I pose a rather insightful question in this regard: If the energy is supreme, boundless, and infinite, how can it be divided into two or more entities? If something is supreme and infinite, it necessarily must be singular. This leaves no room for doubt; then, what underlies the conflict? Why draw lines between 'your God' and 'my God'? Isn't God simply God, and energy just energy?

There is a profound unity in this truth, transcending notions of superiority or inferiority. These distinctions emerge merely from our own limited perspectives, yet the essence remains undivided and boundless. Perceiving reality holds no inherent complexity. It's as straightforward as opening your eyes and observing. However, we humans tend to complicate matters ourselves. We possess filters in our minds through which we perceive the world.

I harbor no hostility towards anyone. In all honesty, I don't have any qualms with any religion, including their rituals and methods of worship; fundamentally, we all honor the same divine presence, albeit through various practices.

My perspective is straightforward: once you strip away the layers of belief from your mind, you will swiftly encounter the unadulterated reality. Consequently, conflicts will cease, and your life will overflow with bliss.

Now, permit me to guide you even further. Together, we will embark on a journey into the depths of spirituality, reaching its core where doubt, uncertainty, and illusion hold no sway.

CHAPTER 21

THE SUPREME TRUTH: GOD, SOUL, AND MORTALS

At the core of Hindu scriptures lies the depiction of three entities that govern the entirety of existence: Brahman, Aatma, and Prakriti, or God, the Soul, and Matter. God is the Supreme Energy, the Source of this existence which is known by several names. The soul serves as the vital essence responsible for the life and functioning of all living beings, including humans, animals, birds, plants, insects, microbes, and other animates. The soul is referred to as Aatma; yet, when it merges with any form i.e. Jiva, it is identified as Jivatma or the Being. The matter is known as Prakriti, which is accountable for the existence of every form within the cosmos, encompassing celestial entities such as the sun, moon, earth, stars, and other planetary bodies, along with elements such as water, fire, air, soil, and other non-living forms.

Throughout history, an array of philosophies and theories concerning the existence of God, the material world or matter, and the soul have surfaced and been disseminated across the world. These philosophies and theories serve as the cornerstone for all religions and sects that have prospered on this planet. Using their intellect and knowledge, the philosophers of different eras endeavored to elucidate to others what they comprehended, realized, and experienced regarding God and the reality of the cosmos through their philosophical frameworks.

Four of these philosophies resonated deeply on a large scale in Bharat, leaving a lasting impact. Even in this modern age, these four philosophies endure, embraced by individuals knowingly or unknowingly. Almost every religion and sect that acknowledges the existence of God aligns with one of these philosophies in some form or another. The following are the four philosophies:

- *Advaita* (Non-dualism)
- *Dvaita* (Dualism)
- *Traita* (Trinitarianism)
- *Vishistadvaita* (Qualified Non-dualism)

Vishistadvaita (Qualified Non-dualism): It is a principal branch of the Vedanta philosophy (profound interpretation of the Vedas) in Hinduism. Ramanujacharya is renowned as the propagator of the Vishistadvaita philosophy. In his perspective, Brahman (Supreme Being) stands as the Supreme Reality; the cause and creator of all within the existence. The Brahman is the only existent entity, while the Aatma and Prakriti emerge as manifestations of this supreme entity, each with distinct identities, intimately connected to and dependent upon it for their existence. The Brahman possesses a certain form and all the forms arise from it. The objective of every Jivatma or individual soul is to attain liberation from all bondages through devotion and surrender to that Supreme Entity.

In essence, as per the philosophy of qualified non-dualism: There exists one entity who has manifested everything from within itself. This divine entity represents the ultimate reality. Just as that Divine Being is real, so is creation, as the entirety of creation is essentially an extension of God and not separate from it. The salvation of a being can be attained by dedicating oneself to the divine form of God.

Traita (Trinitarianism): This philosophy was propagated by Swami Dayananda Saraswati who was the founder of Arya Samaj. According to the Traita philosophy, there are only three eternal entities: Ishwar (God), Prakriti (matter), and Aatma (soul), which function independently in this creation. Ishwar is omnipotent, omnipresent, omniscient, formless, and symbolized as ॐ or 'AUM', representing the eternal and immortal essence that neither begins nor ends. The soul or Aatma resides in all living organisms whether it's humans, plants, animals, birds, insects, microbes, etc. The Aatma shares the same immortal, formless, and eternal nature as God; it plays the role of both the performer of actions and the recipient of their consequences, embodying the intricate dance of karma. It transitions from one body to another following the death of a being, influenced by its past actions. Therefore, it keeps on dwelling in the world till it attains liberation. The purpose of Jivatma is to become liberated from the cycle of birth and death and unite with Paramatma, the Supreme Soul (God). Prakriti is the element from which the physical world is formed; it functions in the form of three qualities: Sattva, Rajas, and Tamas. Ishwar is the creator and originator of all that exists in this universe, having formed the entire cosmos through the fusion of these three qualities of Prakriti. However, these three entities, Ishwar, Aatma, and Prakriti function individually in this existence.

In essence, according to the Traita philosophy: There are three different realities; one is God which is Paramatma or the Supreme Soul. The second is the Aatma or Jivatma which is the individual soul, and the third is the cosmos or Prakriti which is the material world that we perceive through our senses and intelligence. One is the worshipper, the second is one who is being worshipped and the third is the medium through which the worship occurs. Similarly, one is the observer, the second is the object and the third is the medium through which the observation takes place.

Dvaita (Dualism): This philosophy was propagated by Madhvacharya. As per the Dvaita or Dualism philosophy, there are two separate entities that exist in the creation. One is Aatma and the other is Paramatma; one is the individual soul and the other is the Supreme Soul. There are no similarities between these two. The Paramatma reigns as the supreme, independent force, crafting all that exists within this creation, while the Aatma remains reliant upon the Paramatma for its very being. God or the Paramatma exudes a captivating form adorned with boundless virtue. Every living being possesses a distinct soul, each one inherently unique. The Aatma serves as both the doer of actions and the recipient of their consequences; the sheer purpose of the Aatma is to serve the Paramatma. Devotion is the only path to attain salvation, hence by surrendering at the divine feet of God, one can attain liberation.

In essence, as per the Dvaita philosophy: There are two ultimate realities in this existence, God and the soul. These entities are fundamentally distinct, incapable of equivalence: one embodies energy, the other embodies supreme energy; one is the worshipper, the other the worshipped; one is subjective, the other objective. One is the observer, while the other is the observed. God cannot exist without form or attributes. The ultimate purpose of each individual soul is to merge with the Supreme Soul.

Advaita (Non-dualism): This is a profound philosophical concept rooted in Hinduism, particularly prominent in the Vedanta philosophy. Adi Guru Shankaracharya was the propagator of the Advaita philosophy. According to this philosophy, in the vast tapestry of existence, Brahman reigns as the solitary essence, the epitome of reality, while this vast cosmos is but a captivating illusion, or Maya spun from Brahman's boundless being. All that manifests within this magnificent creation is simply an expression of Brahman; the Aatma and the Prakriti both are the manifestations of Brahman. 'That' is the Supreme Soul which resides in all the living beings. Attaining the realization that God constitutes the ultimate reality of this creation, and all else is mere illusion or Maya, leads to Moksha, or liberation.

In essence, according to the Advaita philosophy: There is absolute unity and absence of segregation within this creation. There is no differentiation between God, soul, and matter; the Aatma reflects the essence of the Paramatma. Likewise, there is no distinction between the observer, the observed, and the medium of observation; they are unified as one. The apparent differences are merely illusions. There exists no duality in this massive existence; the creator and creation are inseparable. The soul and the supreme soul, energy and supreme energy, are indistinguishable. The worshipper and the worshipped are unified as one. It is the singular entity manifested in diverse forms and attributes. Duality is merely a mirage conjured by our minds as a result of ignorance. Realizing this truth leads to salvation.

Upon close examination of these philosophies, at their core, they all converge toward the same essence, albeit approached through diverse perspectives. Let's assume, for instance, a band of adventurers embarking on a journey and stumbling upon the serene beauty of water flowing in a river for the very first time. As one of them touches the water and feels a refreshing coolness, they proclaim: 'It possesses the attribute of coldness'. Another individual consumes it and claims: 'It possesses the capability to quench thirst'. Someone jumped into it and observed: 'It possesses cleaning properties, another observed some fishes, frogs, and turtles swimming in it and claimed: 'It is the living place for some bizarre living organisms.'

None of them were mistaken about the water; they simply perceived it through the lens of their own experiences and intellect. Similarly, all these philosophies are logically sound within their respective domains, as long as they do not contradict one another. Although the reference of all these philosophies is the Vedas and Upanishads, the chaos begins merely when these philosophies start contradicting each other thoroughly.

As mentioned earlier, our ancient sages and seers have depicted concepts in various scriptures in a manner that unravelling their essence without thorough study is akin to attempting to boil an ocean. Those who delved into the study of scripture to comprehend God and the truth of creation interpreted their perceptions, experiences, and knowledge as Absolute Truth. Following that, they proceeded to pen numerous commentaries and interpretations in subsequent texts.

However, it's crucial to acknowledge that their perception was merely a glimpse of the supreme reality. They failed to grasp the profound essence of the Vedas. Understanding and perceiving the ultimate source, the Supreme Being, or God is akin to counting the stars in the night sky or measuring the sky—a task beyond measure. For the infinite knows no bounds; it transcends limitations and remains beyond the reach of finite comprehension or resources.

In ages past, as the great sages and wise scholars sought to articulate the essence of the Supreme Being, they confronted their own limitations in attempting to encapsulate its nature. Thus, they reverently denoted it as 'That', acknowledging its inherent genderlessness, the wellspring from which all genders originate. 'That' transcends forms, yet all forms originate from it. Devoid of color, 'That' is the source from which all colors radiate, akin to colorless sunlight giving rise to the spectrum of seven hues. 'That' is devoid of fragrance, yet all aromas derive from it. 'That' remains unseen, yet it governs visibility. Without a defined identity, 'That' shapes the identity of all. 'That' echoes the silence from which all sounds arise. 'That' is the ultimate cause, yet it lacks a cause of its own existence.

Beyond attributes, 'That' serves as the genesis of all attributes. It is inaudible to ears, yet it grants ears their auditory prowess. Invisible to eyes, yet it bestows upon them the gift of sight. 'That' remains untouched, yet it imparts the sensation of touch. Unfathomable and transcending fantasy, 'That' endows us with the ability to think and fantasize. Although it cannot be stored in memory, it is due to it that we possess the capacity to retain things in our memory. Imperceptible to the senses, yet we perceive everything through its influence. Beyond contemplation as it exists beyond thought. 'That' cannot be divided, yet all divisions arise from its essence. 'That' transcends the notions of beginning and end, serving as the genesis from which everything emerges and the ultimate destination into which everything merges. 'That' exists without a creator, yet it is the creator of all. Unnamed and yet encompassing all names, it is the essence of identity. It resides in no single abode, yet its presence is the heartbeat of every corner of the cosmos, pulsing with the rhythm of existence itself. 'That' resides beyond the realms of time and space, yet time and space find their existence within its boundless embrace. It bows to no master, yet it is the sovereign of all sovereigns. 'That' remains motionless, yet everything moves because of its influence. It transcends change, yet change occurs in nature because of it. Beyond the action, everything functions because of its inherent nature. Infinite in essence, yet all finite entities are encompassed within it. It is unmanifest, yet everything that exists is a manifestation of it. Absolute nothingness, from which the entire creation emerges.

Words are not ample in encapsulating the entirety of the Supreme Being, hence the sages expressed it as 'Neti-Neti', denoting 'neither this nor that,' as a means to convey its ineffability. If I strive to decode this expression, particularly found in Advaita Vedanta, it indicates that whatever one conceives, believes, expresses, or perceives about 'That' or the Supreme Being, it is not the absolute truth as it transcends the mind. Our notions and perception concerning the Divine merely capture a fragment, akin to a tiny bubble adrift on the surface of water. The bubble, although composed of water, does not represent the entirety of water's absolute reality; rather, it is merely one of numerous manifestations of water.

Similarly, the Divine can be experienced only in various manifestations, but none of them portray its absolute essence. To convey anything about an element, we must first define its boundaries. Therefore, 'That' cannot be articulated in any way; any attempt to express a specific aspect of it confines it to finite boundaries and there exists no approach to limit the infinite. This physical body has certain limitations, how can one even think to comprehend the essence of the infinite with their finite mind?

Nevertheless, if one attempts to do so, they will inevitably misinterpret it, falling into the same delusion as others. Thus, if one asserts that God is formless, it cannot be refuted, for 'That' is infinite, devoid of definite form. Similarly, if one suggests that God possesses a form, this too holds true, as every form is a manifestation of the Divine. Likewise, proclaiming the world as an illusion finds truth, as all is in constant flux, while eternal truth remains immutable. Conversely, affirming the world's reality is also valid, as the source of creation is genuine and resides within its creation.

The challenge arises in understanding; when one claims their perception as the ultimate truth, dismissing all else as nonsensical, they limit comprehension. What they express about God may hold truth, but dismissing other perspectives as false creates a barrier to deeper understanding.

Now, if you have truly pondered my words, certain questions are likely stirring within you. You might be wondering: If everything we know about God is not true, what's the significance of worshipping deities or engaging in holy rituals? Was all our past devotion in vain? How do we attain liberation? What about life after death? And what about our karma? If God defies description and explanation, why are scriptures filled with teachings about it? What is the purpose of studying these scriptures?

Such questions naturally surface in the mind when one possesses a genuine curiosity and a sincere desire to uncover reality. To unlock all the answers and find true clarity, we must delve into the depths of our ancient scriptures.

To unravel these answers, we must begin by contemplating the essence of 'Aatma'. This singular element serves as the foundational source of the misconception that has led humanity astray for ages. In the past, people failed to grasp the true essence of the Aatma, leading them to wander from one master and sect to another in search of peace, both while living and beyond.

Consider this: What if I were to challenge the very notions of birth, death, afterlife, and liberation, suggesting they are but illusions? And what if, in that revelation, the boundary between your 'I' and another's dissolved into the vastness of existence?

In the contemporary world, numerous self-proclaimed spiritual leaders are manipulating individuals through emotional manipulation, invoking concepts of God, death, sins, virtuous deeds, rebirth, karma, and other facets of spirituality. It's crucial to closely examine these concepts, as they impact every individual's perception.

In the distant past, during the era of great sages and seers, the scriptures were authored, and they eloquently referred to beings as 'Aatma', a testament to their profound wisdom. The term 'Aatma' originates from the Sanskrit word 'Aatm' signifying 'the Self'. In all truthfulness, the cornerstone of metaphysical aspects of life revolves around this fundamental concept.

In this era, the term 'spirituality' encompasses all the metaphysical dimensions of life. However, it's an English term that finds its origins in the word 'Spirit', adding a layer of complexity as spirit denotes something ethereal. Therefore, the word spirituality doesn't represent the essence of all metaphysical facets. On the other hand, in our Vedas, these metaphysical aspects are referred to as 'Adhyatma', a fusion of 'Adhyan' signifies 'study', and 'Aatma' signifies 'the self'. Thus, Adhyatma essentially implies the 'study of the soul' or it is also termed as 'knowledge of the Self'. In a nutshell, spirituality is loosely interpreted as Adhyatma, though the term doesn't fully encapsulate its timeless essence.

The term 'Aatma' has been subject to misinterpretation by scholars over the years, resulting in an array of differing perceptions. Consequently, individuals hold various beliefs about it in their heads. Some assert that each person harbors an individual soul or Aatma within their body, suggesting the existence of numerous souls on Earth; this soul resides in our bodies in the form of pure radiation. Some adhere to the notion that when individuals pass away, their souls depart their bodies as transparent entities, meandering without direction in search of new hosts. Others subscribe to the idea that after death, souls transition to realms of paradise or inferno, where they experience the consequences of their actions. Alternatively, there are those who believe that souls may transform into malevolent beings posthumously, menacing the living, and so on.

In the Bhagavad Gita, we discover that Lord Vasudev Krishna has precisely portrayed the fundamental nature of the soul in just two verses. By reflecting on just these two verses, individuals can swiftly dispel any misconceptions they may have nurtured regarding the soul. In the first verse, the Lord says to Arjun:

'Na jayate mriyate va kadachi
Nayam bhutva bhavita va na bhuyah
Ajo nityah shasvato aym purano
Na hanyate hanyamane sharire'

Bhagavad Gita: Chapter 2, verse 20

The soul is neither born, nor ever die; it is eternal, immortal, and ageless. It does not perish when the body perishes.

When the Lord Himself lucidly explains that the Aatma, known as the soul or the Self, is eternal and immortal—neither born nor perished, neither growing nor diminishing—then whose birth and whose death ought to concern us? Our intense preoccupation with our physical bodies causes us to associate our identities solely with these forms, hence we perceive ourselves as being born and dying.

Driven by ignorance, we have crafted a fabricated self-image in our minds and strive to preserve it, thereby instilling a fear of its dissolution; our identification with our physical bodies leads to various thoughts and beliefs in our minds. However, the reality is that our true essence is immortal; we are eternal entities. Existing since the dawn of time and destined to endure for eternity, our true selves transcend the transient forms we perceive. If we neither come into existence nor cease to be, then what significance do notions of an afterlife or rebirth hold? What significance does our liberation carry?

In truth, there is no need to pursue liberation, for we are inherently liberated beings. Our bondage lies in the misconception that we are the physical body and its associated possessions. It is we who have constructed erroneous beliefs about the Self, thus entangling ourselves in mental chains. There is no salvation awaiting us after death; it's a misconception. Even death itself is illusory; in reality, nothing truly perishes in this existence.

Modern science acknowledges that nothing in the cosmos truly dies; there is no method to completely eradicate something. Instead, one form transitions into another. Energy cannot be created nor destroyed; it merely transforms from one state to another. When the body perishes, it transforms into the elemental components from which it originated—Water, Air, Fire, Earth, and Ether. Thus, what we perceive as death is simply the continuous process of change occurring within this creation.

In this cosmos, destruction and creation occur concurrently, perpetually continuing for eternity. When a form ceases to exist, it seamlessly transitions into another. The end of something marks the beginning of something else. Thus, there exists no distinction between birth and death, destruction and creation; they are inherently intertwined. What we perceive as beginnings or endings are simply the shifts between forms within this eternal flux.

The soul neither perishes nor is it born, so what truly defines the identity of a soul? What is the origin of the Aatma or the Self? Who, indeed, am I? These inquiries signify the core of the journey toward self-realization, the pivotal step in uncovering the ultimate truth. While unwinding all these queries in another verse of the Bhagavad Gita, Lord Vasudev Krishna says to Arjun:

'Aham atma gudakesha sarvbhutashaya sthitah

Aham adish cha madhyam cha bhutanam anta eva cha'

Bhagavad Gita: Chapter 10, verse 20

O Arjun, I am the Aatma, or the soul that resides in the heart of all beings. I am the beginning, middle, and end of all beings.

Therefore, the soul itself embodies the essence of God; the Aatma is the Paramatma. Your reality is not distinct from the Supreme Reality; you are the Ultimate Truth. You are a fragment of God, not apart from it; you are, in essence, 'That'. Within every being, there isn't a separate individual soul; rather, there exists only one soul that resides within all. This soul extends beyond beings and permeates everything; it is boundless and infinite. It remains stationary and unaltered, neither moving nor transitioning between bodies. Like a lamp in a room, it casts illumination upon all within its vicinity. Similarly, it resembles the space; omnipresent and all-encompassing.

In this manner, you are the cosmos itself, and you are also the very origin of this cosmos. Your limitation lies in the belief that the Aatma and the Paramatma are separate entities. It's all part of the Maya's (illusion) play, causing things to appear distinct, but in reality, it's the same energy operating within this creation.

Throughout existence, there exists a fundamental unity; it is all interconnected. Day and night reflect each other, as do good and evil, happiness and sorrow, pain and pleasure, negative and positive, observer and object, consciousness and its object. One cannot exist without the other, akin to two distinct viewpoints of a singular entity. You can only describe something as Black if there is White elsewhere to contrast it with. You can only experience light when you possess the experience of darkness. In the same vein, the fire that offers warmth in the cold of winter, the fire utilized for culinary tasks, the fire that banishes darkness, and the fire that consumes all are indistinguishable.

Whether you believe it or not, accept it or not, are aware of it or not, you are inherent 'That', the Supreme Entity. You serve as the ultimate cause. The truth of your existence, the fabric of creation, and the divine essence are unified. Recognizing the truth of any aspect encompasses the truth of all, embodying the essence of the Vedas, Upanishads, and Adhyatma. This awakening marks the path to enlightenment.

By venerating various deities, we honor the singular Supreme Lord, recognizing these divine manifestations as pathways to connect with the formless essence. To grasp the infinite, it's essential to explore the finite realm initially. You must surpass the limitations of the finite to truly understand the infinite. It's akin to comprehending what lies beyond the confines of the body by first understanding the body itself. Therefore, worship, prayers, and penance are not futile; they are the means to transcend; finite is the path to the infinite. The limitations belong not to you, but to the body you inhabit. It is just a medium through which you can evolve and realize the Ultimate Reality.

Regarding everything I have conveyed thus far, if it doesn't resonate with you or align with your experiences, you essentially have two options: either to believe it or to reject it. Even with the earnest desire to do so, I lack the capacity to validate it; therefore, it's utterly in your hands. Nonetheless, I'm resolute in underscoring a fundamental truth: without firsthand experience, all comprehension of a subject is but empty dialogue, and dialogue, without the grounding of experience, carries little significance. Arjun himself expressed to the Lord, "I have faith in your words, yet I yearn to tangibly experience it."

Similarly, if you are thirsty and I begin describing the qualities of water instead of offering you actual water, it will not quench your thirst; a thought of water cannot quench the thirst.

I genuinely don't want you to take anyone's word, including mine. Instead, I encourage you to venture out on your own and experience life firsthand. It's through your own exploration that you will discern what's real and what's not. Other people's words and experiences won't change your life. You can't find your true essence by following someone else's path. You can't become like the Buddha by imitating someone else, nor you can become like Swami Vivekananda by walking on someone else footprint, you can't become like Ramana Maharishi by chasing others. Similarly, you cannot aspire to be like Kabir by tracing someone else's journey.

While the lives of enlightened beings can serve as inspiration, each individual must chart their own course and their own unique journey. It is only through this individual exploration that one can attain the ultimate truth—a truth that transcends realization, perception, observation, comprehension, expression, inquiry, hearing, and aspiration. At that point, only boundless bliss will remain, and you will reside in it for eternity.

Experiencing that doesn't demand sitting in the Himalayas or any particular place, renouncing everything, enduring extreme penance, or waiting for an extended period. It can happen to you in an instant. It doesn't matter where you are, or what you do, it will happen to you anyway. Just sit and observe inwardly, without any filters or preconceived knowledge, setting aside all your beliefs and notions. Over time, the false sense of Self will fade away, leaving only the truth within you.

The path of self-discovery isn't a linear path toward a goal; it's not about reaching a destination someday. There is no endpoint; it's an eternal voyage. Walking this path doesn't lead to gaining something; instead, it's about shedding everything. This path will perish you thoroughly. You relinquish everything, false identities, beliefs, and notions, leaving behind only your true Self. In realizing this, you won't become infinite, because you already are infinite in actuality. You are experiencing the world through an instrument, mistakenly identifying yourself with it. This misconception binds you, leading you to believe that you are limited and separate.

On the path of self-discovery, the destinations reached by the great beings such as the Buddha, Mahavir, Rumi, Shankaracharya, Nanak, Meera Bai, Kabir, Kinaram, Ramakrishna, Tulsi Das, myself, and countless other enlightened beings, are merely certain points within the infinite, akin to touching different-different drops from a vast ocean. It is an eternal, endless ocean; the deeper you explore, the more you uncover.

Whatever I have described about the Supreme this far, is not the absolute truth. 'That' is beyond depiction. Words are the worst medium to utter something about 'That'. Explore silence, become silence; you will reach closer and closer to 'That' gradually.

The speck was always interconnected with the dune, it was never isolated from it. In fact, the speck was the origin of the dune itself, or you could say the speck embodies the dune.

I appreciate your journey alongside me thus far, yet this isn't the final chapter; there is much more to discover, discuss, and encounter ahead. If you are reading these words, it's a testament to the grace of the Supreme, beckoning you to awaken the dormant spark within and cast aside the veil of ignorance. Move ahead and seek your own truth; eventually, we all have to realize it someday.

I don't adhere to any belief, religion, or sect; rather, I'm an eternal seeker. This journey will persist indefinitely because there exists no ultimate conclusion, as every ending marks the genesis of something new. There will always be something that remains unknown to you.

May Lord Ram bless us all.

To be continued...